Engraved by H.W. Smith

Hosea Ballou.

BIOGRAPHY

OF

REV. HOSEA BALLOU.

BY HIS YOUNGEST SON,

MATURIN M. BALLOU.

"He staggered not at the promise of God through unbelief; but was strong in faith, giving glory to God: and being fully persuaded that what he had promised he was able also to perform."

NINTH THOUSAND.

BOSTON:
PUBLISHED BY ABEL TOMPKINS.
1854.

STEREOTYPED BY
HOBART & ROBBINS,
NEW ENGLAND TYPE AND STEREOTYPE FOUNDERY,
BOSTON.

TO THE

SECOND UNIVERSALIST SOCIETY

OF BOSTON,

THIS BIOGRAPHY OF THEIR LATE PASTOR IS RESPECTFULLY

Dedicated,

BY THEIR HUMBLE SERVANT,

THE AUTHOR.

PREFACE

TO THE REVISED EDITION.

LITTLE more than a year since, the first edition of the following work was issued, on the author's part with much diffidence and hesitation, but the endorsement which a lenient public has given to it has much encouraged and gratified the writer. He attempted the task with a full knowledge of its peculiarities, understanding how liable a son might be to look upon the character and life of a revered parent with eyes too predisposed to affection, and that degree of appreciation which the ties of relationship would render so prominent. But he has endeavored to record faithfully the history of his subject, and is gratified in knowing how largely it has yielded satisfaction to those for whom it was designed.

Since the first edition was issued, the beloved and honored wife of the subject of this biography has been called to join her companion, in another and better world. Her character and connection with the following record are properly referred to in these pages. Her last days and hours were full of that sweet and holy resignation, that blessed purity and affection of heart, that had so glorified the life of her husband, and rendered his fireside, to him and his children, such a peaceful and happy home. Less than a twelvemonth separated the wife from her departed husband, and all that is mortal of both now rests in the grave together.

The time which has transpired since the death of HOSEA BALLOU, has served only to show how deeply the memory of the man is engraven on the hearts of the entire denomination, of which he was the acknowledged head, and that the principles which he advocated so long, and so strenuously, are growing daily more extended, and more cherished in the world.

We are all taught by experience, and in reviewing the following pages the author sees how much they might be improved by rewriting ; but the work would not then be what it now is, an impromptu record, a *plain home picture* of a father's life, produced under the inspiration of his loss, and written with an eye only to his justification before the world, and not as a vehicle for rhetoric or flowery composition.

Some few trifling errors in the matter of dates, etc., crept into the earlier editions of the work, which are corrected in the present issue, but the book, in all its main features, remains entirely unaltered.

CONTENTS.

CHAPTER IX.

CHAPTER X.

CHAPTER XI.

CHAPTER XII.

CHAPTER XIII.

CHAPTER XIV.

CHAPTER XV.

CHAPTER XVI.

BIOGRAPHY.

CHAPTER I.

INTRODUCTORY.

THE gratitude of mankind has not failed to record with honor the names of those who have been the inventors of useful improvements in the arts, or the authors of scientific discoveries, of brave warriors and wise statesmen; ancient history reveals to us the time when the inventors of letters and the plough, were revered as divinities. If there are any who are actually worthy of being remembered by the world, they are those who have proved themselves, by the lives they have led, and by their holy teachings, to be benefactors of the human family, and true followers of Christ.

It is conceded by all, that biography is a most important species of history. Through its agency, men who have been distinguished for merit, talent, or any peculiar virtue, are remembered, and, though they may be personally lost to us, yet the good influence they exerted during their lives, is made to continue for our benefit. The biography of any eminent individual must be, in some degree, a chronicle of the times in which he lived, and thus, though the production may be of the most humble character, the pages of history are enriched, and the records of the past perfected. We think it was the Rev. John Ewart, M. A., a noted English divine, who set it down as one of the most interesting reflections relative to biographical reading, that we may see and know in heaven, those whose life and excellent works we have read of here. This is, perhaps, rather a peculiar argument, but not inappropriate in this connection.

For our own part, we have ever perused, with the liveliest satisfaction, any book of a biographical character, and believe that such works are almost universally read with avidity and profit. With living men and present measures, there is generally some prejudice or passion connected. But when death has set his seal upon a worthy character, and he has departed from the din and conflict of the world, then we can receive the full benefit of his example. For it is very true that genius rarely shines with full lustre until death hath unroofed it of envy. It will, therefore, be our object in these pages to adhere to those facts best fitted to illustrate the personal character of Mr. Ballou, and to furnish the means of estimating aright the services he rendered to his own and subsequent times, that his memory may remain to us in evergreen freshness and beauty, and thus renew to posterity the savor of a good life.

It is the usual practice with biographers to dwell at length and in explanation upon the discoveries and doctrines of the object of their labors, forgetting, apparently, that these things are almost universally known already, and that the main design of a biography should be to make public and illustrate the private life of those whom the world already knows as philosophers, statesmen, divines, or otherwise. It is said of Mallet, that he wrote the life of Lord Bacon, and forgot that he was a philosopher. But this is rarely the case, for it is the prevailing custom, and has ever been, to forget the man in the remembrance of the philosopher. It is the traits of personal character, those slight, yet important incidents and anecdotes which mark the individual's every-day life, that, when preserved and recorded, form the great interest and charm of biography. Plutarch, the writer of half a hundred lives, in that of Alexander says: — "As painters "labor the likeness in the face, so must we be permitted "to strike off the features of the soul, in order to give a "real likeness of these great men."

Hence, biography written in a true spirit, while something quite different from history, is, nevertheless, an important supplement and aid to it, throwing light into its dark corners, and explaining its obscurity. For the historian, in the spirit of the painter or poet, must dispense with all the minutiæ of detail which would interfere with the effect of his conception. He has a broad canvas, crowded with many figures, and in the grouping of these, the bringing out of strong points, the handling of the light and shade, many minor points must be obliterated, or thrown into the background. He presents us with truth, indeed, but not with the whole truth. The historian shows us the warrior in the hour of battle, on the field of review, or in the pomp of a military triumph; the statesman in the light of a senatorial victory, as he appears before the broad gaze of the world; the divine clad in his sacerdotal robe, at the high altar, or in the pulpit, at the moment of addressing listening crowds, and swaying the hearts of men by the fervor of his eloquence.

The biographer, on the other hand, dealing with individuals and not with masses, painting portraits and not groups, is permitted a more elaborate finish in the treatment of his subject. He shows us the soldier not only in the hour of battle, but in the privacy of his tent, or in the bosom of his family; the statesman in his study, or unbending from his public tasks in social intercourse; the divine in the daily walks of life, in the discharge of parochial duties, amid the toils and trials common to all humanity. The biographer is often at variance with the historian in treating the same subject. He often shows us the littleness of the great; for many a prominent actor in the world's great drama wears a mask upon the public stage that conceals his real features. Few men are found abroad, beneath the searching light of heaven, with the same aspect of soul, the same undisguised native promptings, visible in every act and word, as characterize them at their own firesides, and surrounded by those who know them most intimately. It is truly going "behind the scenes" to enter the domestic circle, for there the artificial man must be dropped, the cloak that is sometimes worn before the eyes of the world is laid aside, and we have the soul unmasked indeed.

It will be our endeavor, in the following pages, to illustrate the perfect harmony of a Christian character, the daily beauty of whose private life accorded with that of his public career; through whose existence religion ran like a silver thread, linking all its component parts together, — who "showed the path to heaven and led the way." The world is anxious, when it contemplates the memory of such an exalted character, to know the steps by which the subject rose to the situation which he filled, as well as the incidents by which he terminated his noted career. We are gratified to observe such characters in the private walks of life, to follow them into their families and closets, and to discover thus how those who challenged the respect and admiration of the times in which they lived, conducted themselves amid those cares and duties common alike to the humble and the exalted. These remarks will introduce the reader to the plan of the present work.

CHAPTER II.

BIRTH AND PARENTAGE.

HOSEA BALLOU was born, April 30th, 1771, in the town of Richmond, New Hampshire, a small village situated in the county of Cheshire, in the southern part of the State; at that time little more than an uncleared wilderness. The site of his birth-place is now a most attractive and lovely valley, scooped out from the rough hills and mountains of the Granite State, and known as Ballou's Dale; surrounded by the most romantic scenery, the beauties of which he used to dwell upon in after years, and to sing their praise in verse. The neighboring country is of a bold and rugged character, and is to this day but thinly settled. It was here that he first drew breath in an humble cottage-home among the hills.

The influence of nature in the formation of character has been much insisted on by metaphysicians, and not without ample reason. The qualities of men are found to assimilate very closely to the characteristics of the country they inhabit. Thus the mountaineer is bold, rugged, hardy, independent, and fond of liberty. In Europe, surrounded on every hand by despotism, Alpine Switzerland has preserved its political independence for ages. But especially is the power of natural scenery witnessed in the nurture of deep religious feeling.

"The groves were God's first temples."

The first prayer uttered by man was breathed to his Creator in a garden, among the olive trees of Eden. The disciples of our Saviour listened to their Lord in the deep wilderness, in the awful solitude of rugged mountains. In the heart of mighty forests and by the shores of ever-rushing rivers, the littleness of man, contrasting with the grandeur of creation, speaks to his awakened soul of the omnipotence and goodness of God. Where men are banded together in great cities, in the midst of splendors and triumphs of art, they are apt to feel a pride and self-reliance which abandon them in the face of nature. Apart from the frequent spectacle of man's handiwork, the dweller in the country learns how all human skill is impotent to imitate the smallest feature in the great work of creation; to create the lightest blade of grass that bends in the summer breeze; to fabricate even the minutest grain of sand that sparkles by the river shore. Then, as he lifts his eyes from earth to heaven, and beholds at night the starry host above him wheeling unerringly upon their appointed courses, his mind cannot but acknowledge the existence of God, and the immeasurable greatness of his attributes.

It will be seen, in the course of this narrative, that the influences we have alluded to must have produced a powerful effect upon a mind constituted like that of the subject of this biography.

In relation to the genealogy of the family, we have it in detail as far back, on the paternal side, as his great-great-grandfather, Matteaurian Ballou,—so the name was spelled by him,—who came from England, though a Frenchman by descent, about the year 1640. He occupied a portion of a royal grant of land, about that time purchased from the Narraganset tribe of Indians, by the agent of the crown. This tract was situated in the present State of Rhode Island, where descendants of the family still reside. This Matteaurian Ballou's oldest son was named John, whose second son was named Peter, who, also, had a son named Matteaurian, who in turn had eleven children,—six sons and five daughters. The youngest of the family was named Hosea, the subject of these memoirs.

His father, Rev. Maturin Ballou, was remarkable for his unostentatious manner, his forgiving spirit and meekness, and the strict consistency of a life devoted, as he truly believed, to the service and glory of his Divine Master. He remained a highly respected and influential member of the Baptist church until the time of his death, at the age of eighty-two years. When his son differed from him so materially in faith, though it sorely grieved the parent's heart, it never for one moment influenced him in his affection for his child. His conduct towards him was uniformly kind and solicitous, as was also the son's regard for his father of the most loving and respectful character. Whenever referring to his father, the subject of this biography never failed to do so with that respect and honor for his memory that was ever cherished by him, and which formed a beautiful trait of his character.

In this connection it may not be inappropriate nor uninteresting to say a few words concerning the brothers and sisters of Hosea, the youngest member of the family. Benjamin, the oldest, was a man of strict integrity, and possessed a penetrating and powerful intellect. For some years the power of early influences and associations moulded his life, and he preached the Baptist religion, but was subsequently converted to Universalism, by his younger brother, Hosea, and lived and died in its faith, continuing to the good old age of eighty-two years. This was the grandfather of Rev. Dr. Ballou, of Medford, Mass.; Rev. William S. Ballou, of Strafford, Vt., and Rev. Levi Ballou, of Orange, Mass. Maturin was the second son, who was also a Baptist minister, of strict morality and honorable career, but who died at the early age of thirty-five years. In his manuscript, Mr. Ballou says, relative to this brother: "He grew very liberal in "his sentiments towards the last of his labors, and was "one of the most loving and devout Christians that I "ever knew." David was the third son, and he also preached the Baptist faith, but, like the eldest brother, was ere long persuaded of the truth of the doctrine of universal salvation, which he preached for many years, possessing a strong and well balanced mind, and powerful argumentative abilities. He died at the age of eighty-two. This was the father of Rev. Moses Ballou, of Bridgeport, Ct. The fourth son was named Nathan, a man of remarkable mental and physical strength, who gave his attention mainly to agricultural pursuits, and who lived to be nearly eighty years of age. This was the grandfather of the present Rev. Russell A. Ballou, of West Bridgewater, Mass. Stephen was the fifth son, and combining many of the best qualities of his elder brothers, and possessing a most upright and conscientious disposition, was yet remarkable for the endowment of a large degree of native wit and good humor. He also devoted himself to agriculture, and lived to nearly the age of seventy. All of these brothers were possessed of a handsome competency, realized by their own economy and industry. The daughters were variously espoused, and lived, all but one, who died at the age of twenty, to be venerable and honored in years, and with a numerous offspring.

On the maternal side, these children were descended from Lydia Harris, daughter of Richard Harris, who, like his ancestors, was a Quaker. His forefathers came to this country to escape the persecution of the seventeenth century in England, when the infatuated and tyrannical Charles was oppressing his subjects by restricting the freedom of industry, and billeting soldiers upon the people in times of peace; when the private papers of citizens were searched on mere suspicion, and when the bigoted Laud ruled with as high a hand and reckless a purpose in the church, as his royal master did in the state. Citizens claiming the right of freely uttering what they honestly believed to be true, on the subject of religion, were fined, whipped, and imprisoned. Ministers and educated citizens were branded on the forehead, their noses slit, and their ears cropped, for dissenting from Popish rites and ceremonies. To escape such intolerable persecution, Quakers crossed the ocean. But, alas! persecution followed them even in the wilds of America. Individuals who had left home, friends, country and all, to gain the privilege of worshipping the Almighty after the dictates of their own consciences, did not hesitate to deny others that privilege for which they had themselves sacrificed so much, simply because they differed from them in form of faith.

We should not omit to mention in this place the remarkable degree of affection that ever actuated the subject of this biography towards each and all of the members of his father's extensive family; and this feeling was reciprocal too; especially have we personally observed this on the part of the brothers, whom he frequently visited, through the entire period of their lives. Much older than himself, as far back as our memory of them extends they were venerable and grey-haired men, and treated Hosea more like a son than a brother. Their meetings together, from time to time, were reünions of great satisfaction and happiness. Fully admitting his superior scriptural knowledge and judgment, they delighted to converse upon the theme of religion, and mutually to express the strength of their faith and the joy they found in believing. It was this younger brother who converted them to the belief of God's impartial and free grace, and they died at last with their minds freed from every doubt as it regarded the subject. One or two of these brothers had believed what was called Universalism quite as early as had Hosea, but they had believed it as it was then taught on the old Calvinistic principle, which made it in reality anything but Universalism. It was from this ill-defined platform, this faith of inconsistencies, that Hosea brought their minds to embrace that creed which is now acknowledged as the doctrine of the Universalist denomination. When he spoke to them and of them, it was with that tender and affectionate regard with which his heart was ever filled to overflowing.

We have taken some pains to state the foregoing facts of genealogy thus carefully, merely for the sake of completeness, and not for the purpose of establishing the fact that the family is "an old one." The idea that to be able to trace back one's pedigree any great length of time, imparts any degree of merit or distinction in itself, is a palpable absurdity, inasmuch as the further back we refer ourselves in our origin, the more nearly do we approximate to the same ancestry with the veriest serf in the world. Sir Thomas Overbury said of a man who boasted of his ancestry, that he was like a potato plant, — the best thing belonging to him was under ground! Mr. Ballou was no pensioner upon the dead. The laurels that surrounded the brow of his riper years were self-earned, and worthy of emulation.

CHAPTER III.

EARLY LIFE.

THE life of Hosea Ballou may be said to have commenced with one of the saddest of bereavements, for at the tender age of two years he had the misfortune to lose his maternal parent, who died, leaving him the youngest of eleven children. Thus it was his unhappy lot never to know the fond regard and pure affection of a mother, that holiest tie of humanity. Concerning this matter, Mr. Ballou says, in the brief memoir or outline of his life with which he has furnished us, "My mother "died when I was about two years old, and, of course, I "do not remember her; but from all I can learn of my "mother, I am satisfied that she was of a most tender and "kind disposition. But the treasure was gone before I "could realize its value." The care and guidance of the family then fell upon the father, whose means for providing for his children's necessities were of the most simple and limited character. This parent, a pious and devout preacher of the Calvinistic Baptist denomination, endeavored, to the best of his ability, to bring up his large family to fear and serve a God who was merciful to those whom from all eternity he had elected to be heirs of eternal life, but who was full of holy wrath towards the greater portion of mankind; — a faith which the honest parent little thought, at that time, his youngest son, through the instrumentality of Providence, would so successfully battle against in the spiritual warfare of after years.

In this connection, Mr. Ballou says: — "We were all "taught, and in our youth all believed, that we were "born into the world wholly depraved, and under the "curse of a law which doomed every son and daughter "of Adam to eternal woe. But at the same time God "had made provision for a select number of the human "family, whereby they would be saved by the operations "of the divine Spirit, which would result in what was "called conversion, sometime during the life of those "elected. Those who were not elected would remain "without any effectual calling, die, and be forever "miserable. When I was a youth it was the sentiment "of all Christian people, as far as I knew, that not more "than one in a thousand of the human family would be "saved from endless condemnation.

"Youth were taught to be moral, but that morality was "no security against divine wrath. The conversion of "the soul from the state of nature in which all men were "born into the world, was the only security. One of the "worst things ever taught to youth was, that in this "world there is more enjoyment in the ways of vice, "iniquity, sin, and unrighteousness, than in the ways of "obedience to the commandments of God. But we were "taught at the same time that the wicked were running "an awful risk, for should they die without repentance, "their everlasting condemnation was sure. All the risk "there was, lay in the possibility that death might be "sudden, and give no time for repentance. But the fact "that there is *in* the way of strict morality, *in* the path "of true religion, *in* the road of righteousness, all the "rational enjoyment which our nature is capable of, and "that any departure from right is an equal departure from "true happiness, was not taught, to my knowledge, at 'that time. Nor did I ever understand this great truth "until taught it by the Scriptures, and my study of them, "and by my own experience."

It was the conscientious belief of Mr. Ballou's father that he ought not to receive any remuneration whatever, either pecuniary or otherwise, for his professional services; and, as he devoted himself with the utmost zeal and the most untiring assiduity to his calling, and was possessed of little or no personal estate, his family were all obliged to labor very hard, merely to obtain a simple subsistence. But "even in this was Heaven ordinant." Thus, from his earliest childhood, Mr. Ballou was accustomed to toil and labor, and this too under the hardships of a scanty supply of food and clothing. So destitute even of the most ordinary articles of raiment, or the means of procuring it, was his father's family, in the times of his boyhood, that many a long week has he passed without an under garment of any kind upon his person, and without shoes or stockings for his feet, even during the inclemencies of winter, when his employment would frequently call him abroad for a large portion of the day!

Notwithstanding all these privations and hardships, there was no repining; the rich glow of health was upon his cheek, and a light and happy heart, in spite of iron fortune, throbbed in his young breast. Though such was his early experience, and such the vicissitudes of his youth, yet in subsequent years he was destined to enjoy freely of the liberal bounties of Providence, and, through his own frugality and industry, to be able to give with open hands in charity to others. In these years of prosperity and honor, when revered and beloved by a whole denomination, and when ranked among the most powerful intellects of the age, did he forget, or desire to conceal, the humble character of his youth, its hardships and trials, or the companions of his early days? Let those answer to whom he has related these things in censure of false pride and the vanity of the world. Would it become us, then, who have seen and realized the full bent of this noble spirit in him, to fail to speak clearly of these matters? We opine not, and therefore these records will be found to be full and complete.

The reader will probably agree with us, that there is something exceedingly striking, as well as most affecting, in the domestic circumstances to which we have alluded. The character of Mr. Ballou's father reminds us of one of those stern old Cameronians of Scotland, so well described by one of the first writers of the age. With but little sympathy for his creed, we must nevertheless respect his sincerity; nor can we wonder at all, with his education in the faith which he preached, and hampered by the illiberal spirit of the period, which seemed to mildew every generous prompting of the human heart, that he clung to it with inflexible tenacity. But we must contemplate with unqualified admiration the heroic self-denial, the martyr-like firmness, with which this servant of the Lord pursued what he believed to be the path of his duty, amidst circumstances of such extraordinary deprivation. Truly, he abandoned all to serve his Master. His severest trial must have been to witness the privations of his family. A man can endure in his own person what it costs him agony to witness inflicted on those nearer and dearer to him than life itself. The struggles of that little flock, bereft of a mother's tender care and guidance at the very time when they most required it, must have given many an anxiously painful day and night to a father's heart. Yet we have seen how they were sustained.

This is probably by no means an isolated case of trial. It is but a type of the condition of many of the early settlers in a new country,—in short, a picture of American pioneer life. It is from such beginnings, and under such circumstances, that the most useful and energetic of our countrymen have sprung. It is not to the lap of luxury that we are to look for the source of manly character and manly virtues. The rough nurture of his early years most unquestionably fitted Mr. Ballou for the battle of life which he was destined to fight. It trained him for the long and severe journeyings of his apostolic missions, and it warmed his sympathies for the poor, while it gave him that indifference to ease and luxury which so largely conduces to true mental independence. It taught him also to rely under Providence upon himself; and these early privations, while they strengthened and indurated him, rendered the honorably acquired competence and comforts of his later years in life doubly grateful and acceptable.

Notwithstanding this stern experience of his tender years, and in spite of every hardship, and the severe labor he was obliged to perform under such unpropitious circumstances, still he grew up strong, healthy and vigorous, both in mind and body, possessing a form and face of manly beauty, with expression and intelligence reflected in every feature. In stature he grew to be six feet high, his figure very erect, with finely formed limbs, and a bright, clear blue eye. His whole appearance indicated good health even to advanced old age, his constitution being naturally excellent, and his frugal and temperate habits seconding the kindly purpose of nature. Heaven had marked him for its servant, and breathed into his soul a spirit of energy and unflinching perseverance, that no hardship could quench or diminish. Christ chose his disciples from among the lowly fishermen of Galilee; God herein took an humble but faithful follower from a cottage amidst the mountains.

Although descended from a devout and eloquent preacher of the Scriptures, the reader will at once observe that Mr. Ballou was not indebted in the least particular for the future lustre of his reputation as a powerful and original thinker, writer and teacher of the gospel, to his birth, or early condition in life, but that, on the contrary, he was literally a self-made man, owing his position strictly to individual merit alone. Enjoying none of the educational advantages resulting from wealth, or even from a simple competency, yet he steadily rose above every impending obstacle in his path, to the truly enviable position which he attained in the hearts of thousands upon thousands who were led through his teachings, both orally and through the productions of his prolific pen, to see their God and Father as he is in all harmony and beauty. Thus it is that poverty of condition and wealth of intellect go often hand in hand.

"Where, in modern history," asks Rev. A. R. Abbott, in his late eulogy upon Mr. Ballou, "can another "instance be found of a man laboring under such disad- "vantages, in the face of such opposition, and yet perform- "ing such a work? Those who have heretofore accom- "plished much in that field, have had all the advantages "which the most thorough culture of their times could "give. Like the giant of Gath, they have taken the "field encased in polished armor; he, like the stripling "of Bethlehem, came to the contest with only the shep- 'herd's sling and the smooth stones from the brook."

As no general rule can be adduced for the formation

of human character, so long as the power of early association, the influence of education and example, each and severally produce in different individuals exactly opposite effects, so no general rule can be applied as to the result of certain accessory circumstances. Therefore we deduce no result from the mere fact of Mr. Ballou's father having been a professed minister upon the character of his son, having no belief that genius is hereditary, or that paternal authority can influence its natural course. Indeed, the reader is doubtless well aware that the opposition of a father to the natural bent of his child, rarely fails more strongly to develop the original taste and purpose, generally arousing in the end a spirit of resistance, that is pretty sure to strengthen by opposition.

Before the age of sixteen, by the utmost perseverance, ingenuity, and industry, the subject of this biography had learned to read and write with facility, almost entirely by his own unaided exertions, or with little assistance of any kind; for had there been a school in the neighborhood of Richmond, which was not the case, he could have found no time to attend it, being ever laboriously engaged from morning until night. He learned to form the letters of the alphabet in the following ingenious and original manner, which he related to us when a mere child, we were making the first advances in the use of the pen. After not a little thought and sober calculation as to how he should accomplish his purpose, — for pen, ink and paper were luxuries his father's means could not command, — for paper he substituted thin pieces of birch bark, neatly prepared for the purpose by his own hands, and for pen and ink he used coals taken from the fire. With these rude materials, after the labors of the day were over, seated on the floor, by the light of the fire,—for candles were too expensive to be afforded in the frugal household of his father,—he taught himself to write. A student, actuated by such resolution and determination of purpose, must soon become a proficient, in defiance of every minor obstacle; and thus he speedily improved with these humble means.

Some further idea of the limited means of his father's family, and the extraordinary disadvantages under which his early progress was made, may be gathered from the fact, that the only books the house contained, or in fact that the family had access to at all, were a Bible, an old dictionary, and a well-thumbed pamphlet of the scriptural story of the tower of Babel. A newspaper in the days of which we write, in the town of Richmond, would have been considered a most rare curiosity. Perhaps this very dearth of literary material led Mr. Ballou to be the more intimate with that volume

> "Within whose sacred pages lies
> The mystery of mysteries,"

with which alone no student can be poor, without which the largest library is incomplete. It has been remarked of the sacred volume, that, as the face of nature is bedecked with colors and adornments to render it agreeable to the senses, so its pages are filled with that luxury of poetry and language and incident which commends it to every imagination. Even the half-unbelieving Byron confessed that nothing in literature was finer than the poetry of the Old Testament. Thus the word, like the bow of promise, is gilded with the fairest hues. The solemn march of historical narration, the sublime hymns of triumph, praise and rejoicing, the records of battles and heroic deeds, the familiar narrative, the interesting parable, the pithy proverb, the terse and vigorous delineation of character, the sublime visions of inspired prophecy, are all there. Of almost every style of literary composition there is an example, captivating alike to the humblest reader and the most cultivated critic. It is the beginning and the end of learning. In the midst of the sublimest flights of human genius, amid the most burning words of modern eloquence, introduce a passage of scripture, and how poor will seem the language and the thoughts by which it is surrounded!

Need we count that house poor in literary possessions which contains a Bible?

If it be true that there are certain ennobling qualities, to produce which a soil of privation and poverty is requisite, the reader is doubtless already prepared to allow that Mr. Ballou was not deficient in the necessary experience for their possession. A lack of those advantages which are enjoyed in the "schools of human learning" did not lead him in the least to undervalue the humble opportunities for acquiring mental discipline and useful information that every-day life graciously affords to all. But the clear, free river of knowledge and unbounded information, that now pours out its wealth at the feet of the people, was then undiscovered. It has been left to these more modern and favored times for inventions in the arts to so revolutionize the means of disseminating knowledge, as to lay the wealth of wisdom at the poor man's door.

At the age of sixteen he left the paternal roof for the first time, and made a journey on foot to Guildford, Vt., a distance of about forty miles from Richmond. Here he visited an elder brother, and, after working with him upon his farm through the season, returned to his father's house again in the fall. About one year from the time of his visit to Guildford, he visited another brother who resided in Putney, Vt., where he also labored for a season upon the farm, employing all his leisure moments to the improvement of such simple means as were within his power to command, aided by the greater experience and better mental cultivation of his brother. He remained through that season only at Putney, however, and returned again in the fall of the year to Richmond.

At the age of eighteen he went to Smithfield, R. I., where many of his relations, on the paternal side, were settled. Here also he devoted himself to constant labor during the day, and to the eager perusal of any and all books to which he could obtain access, during the evenings and a large portion of the nights. He remained in Smithfield but about six months, again returning to the place of his nativity. In making these changes he was almost solely actuated by a desire for instruction and general information, and this being his great aim, we have seen how much he improved every available means to consummate it, and thus his exploring and impressible mind was not a little enriched. The time passed at home during the intermediate and subsequent periods to those referred to, was employed by him upon his father's farm, in the tilling of the soil, and in constant efforts to improve his mind. Those who were older than himself were earnestly questioned for their experience. Those who had enjoyed any educational advantages were eagerly sought after, and regarded by him as favored beings, and their conversation listened to with avidity.

The improvement and development of a mind in this condition, a healthy mind in a healthy body, is exceedingly rapid. It is then

> "Wax to receive, and marble to retain."

It seizes eagerly on all the food placed before it, and rapidly digests every acquisition. The condition of a mind with every appliance for improvement at hand, is not unlike that of a person with every variety and quality of food set before him for the gratification of a bodily appetite. Repletion, satiety, and indigestion, follow in one case precisely as in the other. Many of our modern students are crammed and gorged with study. The mental appetite is over-indulged; and an attempt to master too much is doubtless the besetting literary sin of the present day. The cases of mental dyspepsia are as common as those of the body. Sound scholarship consists not so much in the quantity of material consumed, as in the quantity properly prepared for intellectual nurture. A man may possess a fund of encyclopedic knowledge, and yet his mental powers may be weakened by the very process of grasping so many details. He may be good authority to appeal to, but will hardly prove a sound thinker or a good logician. "Not many, but good, books," was the golden advice of a wise man on the formation of a library. Self-made men, like Mr. Ballou, are apt to make judicious selections in culling the great field of knowledge, while those who pass through a regular, systematic, academic training, are often forced to fill their minds with a mass of matter for which they have no use, and to waste much time in questionable acquirements, simply because in so doing they comply with the requisitions of a prescribed formula.

It was customary for the young men of all classes in those days to pursue athletic exercises, such as pitching the bar, leaping, wrestling, and the like, these being regarded as the surest tests of bodily strength. Possessing a powerful and active frame, he was ever the victor in those sports; and from his marked success among his comrades in this respect, and his fair and impartial disposition, he was universally the umpire in all disputes growing out of these and like contests for superiority that arose between one and another. In the matter of his physical strength, particularly when young, he ever cherished a laudable degree of pride, and delighted in accomplishing a large amount of work within the hours devoted to labor.

In this connection, Mr. Ballou says: — "I have the "comfort, even in my old age, of remembering that I was "deemed in our family circle to be a good child, and "marked for giving evidence of being less averse to "necessary labor than others. Though this contributed "somewhat to make me proud, and to think well of my-"self, in other respects it was of some advantage to me "to be held in esteem by my mates, who ever showed "that they had a peculiar regard for me."

Mr. Ballou undoubtedly owed the vigorous health which carried him through the exertions of a life protracted beyond the allotted span, to the athletic training of his youth, in his labors and in his sports. One of the besetting sins of the present mode of education is the almost total neglect of physical training, and the forcing system applied to the mind at the expense of the body. We hear much about sanitary reform and the necessity of exercise; we write and read voluminous treatises on the best mode of preserving bodily health, and almost all of us can talk learnedly upon the subject, and yet in practice we set at naught all our elaborate theories. How rare it is to see a vigorous, ruddy-cheeked student. The ancients were wiser than ourselves in this respect, for with them mental and physical training went hand in hand. A popular form of instruction was that given orally in the open air; and thus, during the very hours of study, the frame was submitted to the healthy influence of pure air. The subject of these memoirs often referred to the pale cheek, stooping form, and defective vision which are characteristics of the American student, and he never failed to inculcate on all proper occasions the preservation of health as a high moral duty.

While of tender age, and in each successive year, he evinced an ardent and constantly increasing desire for scriptural knowledge; and the earliest dawnings of his young mind among his brethren were of a character that gave promise of the Christian grace and excellence to which he attained in after years. It is interesting and curious to trace the unconscious, and, so to speak, the providential adaptation of the early life to the future calling of riper experience. Mr. Ballou says, in relation to this subject: — "I was remarkably inquisitive, even "when a mere boy, about doctrines. I was fond of "reasoning on doctrinal points, studied and talked much "upon the subject of free will and necessity. I well "remember to have surprised my honored father with "such a question as the following: 'Suppose I had the "skill and power out of an inanimate substance to make "an animate, and should make one, at the same time "knowing that this creature of mine would suffer ever-"lasting misery,— would my act of creating this creature "be an act of goodness?' The question troubled my "father, and I let it pass without an answer."

These frequent questions had the effect of causing the father much uneasiness of mind, and he used often to express great solicitude and fear for the present and future welfare of his son. Many were his endeavors to convince Hosea of the dangerous character of the sentiments that seemed to be springing up spontaneously in his heart, but the unprofitable nature of these efforts soon became apparent, from the fact that the simple, natural arguments of the son confounded the father. Boy as he was, he yet would not take the assertions of faith for argument, but insisted upon reason, and understanding at all times the "root of the matter."

To the honor of this truly pious and devout parent, it should be remembered, however, that these controversies never elicited an unchristian spirit, or the least anger towards his child. This was a natural and beautiful characteristic of his father's disposition.

CHAPTER IV.

BECOMES A PROFESSOR OF RELIGION.

At the age of nineteen, there being what was termed a reformation in the town of Richmond, Mr. Ballou was induced, believing it to be his duty, to become a professor of religion, and accordingly at that time he joined the Baptist church, of which his father was pastor, in the month of January, 1789. It is very evident that he was partly induced to this circumstance by the bearing of external circumstances and the immediate associations about him, such as observing the conduct of others of his own age, who at that time made a formal and public profession of faith, and also by what he knew very well to be his father's earnest desire. It seems, therefore, that these matters, rather than any earnest mental conviction of faith, were instrumental in leading him to join the church as he did, — inasmuch as none of those objections which he had often made to his father's belief, had yet been cleared up to his mind.

But this joining of the church was plainly of immediate

advantage to him, as it led him to think still more seriously and earnestly upon the subject of religion; but, owing to early prejudices, and his limited means of acquiring information, or of possessing himself of any books upon such subjects as would have been useful to him, his progress towards the light of truth was but slow. Mr. Ballou says, in relation to this conversion: — "I was "much troubled in my mind because I thought I did not "stand in such fear of the divine wrath as I ought to do, "or as others had done before they found acceptance with "God. I well remember that as I was returning home "from a conference meeting, one evening, when about a "quarter of a mile from home, being alone, I stopped "under a large tree, and, falling on my knees, prayed as "well as I could for the favor I sought." His connection with his father's church, though it continued but a short period comparatively, seems to have made no slight impression upon his mind and feelings, for he says: — "I have always felt towards this people (the Baptist "denomination) as one feels towards his family, and "though the religion of Christ consists in love to all "men, I have a peculiar feeling for the Baptists."

In his researches and reading concerning the creed that he had now publicly professed, he found it impossible to bring his heart to conform to the doctrine of eternal reprobation, and this in itself, as he afterwards remarked, was an evidence of no inconsiderable importance, to his mind, that it could not be true; for why should his Heavenly Father have implanted in his heart an earnest desire for the salvation of all mankind, unless that desire was susceptible of gratification, as is every appetite, mental or physical, with which we are endowed by nature? Such thoughts caused him much and incessant anxiety of mind, because the very fact of his entertaining them, if the doctrine he had professed was true, endangered his eternal salvation; while, on the other hand, if this creed was not that taught by God's revealed word, then he was needlessly suffering, to a degree that greatly depressed him.

No wonder that this double incentive led him to search the Scriptures with the utmost care and attention, and to weigh and decide in his own mind the relation that one portion bears to another, and finally, with the help of Heaven, to make up his mind as to the true spirit and doctrine of the whole. The reader can easily imagine the fervent prayers he uttered, the sleepless nights he passed, and the arduous study he performed, in his search for the light of truth. After all this anxious solicitude, this solitary mental struggle, this prayerful communication with Heaven, he at length declared himself a believer in the *final* salvation of the whole human family.

Great was the surprise, disappointment, and chagrin of his father and friends generally. Being looked up to by the young men of his own age as a sort of leader in their secular plans and games, the influence of his example was greatly feared as operating upon the younger portion of the church; and as his joining it had been the occasion of much rejoicing at the time, so his declaration of unbelief in its faith was the cause of a proportionate degree of sorrow. His new declaration was at once pronounced to be downright heresy, and he was accordingly excommunicated from his father's church. the document with which he was honored on the occasion carefully stating that nothing was found against him, but that he believed in the doctrine that God would finally save all men.

In relation to this subject, Mr. Ballou says: — "Above "all else, my theological bias of mind predominated, and "engrossed most of my attention. As I had formerly "been in the habit, while with the Baptists, of speaking "in their meetings, and of offering up prayer at conference "meetings, I now sometimes spoke my sentiments at "meetings in my brother's house. The church of which "I was still a member thought it a duty to call me to "answer for the course I had taken, and I was called "upon to meet the accusation of believing in the salvation "of all men. I attended, but did not feel it my duty to "deny the charge, or to renounce my belief. I was "therefore excommunicated from the church, my letter "of excommunication carefully stating that no fault was "found in me, my belief in the salvation of all men "excepted. I shall ever remember the tears which I "shed on this solemn occasion."

It was about this period that Mr. Ballou, ever in search of improvement, possessed himself of some book of a liberal religious character as to the sentiments it inculcated, when his father, chancing to see him reading it, told him decidedly that he would not have Universalist books in his house. Promptly acquiescing, as he always did, in his father's directions, a few days subsequent, the parent, on returning home, found Hosea reading a book beside the wood-pile, out of doors. "What book are you reading there?" he asked. "A *Universalist* book," replied the son, respectfully. An expression of dissatisfaction escaped the father, as he turned away and entered the house. Watching until his son had placed the book in the wood-pile, and left the spot, the parent resolved to possess himself of it, and perhaps even destroy it. But, lo! when he opened it, he found it was the Bible.

In an article written many years subsequent, relative to his conversion to the faith of God's impartial grace, Mr. Ballou says: — "I found, when conversing upon the "subject, that my Calvinistic tenets could be made either "to result in universal salvation, or to compel me to "acknowledge the partiality of the divine favor. This "gave me no small inquietude of mind, as I was unable "to derive satisfaction from sentiments which I could not "defend. That which more than anything else contri-"buted to turn my thoughts seriously towards the belief "of Universalism, was the ardent desire with which I "found myself exercised that sinners might be brought "to repentance and salvation. I found it utterly impossi-"ble to bring my feelings to consent to the doctrine of "eternal reprobation, and I was compelled either to allow "that such feelings were sinful, or that my Heavenly "Father, in giving them to me, had implanted an evidence "in favor of the salvation of all men, the force of which I "found no means to resist."

As to Mr. Ballou's having been brought up in the faith of Calvinism, it was not without its benefits upon his after life, for it gave to him a most unlimited and perfect knowledge of the various items of faith professed by that sect, as well as the common tenets of all those who believe in the partial salvation only of the great human family. Owing to an early desire to understand the doctrine of Christianity aright, while yet of tender age he became familiar with the arguments used in support of predestination, election, reprobation, the fall of man, the penal suffering of Christ for the elect, and many other items of creed relating to the moral agency of man. Concerning this subject, Mr. Ballou says: — "As to the doctrine of "Calvinism, in which my honored father was a believer, "and which doctrine he preached until nearly the end of "his public labors, my acquaintance with its various "tenets, while quite a youth, was by no means very lim- "ited, owing to the pious endeavors of a parent whose "affection for his children rendered him extremely "anxious for their spiritual welfare, and to an early "desire of my own to understand the doctrine of Chris- "tianity correctly." It was necessary that he should understand these matters as he did, and as he could only do, by serving an apprenticeship to them, so to speak, in order the better to enable him to refute them in after years, when he should be arrayed in a moral conflict against them. Thus the pious and well-meant endeavors of his parent to inculcate the principles of his own faith in the mind of his child were but a part of the well ordained purpose of the Almighty, in raising up an able champion for the gospel of truth.

Mr. Ballou says, referring to the period just previous to his declaration of faith and consequent excommunication: — "In the spring after I joined the church in Richmond, I went, with my brother Stephen and our cousin "Jeremiah Harris, to the town of Westfield, in New "York. This town is now called Harford. Here we "labored together during that season, attending Elder "Brown's meeting. He was of the Baptist order. Even "before I left home my mind had become somewhat "shaken in regard to the doctrine of endless punishment. "I found it utterly out of my power to reconcile it with "what all Christians professed of love to the unconverted; "nor could I reconcile it with many plain declarations of "Scripture; but I was by no means persuaded that salvation was for all men. My brother, knowing that I "had trials of mind on this great subject, expressed a "desire that I should have a conversation with Elder "Brown relative to it, hoping thereby that my doubts "would be removed. A conference was therefore appointed, at the house of one of the elder's deacons. "There were a number present, and the elder requested "me to name some passage of Scripture which to my "mind favored universal salvation; expressing at the "same time perfect confidence that he should be able to "show me that the passage did by no means favor such "doctrine. I opened to the fifth chapter of the Epistle "to the Romans, and read the eighteenth verse, as fol-

"lows: — 'Therefore, as by the offence of one judgment "came upon all men to condemnation; even so by the "righteousness of one the free gift came upon all men "unto justification of life.' The elder did not appear to "be at all acquainted with the text, for, instead of direct- "ing his remarks to it, he seemed to wander far off, and "to talk very loud, and nothing to the subject. When "he paused, I again read the text, and asked the elder if "the same *all men* mentioned in the first part of the text, "were not mentioned in the last? This simple question "seemed to embarrass his mind; he was evidently out of "humor, and manifested a bitter spirit, which being dis- "covered by my brother, caused him to desire that the "conversation should close, and it did. This circum- "stance tended rather to strengthen my mind in favor of "universal and impartial grace, and to induce a more "thorough examination of the Scriptures and the subject. "I had no other book than the Bible, and all my early "education lay like a broad sheet to cover that book from "my vision. But one or two passages were found, and "from them I found my way to others which seemed to "agree with the first, and it was not long before I was "astonished at my ignorance of the Scriptures. The "Bible was no longer the book it had been to me. I "became entirely convinced of the truth of the doctrine "of Universalism."

It was therefore in the town of Westfield, N. Y., that Mr. Ballou came fully to believe in the final salvation of all mankind. We do not mean to be understood that he came at once to the full belief of the doctrine that he afterwards taught, but that he made at this time the earliest and most important advance towards the belief which he subsequently declared, and which has since become the creed of nine-tenths of the Universalist denomination. At this period he believed the doctrine, as he says he preached it not many months afterwards, being the fall before he was twenty-one, "when I began "to speak in public," he says, "believing and preaching "universal salvation, on the Calvinistic principles of "atonement and imputed righteousness." The few Universalists that then existed, having obtained proof, to their satisfaction, that none of the human family would suffer endless punishment, thought they had sufficient cause for rejoicing, and seemed to be content to rest their discoveries there. Further *progress* upon this subject was left for Mr. Ballou to make and promulgate, as by careful and unaided research he should come more fully to understand this most important subject.

"At this time," he writes in his manuscript before us, "fully realizing that the basis of all spiritual knowledge "was the Bible, that blessed book was ever with me, and "not one moment in which I was freed from necessary "labor was occupied save in its perusal. I learned to "love it, to consult its pages with reverence, and prayer-"fully, that I might rightly interpret its true meaning. "I became very familiar with the various important pas-"sages, which frequently gave me great advantage in "controversy, at that time, on points of faith; for it was "the practice of those days to blindly give credence to "such faith as was taught from the pulpit, and, leaving "the minister to reason for the whole congregation, they "themselves rarely consulted the holy text, in a spirit of "inquiry, though they deemed themselves most devout "and reasonable Christians. By individual and careful "explorations, I found my Bible was able to teach me "all I desired to know, and that, at the outset, I had "been miserably deceived in my early impressions of "God's word, by not examining and weighing the subject "matter of divine revelation for myself. But such is "the force of habit that those early impressions were at "first constantly recurring to my mind, and acting as "stumbling blocks in the way of my onward progress."

It is often said that Rev. John Murray was an earlier preacher than the subject of this biography; that he is called the father of Universalism in America; and that Mr. Ballou received his opinions direct from him. But those persons who say thus, or entertain themselves such an idea, are mistaken; indeed, as often as this remark is made, it must always be by those who have thought little, and known less, of the history of Universalism. No one venerates the memory of Rev. John Murray more than the author of this memoir, who, indeed, out of respect for his Christian virtues and excellence, bears his name; but these records must be faithful in all respects. So far from Mr. Ballou's having obtained the opinions which formed the great and distinctive features of his doctrine from Murray, that venerated minister did not believe the creed of Universalists as taught by the subject of this biography, namely: *that the Bible affords no evidence of punishment after death.* Even at the time of Murray's death he held most tenaciously to his early belief; and he ever preached the doctrine on the old Calvinistic principles, between which and the doctrine promulgated by Mr. Ballou there is a wide difference.

While in the town of Westfield, a serious accident occurred to Mr. Ballou, by which he nearly lost his life, being, by some accident, most fearfully scalded. After much suffering from the injury thus received, he perfectly recovered, and soon after returned once more to Richmond, being not yet twenty-one years of age. He now first commenced the study of the English grammar, and attended for a period a school kept in the Quaker meeting-house in his native town.

Mr. Ballou says of this first attendance at school: — "It was a private school, the first one ever opened in the "town, and was supported by a few young people with "whom I united; and here I obtained the first instruction "in English grammar. I now set myself to work in "earnest to obtain learning. I studied night and day, "slept little, and ate little."

At the close of this school, being actuated by an earnest desire to obtain knowledge, and realizing more than ever the immense advantage it bestowed, he determined, for a period, to devote his entire earnings to this end; and, in pursuance of this purpose, he immediately entered the Chesterfield (N. H.) Academy, where, by industry and incessant application, allowing himself but a brief period of time out of the twenty-four hours each day for sleep, in a very short space of time he acquired a good knowledge of the ordinary branches of an English education of those days. The tuition received by Mr. Ballou at this academy was the first worthy of mention that he had ever enjoyed, and was of vastly more importance to him than all he had been taught before, or had himself acquired, as it regarded the rudiments of his native language. Fortunately, the instructors employed were men of sound ability, and consequently from his studies here he realized most important and lasting benefit.

It was not alone the additional theoretical knowledge that he acquired here that we refer to as being of so much advantage to him; it was also that which he saw and realized while at this school. It was the spirit of emulation that was imparted to his disposition by observing others in their progress, as it regarded mental culture, and the acquirement of useful knowledge. His early associations had been among that class who had paid but little attention to mental cultivation. He had enjoyed but a limited opportunity thus far to judge of the incomparable power and importance of education; but now he realized it at a glance, and, determining to let no means within his power remain unexercised in the great purpose of obtaining knowledge and of cultivating intelligence, he gathered his golden harvest from every available source, and stored it in the cells of his brain.

We have heard him refer particularly to this period, as having devoted the hours of the night, as well as those of the day, to enable him to keep pace with more experienced minds and better cultivated intellects, and how apparently gratified the preceptor was to see him able and thorough in his recitations, knowing the strong disadvantages under which he labored. It was his good fortune to make the acquaintance of the teachers on good terms. They seemed prepossessed in his favor, and were exceedingly kind, and even assiduous, in rendering him every needed assistance in his studies. This was of unquestionable advantage to him, and made him, if possible, more attentive than he would otherwise have been as to studies and recitations, that those who had been so kind to him might see that their labor was not thrown away. "I well remember," says Mr. Ballou, "the kindness and "consideration exercised towards me by Professor Logan, "the principal of the academy, who seemed resolved that "my tuition should be of real benefit to me." And thus, indeed, it really proved, forming a foundation on which to rear a structure of useful knowledge, and the better to enable him to arrange and discipline his mind.

On leaving the academy, he obtained a certificate testifying to his sound moral character and ability, which document proved of considerable benefit to him afterwards in obtaining various situations as a teacher. Schools for the young were then kept but a short period at a time in New England, and thus the teacher had often occasion to change the field of his operations. Though thus engaged in the calling of a school-master, his mind, he has frequently told us, was at all times, when not immediately engaged with his pupils, occupied with the one great subject that had already taken such root in his heart, — that of religion. His Bible was ever in his hands or about his person for frequent reference, and his earnest and constant prayer to Heaven was that he might be able rightly to comprehend and analyze its doctrinal teachings.

He found his daily increasing knowledge of the Bible to be of great advantage to him, as he says himself, in argument with others, and also as it regarded properly weighing and arranging in his own mind its various parts, and the bearing each sustained to the other. The early knowledge thus obtained of the holy text never left him, and was retained with most marvellous power and correctness through his entire life.

CHAPTER V.

COMMENCES TO PREACH.

WHILE Mr. Ballou was yet but twenty years of age, he made one or two unsuccessful attempts to preach a regular discourse. That is, he delivered sermons once or twice at the period referred to, before small assemblies of his personal friends and relations. But so far from satisfying himself in relation to his ability for public speaking, he was quite disheartened by the result that attended these his first efforts. Yet, by the constant solicitations of those who were curious to hear him discourse upon the topic of his peculiar views, he continued to speak, despite of the advice of his immediate friends and relations, until he not only soon satisfied himself as to his abilities, but also received the cordial approval of a large number of those who would, at the outset, have discouraged him entirely.

In relation to this period of his life, Mr. Ballou gives us his own words, and to the point. But the reader will please to mark that when he speaks at this period of

Universalists, he refers to those who thus called themselves, but who would, in these days, be more properly denominated Restorationists. The correctness of this statement will at once be seen from the fact of his saying that he met John Murray, etc., at the first *Universalist* convention which he ever attended, while those who are acquainted with that honored teacher's tenets of faith are aware, as we have already stated in these pages, that he lived and died solemnly believing in a state of future suffering or punishment, and more latterly during his life he sustained many controversies with Mr. Ballou on this very subject.

"In September of the year preceding my beginning to "preach," says Mr. Ballou, "I went to Oxford with my "brother David, to attend the first Universalist conven-"tion I had ever met with. Here I saw John Murray "for the first time, and George Richards, and some other "public preachers. The next summer after I was twenty "years old, I labored with my brother on his farm, and "late in the fall made my first attempt to preach. This "was on an evening, and at the house of Deacon Thayer, "in Richmond. Mr. Thayer had been a deacon in the "Baptist church, but had become a Universalist, and "still retained his office with the last-named denomina-"tion. My brother and Rev. Caleb Rich were present "to hear my first attempt to preach; and, according to "what I could learn, they had their doubts whether I "had a talent for such labor, but were not without some "hope. The second time I attempted to preach was in "the town of Brattleboro', Vt., where my brother "preached in the daytime, and I undertook to speak in "the evening, being overpersuaded to do so; but this "attempt was a failure, and I was greatly mortified, and "thought, for a time, that I would not engage in a work "for which I was not competent. However, it was not "long before I became encouraged to try again, after "which I met with no remarkable failure to produce dis- "couragement."

The comparative failure of Mr. Ballou's earliest attempts at public speaking, although soon afterwards followed by complete success, is not at all surprising. It is exceedingly rare to find the first efforts of orators satisfactory to themselves and to their friends. The first attempt of Richard Brinsley Sheridan, the most brilliant orator of his time, — if, perhaps, we except Burke, who was, however, more distinguished by the eloquence of his diction, — was a complete and decided failure. But, knowing himself, he declared emphatically that "it was in him, and must come out." When General, then Colonel, Washington rose to respond to a complimentary address of the legislature of his native colony, he found it impossible to express himself; and the first efforts of the illustrious and lamented Henry Clay gave no promise of his future eminence. It would be easy to multiply illustrations of the fact that it is only step by step that fame and honor are attained. No one springs at a bound to the summit of his reputation and usefulness. It is only shallow pretenders who sometimes shine with a false lustre at the outset of their career, soon to sink into utter insignificance. But the true man, the man of sterling genius and worth, conscious of a high mission, and confiding in Providence for the energy and inspiration necessary to fulfil it, is not daunted with the obstacles that present themselves at the outset of his career. They are regarded as trials and tests as to his adaptedness to the purpose for which he is created. From every rebuff he acquires new strength; he puts forth redoubled energy, until at last he triumphs over every impediment, and stands forth in the full energy of his being.

Had not Mr. Ballou been prompted by such a spirit as this, had he not been possessed of an extraordinary vigor of character, for which he was ever remarkable, he would hardly have persevered in his attempts to preach under these discouraging circumstances. It will be remembered that he did not sit down and compose a discourse which he afterwards read to his audience; this is comparatively an easy task. He spoke extemporaneously then, as he ever did afterwards. In subsequent years he was frequently called upon for manuscript copies of his discourses for publication. But the sermons were not written until after they had been delivered; and it was not his practice to put on paper even the heads of his discourse to take into the desk with him for reference in delivery. Trusting entirely to his powerfully retentive memory, the arrangement of his sermons was as methodical and correct as though penned in the seclusion of his study. We have heard some persons, more nice than wise, speak of his extemporaneous delivery as an objection, and find fault because he did not write his discourses, and thus deliver them from his notes in the pulpit. We have a word to say in relation to this subject, since it has been thus referred to.

To speak extempore and at the same time to speak well and to the purpose, to arrange certain points and arguments mentally with nice precision, so as to deliver them with fluency and effect, must require a strong and healthy intellect, a powerful and original mind. But a man with an ordinary degree of mental cultivation, who cannot write a discourse and read it afterward, must be singularly deficient in his intellectual capacity. It is impossible for an audience to feel so deep an interest in the service as that which is felt in listening to the spontaneous outbreakings of a warm and ardent mind while it is engaged upon the holy theme. The speaker must invariably grow enthusiastic in so glorious a cause as he advocates, and his audience necessarily partake of his feelings. But when there is any particular degree of spirit or animation evinced by one who is reading his discourse *verbatim et literatim*, it is of necessity a preconcerted exhibition, and as such must fail of its effect with the majority. It may be said that no man can lay out so well his matter, nor give so good and sound an argument, spontaneously, as when he commits his ideas to paper. This, as a general thing, must be conceded, for there are comparatively few intellects sufficiently powerful to adopt the opposite course.

The advantages of extemporaneous speaking are doubtless many. It enables the individual to place himself in closer contact with the feelings of his audience, giving him the power to take advantage of any bright thought that unexpected impulse may impart. An experienced commander arranges the general plan of an engagement before going into battle, but he can do no more, for circumstances must guide him in the conflict. He must improve the opportunity to throw forward his forces just at the right moment, not too soon nor too late, as such an indiscretion might change the fortunes of the day, and lose the battle to him who would else have won it. So with the preacher; he must watch the inner man of his hearers, and, as he gains ground in the heart, follow up his influence by well-sustained argument, and strengthen his position by proper means made available at the appropriate moment,— neither too lightly nor yet with too much force, but be guided safely by the strength of the position he already holds in the minds of his audience.

Such things cannot be correctly anticipated, and laid down beforehand, by comma and period, in the study. Mr. Ballou's arguments were arranged with the utmost precision, his reasoning followed in the most logical array, and all the while he was talking to the people in the most unconcerned and familiar manner, as though each respective member of his congregation was sitting by his own fireside and the preacher had happened in. This is the mode of preaching which is effectual, and all the flowers of rhetoric may seek in vain to attain a like influence over the hearts and sympathies of an auditory. The latter mode of preaching may please, but the former will convince; the first will make worshippers, the last admirers. Thinks the reader that the simple fishermen of Galilee — yet the chosen of God — sought by the vain and gaudy ornaments of elegant delivery, and studied eloquence to please the people? No! They preached the holy word in all meekness, striving to exalt not themselves, but rather the name of him who had sent them.

Mr. Ballou says, relative to the period when he commenced to preach: — "Mr. Logan, the preceptor, gave "me a certificate when I left the Chesterfield Academy, "which was sufficient to enable me to get a school in "Bellingham, Mass. Here I taught school during the "other days of the week, and preached on the Sabbath. "When I first engaged in preaching, it was not with the "most distant expectation that I should support myself "by the ministry; but I thought I could keep school "some, and labor some with my hands, and live with but "a little income. From Bellingham I went to the town "of Foster, R. I., where my father formerly lived, and "there my father taught a large school and had good "compensation; and here also on the Sabbath I preached "in the school-house where I taught. From this place "I went to Scituate, in R. I., where I preached and "taught school. My meetings grew very large, and I "was called on to go to different places,— to Smithfield, "Providence, Pawtucket, etc. After I had spent about "two years in keeping school and preaching, I found

"that I had used up all my earnings, had laid up noth-
"ing, except that I had more costly clothing than when
"I first began. And now, at the age of twenty-four, I
"was so much called on to preach that I gave up keeping
"school, and devoted my time to the ministry, receiving
"now and then some compensation for my services."

Mr. Ballou's life as a public minister may be said to have commenced at the age of twenty. From that time, as it became known that he preached the doctrine which was deemed by nearly all to be such a heresy, there were numerous invitations, as he shows us above, pouring in upon him from all quarters, to come and address the people concerning the faith he had espoused. His labors were by no means confined to Rhode Island, but he preached in the neighborhood of Richmond, and in various parts of Vermont and Massachusetts, improving every moment of leisure time in the most careful study of the Scriptures. He no longer preached on the Sabbath only, but also on nearly every consecutive evening of the week. It was easy to gather an audience, anxious and ready to listen to the new and most happy doctrine that the preacher taught, and even at this early period of his ministerial career he began to address those spontaneous mass assemblies that in after years always gathered from all directions to listen to him whenever he appeared. Entirely forgetting himself, and with but one great object in view, that of preaching God's impartial grace, and of convincing all who would listen to him of the glorious truths of Universalism, he counted not the hours of mental labor which now increased upon him, but labored hard and willingly with his hands to clothe himself, receiving but a mere trifle for his professional labors. Pay, at this period, he never demanded, and very rarely expected; he was fully contented with the inward recompense which he realized.

"At this period of my life," says Mr. Ballou, "my "health was very indifferent. I had most of the time a "severe pain in the pit of my stomach, and my appetite "was far from being good, and so debilitated was I in "strength that I have even been obliged to sit while I "preached. It became necessary for me to procure a "vehicle to journey in, being too weak to ride on horse-"back; however, by care and good advice, I gradually "recruited. My travelling for that period was exten-"sive, from Cape Ann east, to the Connecticut River "west, to Richmond north, and New London and Hart-"ford south. All my Sabbaths were employed, and many "lectures were attended during each week. I preached "in meeting-houses when they could be obtained, some-"times in school-houses, sometimes in barns, and not "very seldom in groves and orchards, and often in private "houses.

"To the people, the doctrine I preached was new, and "the opposition lacked not for bitterness; and such was "my condition that I was constantly in conflict, and "never allowed to put off my armor to rest, day or night. "All manner of evil reports concerning me were in-"vented, and the worst of slander circulated, all tending "to make me regardless of what my enemies said. My "answer to all this slander was, while they speak thus "falsely of me, I am in no danger; if I am injured I "shall do that myself."

Theology was a subject of most sombre hue at this period in New England. Calvinism had twined its choking fibres so closely about the sacred tree, that its branches drooped, and its leaves withered in the sunshine of truth. The doctrines taught from the pulpit, while they were listened to as a duty, were yet repulsive to the heart of the hearer, and abhorrent to his very soul. The principle of divine love was clouded wholly from sight by the dark mass of murky error that enshrouded all scripture teachings. The duties of man to his Maker and to himself were held forth under fearful threats, as a penalty for disobedience, but the idea that in the performance of our duty real happiness is alone to be found, while sin most surely brings its own punishment, was never publicly advanced. Sinfulness, aside from the liabilities of eternity, was not held up to be avoided, but rather acknowledged to be pleasant and desirable, while those who trod the paths of righteousness were taught to consider themselves as self-sacrificing martyrs, and told to look for their reward in eternity. It was these obvious inconsistencies that at first challenged the attention of the subject of this memoir. And when he stood up and boldly exposed these palpable errors, when he preached *love* while others preached *wrath* to the people, it is not singular that those who were so diametrically opposed to

6

him in faith should be ready to believe and propagate any stories that might reflect upon his character, and thus detract from his influence as exercised upon those who so eagerly listened to him, and in whose hearts, in the very nature of things, he was sure of an answering and approving sentiment.

It is a matter of regret that Mr. Ballou has left no record of his journeyings and labors during this important period of his clerical career, as such a narrative would have been most deeply interesting to his family and friends. The amount of labor he performed must have been prodigious, and fully accounts for the enfeebled bodily condition to which he alludes. Every fibre of his intellectual frame must have been constantly in a state of extreme tension; for his was not the easy task of preaching on the Sabbath a written discourse which he had taken a whole week to prepare, but, as we have said, he was called upon almost daily to address large audiences and promiscuous assemblies. Nor was his the pleasant duty of the navigator who follows the course of the stream and the tide. He was a pioneer; he preached a new doctrine; and, as he says, "the opposition lacked not for bitterness." It is not surely an exaggeration to declare that Universalism in those days was popularly regarded with as much hostility as Infidelity itself is now. Hence, in addition to the severe fatigue of travel, the necessity of finding constantly new arguments and new illustrations, to sway the minds of constantly changing auditors, he had to battle valiantly, like a soldier of

Christ, against the most vigorous and determined opposition.

In this condition, how mentally and physically trying must have been his incessant labors in his Master's vineyard! Neither by night nor by day could he for a moment lay aside his armor. Standing alone, there was no respite to his exertions. Later in life he beheld a host of able followers ready to relieve him of a portion of his duties. His doctrine was no longer the theme of obloquy and outrage. He outlived calumny and detraction. But it will be seen that even in extreme old age he did not spare himself; he did not suffer sloth to creep upon his spirit, nor rust to gather on his armor. He was still the favored champion of his cause, and ever ready to minister to the spiritual wants of his brethren in the faith.

With the close of his itinerant labors, we now come to another important and interesting epoch in his life.

CHAPTER VI.

BECOMES A SETTLED MINISTER.

THE first place in which Mr. Ballou engaged permanently as a settled minister was in the town of Dana, Mass., in 1794–5. The society here, not feeling able to pay for an engagement which should occupy him the whole time, engaged him for a portion, leaving him to supply the societies in Oxford and Charlton, Mass., also, a portion of the time. Having now become located, and his residence known, large numbers of people from a distance gathered to hear him, not only on the Sabbath, but frequently for several consecutive days of the week besides. Many there were who held his doctrine to be such damning heresy that they counted it a sin even to listen to it; while others of his religious opponents, holding that "there is no error so crooked but it hath in it some lines of truth," came and listened, and the seed not unfrequently fell into good soil, bringing forth a hundred fold.

"Often was I greeted at this time," says Mr. Ballou, "by people who would say, 'Sir, I heard you preach

"a sermon. a few weeks since, from such a text,' nam-
"ing it, 'and I have been uneasy and anxious in my
"mind ever since. If your doctrine is true, I must
"understand and believe it. But, alas! I fear it is too good
"to be true; it is so different from what I have been
"brought up to believe that I cannot divest my mind of
"early prejudices sufficiently to receive it, though Heaven
"knows how gladly I could do so.' Then the individual
"would quote some passages of scripture which seemed to
"him to be insuperable objections to the doctrine I pro-
"fessed, and I would do all in my power to explain these
"passages to his mind, in the way I had myself already
"learned to interpret them. Usually, with the blessing
"of Divine Providence, I was successful, at least in a
"large degree, and on the following Sabbath I was pretty
"sure to find the honest seeker after truth among my
"congregation, and the following Sabbath he would be
"there again, attentively listening to the word, until,
"finally, he came forth and openly espoused the blessed
"doctrine of God's impartial grace. Thus encouraged
"with the growth of the seed that I strewed by the way-
"side, my task was a grateful one to my soul, and I was
"constantly gladdened by the visible fruits of my efforts
"in disenthralling men's minds of the dogmas and
"blind creeds that early prejudice and the schools had
"inculcated."

Let it be borne in mind that at this period he was preaching Universalism on the principle of the final restoration of the whole human family, not having satisfied himself yet that there would be no punishment in a future state of existence, or, indeed, ever thought upon this subject to any great extent. Owing to the very trifling amount of his remuneration from the society in Dana, while he resided there, besides tilling a small portion of land, he was obliged to keep school during the week, and this engagement was often broken into for lecture purposes. His keeping and teaching school was a benefit to him beyond the pecuniary consideration he received, inasmuch as it familiarized him with many branches of an English education which he would perhaps otherwise never have acquired, or at least not nearly so thoroughly as he did by this means.

Uninfluenced by the sneers of his opposers, and the poor remuneration he received for the preaching of his belief, he never for one moment wavered in a steadfast purpose, even at this early period, to preach Christ and him crucified, and the unsearchable riches of God's goodness. In this connection we are reminded of the remarks of the editor of the New Covenant, Chicago, Ill., who, in his obituary notice of the decease of Mr. Ballou, says: —

"But now we are called to mourn the departure of "one who, when our cause had scarcely a name to "live, — when it was the subject of the sneer of the "bigot, as well as of the profane curse of the irreligious, "and even its warmest friends scarcely dared to hope for "its resurrection to honor and respect, — bent the energy "of a giant mind to a life-long defence and promulgation "of the truth, — by his unanswerable arguments turned "the sneer of bigotry into a smile of hope, and the "curses of the profane into blessings, — of one who has "done more in this age for the liberalizing of religious "sentiment than all his contemporaries combined. "Strong in the faith he preached, and steadfastly believ-"ing it must at last triumph, from early youth to "mature old age he has kept on his armor and fought "the good fight of faith, and death even found him at his "post as a faithful sentinel, and in the midnight hour he "could answer, 'All is well!'"

At the age of twenty-five, and while resident in the town of Dana, he became acquainted with the family of Stephen Washburn, in the town of Williamsburg, Mass., and, after an intimate acquaintance of about a year, he married their youngest daughter, Ruth Washburn, who was some eight years younger than himself. His wife, like her husband, had been brought up to habits of industry and economy; she proved a kind, constant, and devoted help-mate through his entire life, sharing with him every joy and every burthen, and, by the influence of a naturally strong and well balanced mind, a cheerful and gentle disposition, exercising a most goodly influence upon his life and labors. She became the careful and prudent mother of a large family, nine of whom lived to rear families themselves during the life of their parents. Through their whole lives there was a remarkable oneness of feeling, and a depth of affection evinced by each for the other, that years served only to increase, and old age to cement the more closely. But of this matter we may yet speak more fully.

Mr. Ballou resided in the town of Dana for about seven years, devoting every spare hour to careful study of the Scriptures, systematizing his time by a careful division of the hours of the day, and permitting himself but a very brief portion of time for sleep.

When we say that he devoted his time so assiduously to study, we do not mean that he occupied himself in the perusal of books alone. He *thought* much, communed with himself alone, and even at that period accustomed himself to a degree of inward or mental communion with himself, that would seem to exclude the world about him, for the time being, from his sense of seeing or hearing. This was more observable in later years, when he often sat long in his study thus, sometimes with his eyes closed, sometimes with their pupils directed to the floor or the ceiling of the room, his lips moving, and at last, having seemingly weighed well some important matter, he would rouse again as if from a trance, and look about him with apparent satisfaction at the result he seemed to have accomplished. Sometimes these moments were followed by the use of the pen for records in his note-book of texts and sermon heads, sometimes by a reference to the Scriptures, and sometimes by a walk in the open air; then his lips would be seen to move, and he would be quite oblivious to all outward circumstances. He studied thus, carefully and deeply. At times he would walk in the fields or the woods while thus occupied; and the family never disturbed him by any remarks, or by calling his attention, while he was thus mentally absorbed. In another part of this biography, reference will be found concerning this peculiarity, as exhibited at a later period of his life, and observed by one who was an inmate of his family, and a student of divinity with him. The family were accustomed to his mood in these matters, but it usually affected a stranger, or one not familiar with him, in quite an impressive and solemn manner; it seemed so much as though he was communing with unseen spirits, and a power that was invisible to those about him or to himself, save through the powers of his mental vision.

It would seem that the little bodily rest which he allowed himself at this period must have induced physical debility; and yet it did not appear to do so. In travelling, a large portion of his short journeyings were made in the evening; sometimes at midnight even, and often before the break of day, in order to fulfil necessary appointments without encroaching upon his arrangements at home. When stopping for his horse to take rest and food, himself much fatigued, he would take his watch from his pocket, and, laying it upon a table near some place where he could find a recumbent position, he would carefully mark the time, and say distinctly to himself, "I "will sleep now for just one hour, when I must awake and "go on." Singular as this may seem, he has told us that he never failed to awake at the expiration of the hour, and, much refreshed, he would mount his horse and press on to fill some professional engagement, perhaps twenty or thirty miles from the stopping-place. At other times, while his horse was eating, he would deliver a sermon, and, having completed it, would, without stopping for any physical refreshment for himself, start off once more on his mission.

"In searching the Scriptures," he says, "to enable "myself to preach as the divine oracles taught, I became "satisfied that those who were then called Universalists "had founded their doctrine on wrong principles, as well "as other denominations. The doctrine of man's native "depravity, of original sin, of the deserts of eternal "misery, of the vicarious sufferings of Christ, by which "he endured, in man's stead, the divine penalty of God's "law, whereby man could escape the punishment due to "his sins, was believed by those who called themselves "Universalists, as well as by Calvinists: also, the doc-"trine of the Trinity, holding that Christ is equal to "God, or, in other words, is God, being the second per-"son in the holy Trinity. All these notions, as it "appeared to me, were essential errors, constituting a "mass of confusion. I soon renounced all these views, "and preached only God, and one mediator between God "and men, the man Christ Jesus. All my brethren "in the ministry, and all our friends, stood on the old "platform, and I found that I had to contend with Uni-"versalists as well as with partialists. But I went to "my work in earnest, laboring, with all my skill and "with all my limited talents, to convince my brethren in "the ministry, and all who heard me preach, that the "doctrines of the Trinity, of depravity, of eternal pen-"alty, etc., were neither the doctrines of the Scriptures "nor of reason. The opposition to my sentiments fast "gave way among Universalists, though even among "them I met with as bitter opposition, in some instances, "as from other denominations. The first time I preached "in Bro. Murray's church, in Boston, was during his "absence in Philadelphia, and I then came out fully with "my Unitarian views, which produced great disturbance. "Some were violent in their opposition, while others, and "not a few, fell in with my manner of explaining the "Scriptures. I was then twenty-eight years of age."

Mr. Ballou says that his declaring his views on this occasion was the cause of "great disturbance." This disturbance was so earnest that some few of the audience, more bitter than the rest, rose in their seats and declared that the sentiments which had been uttered were not in accordance with Mr. Murray's views, etc. Whereupon Mr. Ballou simply informed them that he had been invited, without solicitation on his own part, to preach in that desk; that he came there to preach no one's convictions but his own; that he never had consulted, and never should consult, the taste of his audience as to the doctrine he preached to them; but that he should proclaim the truth, as, by the help of Heaven, he had been enabled to learn it from the Bible, and the truth only!

On the subsequent day Mr. Ballou was formally waited upon by a committee from the Society, who thanked him for the discourse, and a majority coincided also in his peculiar views.

The conclusions as to doctrine at which he arrived

were based upon severe study and profound reflection; and when we consider the age at which he had elaborated and enunciated a creed of such vast importance, a creed so entirely in advance of his contemporaries, we cannot fail to be most forcibly impressed with the extraordinary originality and remarkable precocity of his intellect. Such early vigor and maturity would have been astonishing in one who had enjoyed all the advantages of early training, all the aids afforded by the best theological institutions and instructors; but in one who had passed through so many hardships, overcome so many difficulties, and was so emphatically self-taught and self-made, they can only be regarded as evidences of the highest genius, and the immediate favorable interposition of Divine Providence.

His unshaken faith and inflexibility of conviction are evinced by the fact that he stood firm, not only against the opposing sects, but against the disciples of the improved doctrine which he first preached. It requires not a little energy to confront declared foes; but to contend with friends, to risk the loss of their favor and support, is a trial which few have the boldness to sustain. But the subject of this biography knew not what temporizing meant; his whole life, his whole intellect, all his energies, were devoted to the discovery of truth, and the enunciation of the truth he discovered. Had he stood entirely alone, without one single friend, without one single proselyte, he would have spoken as he did, boldly, earnestly, candidly, the apostle and defender of his faith.

The inspiration of his mission was from on high; neither applause nor opposition changed his views, or in the least affected his serene and constant equanimity.

The patient and unruffled manner in which he always held a controversy has been often remarked of him; himself the mark for all manner of personalities and low reflections, he never descended to such a mode of warfare, being fully content in the justice and power of his cause, and considering that as more than equal to low cunning, or, indeed, any trickery of those who opposed him so bitterly. Flattery would have been equally powerless in effect upon him, for he looked not to man for approval, but to his own conscience and his God. Love of applause is a most natural trait in our dispositions. The hero of a hundred battles feels his heart glow afresh at the grateful meed of praise; the politician reads the glowing accounts of his own eloquence with secret gratification; and who is there so humble that is not susceptible of flattery, who so high in worldly honors that they do not acknowledge the potency of applause? And yet we shall be sustained in the remark by all who knew the subject of these memoirs intimately, when we say, that neither ridicule nor flattery moved him in the least, the single purpose of his life being his Master's business; and he ever acknowledged himself, that he really endeavored to be (and beyond which he aspired not) the servant of all men. Few persons, with his power over the masses, and holding the position that was universally accorded to him, but that would have often brought themselves as *individuals*, with their *personal* interests and desires, before the public; self-aggrandizement will almost always discover itself more or less in prominent public men. But he knew no such incentive; he had one grand object in view, one which he never lost sight of, and which was more than paramount to everything else combined; — it was to inculcate the religion of God's impartial goodness and eternal grace.

In the thirtieth year of his age, he was induced to accept of the invitation of the towns of Woodstock, Hartland, Bethel, and Barnard, Vt., making the latter place his home. While resident here he devoted himself to ardent and constant study, and in the year 1804 produced his "*Notes on the Parables*," one of the most popular and useful books, even to the present day, in the Universalist library. It has passed through numerous large editions, and a new one, at this present writing, is about to be put to press. It is a book containing nearly the same amount of matter as the present memoir in the reader's hand. This book was written and published at a time when Mr. Ballou's health was really suffering from the effects of his unremitting labors, both mental and physical.

"My health," he says, "in those years which I "passed in Vermont, was generally very good. I had "some time, previous to removing from Dana, been "gaining health and growing more corpulent, so that my "uniform weight for several years was about two hun-"dred pounds." But at the time when he wrote the

"Notes," for a considerable period he had been overtasked, and so much so as to materially affect his health. The roads about the country were of a very poor character, and being unable to use a vehicle on many of the routes over which he passed, he was frequently obliged to accomplish his journeys on horseback, which was a severe draft upon his strength. In his first preface to the edition of Notes on the Parables, the author thus refers to the subject of the book:—

"In my travels through the country in discharge of "duties enjoined by the ministry of the Saviour of sinners, I have met with more opposition to the gospel "preached to Abraham from false notions of the parables "of the New Testament, than from any other source. "Often, after travelling many miles and preaching *several* sermons in a day, I have found it necessary to "explain various parables to some inquiring hearer, when "my strength seemed almost exhausted. At such times "I have thought a volume, such as the reader has in "hand, might save me much labor, and I have often "said to myself, If God will give me a few weeks' leisure, "I will, with his assistance, employ them in writing "'Notes on the Parables.' This favor has at length "been granted, though it was by depriving me of that "degree of health that was necessary to the performance "of the journeys which I had already appointed, yet "preserving so much as to render me composed in my "study."

This is undoubtedly one of the most valuable books in

the Universalist library; particularly valuable from the fact of its treating, in the clearest and most forcible manner, upon those peculiar doctrinal points which, more than all others, have been the theme of contention among professed Christians. At the time when Mr. Ballou published this work, his mind was not fully made up as to the subject of punishment after death; but the matter had already resolved itself to this in his mind; that if any suffer in the future state it would be because they would be sinful there. It was not long subsequent, however, that he came to the full knowledge and conviction that the doctrine of future punishment was nowhere taught in the Bible, and this creed he thenceforth ever most assiduously preached on all occasions.

In his preface to the fifth edition the author says: — "On account of so many of the parables being used by "believers in endless punishment to support and enforce "that sentiment, the author of the Notes was induced to "study them with special reference to the question "whether they might not, with more propriety, be ap-"plied in a different manner. Of this fact he became "fully satisfied; even as much so as he is now. But, "though he entertained no scruples on that point, he "was not so happy as to be fully satisfied, in every case, "as to the true intent of the parable. In this situation "he cautiously endeavored not to apply any parable to a "subject which was not found to be embraced in the sys-"tem of truth which the Scriptures clearly and evidently "support. Little harm is done by applying a parable to "a subject to which it was not intended by the author to "apply, provided the subject to which it is misapplied be "a truth clearly supported by either Scripture or man's "experience; but to misconstrue any passage of the "divine testimony so as to give support to what is not "true, is unquestionably no small damage; and if the "error be of magnitude, whereby our Heavenly Father is "represented in an unlovely character, or our confidence "in his goodness diminished, such misconstruction is not "only a reprehensible violence on the Scriptures, but a "dishonor to their divine Author. I am persuaded that "a just knowledge of the parables is almost indispens-"ably necessary to a knowledge of the doctrine preached "by Christ, as much of his public communication was in "this way. It is in the parables of Christ that we learn "the nature of the two dispensations or covenants; the "situation of man by reason of sin; the character of the "Saviour as the seeker and savior of that which was lost; "the power of the gospel as a sovereign remedy for the "moral maladies of man, and its divine efficacy in recon-"ciling and assimilating the sinner to God. It is by the "parables that we learn the unprofitableness of legal "righteousness in point of justification to eternal life; "the absolute necessity of becoming new creatures, in "order to enter the kingdom of God; the true character "of the Saviour as the Lord our Righteousness, and his "divine power to make all things new."

The "*Notes on the Parables*" have unquestionably led thousands of minds to valuable improvement in the knowledge of the Scriptures, and converted many a longing soul to the precious and joyful belief of universal salvation. At the time when these Notes were written, the light which has now become so general and evident to nearly every candid seeker after truth,— the true light of the gospel of Christ,— seemed to be but just dawning; the warm and genial sun of the true faith but faintly tinged the east; but ere long it rose steadily and majestically, until it radiated its noonday warmth, in meridian splendor and beauty. We should remember that the author of the "Notes" enjoyed the use of no other book than the Bible in forming and promulgating his own opinions, which have since become the general belief of the Universalist order. The book is especially lucid and original in its style, and bears in its pages constant evidence of deep and careful research.

In an excellent book lately issued by the publisher of this biography, entitled a Memoir of Rev. S. R. Smith, written by Rev. Thomas J. Sawyer, D. D., of Clinton, N. Y., we find the following incident related, referring to this period of Mr. Ballou's life. It is from the pen of the subject of the memoir, Rev. Stephen R. Smith, concerning whose Christian excellence too much cannot be said.

"By what means the intelligence that Hosea Ballou "would preach on the following Sunday, in a place fifteen "miles distant, could have been conveyed to a very young "man, who did not then know a single Universalist in "the world, is not remembered. He went, however, and "heard a discourse in the morning, from Zech. 6: 13; "and, for the first time in his life, felt that he had "listened to a sermon that neither involved an absurdity "nor a contradiction. The congregation was not large, "and occupied a school-house in the present city of "Utica, then a meagre and muddy village. A larger "congregation was anticipated in the afternoon, and "arrangements were made for the service in the open air, "under some trees, on the bank of the Mohawk river. "There, in due time, a large auditory assembled, and "listened to one of Mr. Ballou's best discourses, from "Deut. 33: part of the 16th with the 17th verse. It "was a glorious day, early in June. The silence of "Sunday was around us; the bright blue heavens above "us, partly veiled by the branches of a few scattering "oaks; the clear, quiet river at our side; the ruddy and "healthy preacher, in all the vigor of manhood, before "us, and pleading the cause of God and humanity with "a group of most attentive hearers. Such a scene is not "to be forgotten; and, altogether, it was one, in every "respect, calculated to make the most lasting impression. "And such certainly were its effects upon the mind of the "writer. For, while it left him without any pretension "to the knowledge or belief of Universalism, as a system "of religious truth, it certainly satisfied him that it was "consistent with itself, and with all that we see and know "of the Deity and his moral government. It is scarcely "to be doubted that similar impressions were made on "many persons in that congregation."

While resident in Barnard, he wrote also his "*Treatise on Atonement*." This book, though written so many years since, is still as popular as when first issued from the press, and has passed, like the "Notes," through several large editions. It is contained in a volume of between two and three hundred pages, and is justly esteemed as one of the soundest productions that has ever emanated from the author's pen, and we may, perhaps, add without apparent arrogance, one of the most thoroughly philosophical and argumentative works of the age. In the Modern History of Universalism, the author, in speaking of the change of opinion generally from the ideas preached by John Murray, Winchester, and other early ministers, says that the belief in the Trinity, atonement, and kindred notions, was discarded through the influence of this book.

"The labors of Hosea Ballou, of this city," says the author, "may be regarded as one of the principal means "of the change. In the '*Treatise on Atonement*,' he "has treated the subject at length, maintaining the sub- "ordination of the Son to the Father, the eternal and "impartial love of God to all creatures, and holding forth "the death of Christ not as the cause, but as the effect "of this eternal principle of the divine nature. The "very wide circulation of this work evinces the high "estimation in which it has been held by the American "Universalists."

We subjoin also the following notice of the "Treatise," because we think it a most truthful critique relative to the book, which we desire to have the readers of this biography to understand. In this review, which appeared not long since in the Evangelical Magazine, the editor says:—

"The decided manner in which the doctrine of vica-
"rious atonement is rejected, the prominence given to
"the belief that Jesus was a dependent being, dependent
"like ourselves on a common Father and God, and that
"he was sent to preach the truth and illustrate its
"requirements, and by his exclusive influence to recon-
"cile man to his Maker, were subjects so new, so start-
"ling, that for a time the work appears not to have been
"very well received. But the important object was
"attained. The public attention, and especially that of
"Universalists, was drawn to the consideration of these
"fundamental and momentous doctrines. The author's
"views were very generally adopted by the order, and
"the book obtained unbounded popularity. It deserves
"this distinction, for it doubtless wrought the great revolu-
"tion that transformed Universalism from the Trinitarian
"hypothesis, with all its concomitants, into the simple
"and intelligible system formed in the doctrine of the
"indivisible oneness of God. It is, perhaps, impossible
"to estimate the influence which this work has had upon
"the so-called Unitarian controversy in New England.
"But this much is quite certain, the 'Treatise' was
"one of the earliest publications that openly and dis-
"tinctly rejected the doctrine of the Trinity, and man-
"fully met the prevailing prejudices respecting that

"subject. But aside from these matters, there is not "another book in the country, on the same subject, that "has been read by half the number of persons, or wrought "conviction of the truth of the doctrine of the Divine "unity in one half so many minds, as this '*Treatise on* "*Atonement.*'"

These notices, as we have just intimated, are introduced here to give the reader, who may not be otherwise acquainted with the "Treatise," a correct and clear idea of the work. Though among the earliest of Mr. Ballou's publications, this book is far from being deficient in any point, either as to sound logical reasoning, or in force and earnestness of style. Simple, yet profound, it is within the capacity of the humblest to comprehend and fully understand, while it cannot fail to challenge the admiration of the scholar and philosopher. It is written in the plain, straightforward manner which so distinguished his after productions, and which never failed to carry conviction with it. "The 'Treatise' has been pronounced by "one of the strongest minds of the age," says the publisher of the sixth edition, "to be one of the soundest "arguments in the English language." Were the author's reputation to rest solely upon this work, we should feel satisfied at the manner in which his memory must be handed down to posterity.

In his preface to the first edition of the book, he says: —"Many circumstances might be mentioned, which, in "their associations, have induced me to write and pub-"lish the following treatise; but I can say with pro-

"priety, that the principal object was that in which I "always find the greatest happiness, namely, to do what "I find most necessary in order to render myself useful "to mankind."

At the time of the publication of this "Treatise," Mr. Ballou had by no means arrived at such a degree of understanding and belief upon the subject of the Scriptures as was the case in after years, and, with wise forethought, he thus speaks his mind in the preface to the first edition: —

"I have often been solicited to write and publish my "general views on the gospel, but have commonly "observed to my friends that it might be attended with "disagreeable consequences, as it is impossible to deter- "mine whether the ideas we entertain at the present time "are agreeable to those which we shall be under the "necessity of adopting after we have had more experi- "ence; and knowing, to my satisfaction, that authors are "very apt to feel such an attachment to sentiments which "have been openly avowed to the world, that their pre- "judice frequently obstructs their further acquisition in "the knowledge of the truth, and even in cases of con- "viction their own self-importance will keep them from "acknowledging their mistake."

Though he was thus cautious (and what judgment, prudence, and cool reasoning are evinced in this paragraph), the only change that experience did bring about, in the author's mind, was, that he became even more fully convinced, as the experience of years ripened the harvest of his wisdom, of the truths of his former belief, and made still further *progress* (a word that he loved and lived up to), in addition to certain points that are but lightly touched upon in the work.

The following letter, relating to this and other works, was elicited by the presentation to Mr. Ballou of a set, in a new and uniform edition with some of his subsequent publications; the constant call for these books, even after several large editions had been exhausted, and a long period of years had elapsed since their first being issued, requiring this fresh publication of them. Mr. Ballou having parted with the copyright at the time of publication, they were of course in the hands of the trade. This letter is introduced here as illustrative of the humble estimate he put upon his own important labors and discoveries, and is also in style very like him. It bears date 1844, and was written, consequently, when he was seventy-three years of age. It was addressed to the editor of the Trumpet, and appeared in the editorial columns of that paper.

"BR. WHITTEMORE: Please permit me to acknowl-"edge with gratitude a favor I have received from Br. "Abel Tompkins, consisting of four volumes of my "writings: my Notes on the Parables of the New Tes-"tament; my Treatise on Atonement; my course of "Lecture Sermons, and my Select Sermons. It gives "me much pleasure to learn that these works have been "so favorably regarded by the denomination with which

"I have had the happiness to hold an unbroken and un-"interrupted connection for more than half a century, as "to warrant this new edition. The improved style in 'which these volumes now appear cannot fail to give "entire satisfaction to all who have a good taste, and will "doubtless facilitate their sale.

"When, more than forty years ago, I wrote my "'Notes' and 'Treatise,' I had never seen any work in "defence of the doctrine of the Divine unity, and the "dependency of the Son upon the Father. When this "circumstance is duly considered, the reader will be "satisfied that the writer must have exerted the limited "powers of his mind to their utmost capacity. This is "all the credit he claims.

"HOSEA BALLOU."

Mr. Ballou has long been allowed the credit, which is also most justly due to him, of having been the first Unitarian writer in this country; for, as he says above, he had never seen any book in defence of the doctrine of the Divine unity when he wrote in favor of those principles in the works referred to. Another evidence of the fact is, that Mr. Ballou's sentiments at that time were considered most strange and novel by all.

"In this Treatise," says Rev. Thomas Whittemore, "Mr. Ballou took the ground that God was never un-"reconciled to man; that man was the party who needed "reconciliation, for God is love from eternity to eternity, "and that God's love to sinners was the cause of Christ's

8

"being sent by the Father to redeem them. He held "that Christ was not God himself, but the Son of God; "a distinct being from the Father, — a *created* being; — "a doctrine which he had believed and preached for ten "years, having commenced to preach it as early as 1795. "He must therefore be regarded as the earliest defender "of Unitarianism the country has produced."

Mr. Ballou says, relative to the doctrine of the Trinity: —"I had preached but a short time before my mind was "entirely freed from all the perplexities of the doctrine "of the Trinity, and the common notion of atone- "ment. But in making these advances, as I am disposed "to call them, I had the assistance of no author or "writer. As fast as these old doctrines were, by any "means, rendered the subject of inquiry in my mind, "they became exploded. But it would be difficult for "me now to recall the particular incidents which sug "gested queries in my mind respecting them."

The reader will at once be prepared to admit that Mr. Ballou must have expended much time and labor in the research and study of the Scriptures, necessary to enable him to write and publish these works, in a cause, and upon a theme, wherein he was a pioneer. He steered his barque into new waters, and was obliged himself to stand ever with the "lead" in his hand, to ascertain the true soundings, and keep thus in the narrow channel of truth. Concerning this matter, he has said, in an article furnished for a work entitled "Modern History of Universalism:" —

"I never read anything on the doctrine of universal "salvation before I believed it, the Bible excepted; nor "did I know, that I can now recollect, that there was "anything published in its vindication in the world. Nor "had I ever heard a sermon on the subject, except in "boyhood I once heard Brother Rich, but concerning "that sermon I realized nothing."

In speaking of his advance towards the knowledge of the truth, after his conversion, he says, in a published article: —

"It may be proper for me to state one circumstance "which had no small tendency to bring me over to the "ground on which I have for so many years felt estab- "lished. It was by reading some deistical writings. By "this means I was led to see that it was utterly impos- "sible to maintain Christianity as it had been generally "believed in the church. This led me of course to "examine the Scriptures, that I might determine the "question, whether they did really teach that Jesus "Christ died to reconcile an unchangeable God to his "own children. You cannot suppose I was long in find- "ing that, so far from teaching such absurdities, the "Scriptures teach that 'God was in Christ, reconciling "the world to himself.' The question concerning the "Trinity was by the same means as speedily settled."

It is an interesting and curious fact that he should have been aided, as it were, by the darkness of error to find the light of truth. The obvious inconsistency in his former belief, made evident by the deist, did not win him to the faith of the latter, but rather led him to investigate for himself, and to find a religion more congenial with the native promptings of his own heart and the evidences of the Bible. His was an exploring mind; he was not content to receive this faith, or that position, because others believed it, or because it had remained so long the unchallenged and unquestioned creed of the church. He must look into the matter and understand for himself, and make all parts of a doctrine to harmonize with each other, before he could reconcile it with his own reason and convictions.

This was a trait of character not alone observable in him as it related to the subject of religion; he applied the same rule to the affairs of every-day life, to political economy and business arrangements. He was always open to conviction, to reason and evidence, but could never embrace blindly any proposition whatever. Because the political party which the nearest assimilated to his views of the proper mode of government adopted this or that policy, he did not by any means consider it his duty to coincide with them, against his sober conviction, and he never did so; on the contrary, as often criticising the measures of one political party as another, and frequently finding much excellence, and principles worthy of commendation in the national policy of both. For this reason he could not be a politician, had he experienced an inclination that way. He was too honest.

CHAPTER VII.

REMOVES TO PORTSMOUTH, N. H.

AFTER the expiration of a period of six years from the time of his first settlement in Barnard, Vt., and during which season he enjoyed an uninterrupted flow of kindness and good fellowship with the societies of his charge, he accepted the invitation of the society of Portsmouth, N. H., to become their pastor, and to devote his whole time to the good of the cause in that place. He had formed within the circle of his professional labors in Vermont a host of kind and warm-hearted friends, and it was a considerable period after the proposition had been made to him, before he could make up his mind to accept it. He did so, at last, however, influenced by several reasons.

First, the large field over which he was obliged to travel, while settled in Barnard, involved not only much physical labor and expense, but also the loss of a large amount of time, that might be devoted to more profitable pursuit. Then the pecuniary emolument offered him at

Portsmouth was considerably larger than he had yet received, and his now growing family rendered such a fact to be a necessary consideration. And yet, let it not be supposed that there was any mercenary trait in his character; such was as foreign to his nature as was deceit, or guile of any sort, as the progress of this biography will show. He realized, also, that, while such a change would diminish his physical labors, it would doubtless enlarge the sphere of his usefulness, bringing him in contact with larger audiences and more miscellaneous assemblages than usually gathered to listen to his public communications in a less thickly settled district.

He says, in this connection: — "I have found through-"out my life, that whatever place I have long tarried in, "I have become greatly attached to, and to the people "with whom I associated. This was peculiarly the case "in Barnard, and among the neighboring societies, with "whom I was, for a period of six years, most agreeably, "and I trust profitably associated. I long weighed the "proposal from my friends in Portsmouth in my mind, "before I could consent to break up a connection which "had afforded me so much real satisfaction. But might "I not render myself more useful by accepting this call? "Was it not the design of my Master to enlarge my "sphere of usefulness in his service? These things I "weighed carefully in my mind, and prayed for counsel "and power to enable me to judge of my duty aright; "until, finally, believing it to be my duty, I accepted the "call of my brethren in New Hampshire, and accord-"ingly removed to Portsmouth."

Duly weighing these matters, he deemed it his duty, as he says, to bid his brethren in Vermont farewell, and he removed to Portsmouth in the year 1809, being in the thirty-eight year of his age. Here he was installed, Nov. 8, the sermon on the occasion being preached by Rev. Edward Turner, then of Salem. Though the pecuniary emolument, before referred to, was somewhat more than he had formerly received, yet it required an exercise of the utmost frugality and prudence to enable him to support his family comfortably. Indeed, this could not be done upon his salary as pastor of the Universalist Society alone, and therefore, in addition to his other numerous and arduous duties, he again taught school for a considerable period, while resident in this place, assisted by Hosea Ballou, 2d, now Dr. H. Ballou, of Medford. If it be true, as Lord Bacon has said, that reading makes a *full* man, conversation a *ready* man, and writing an *exact* man, then teaching certainly embraces the advantages to be derived from all three; and this Mr. Ballou found to be the case, as he has often said.

While resident in Portsmouth, notwithstanding the labors of the week, the necessary preparation for the Sabbath, and the earnest efforts that were required of him upon that sacred day, still he pursued a course of religious investigations into the subject of the holy text, that we are at a loss to know when he found time to consummate. It was at this period that he wrote his "Candid Review," in reply to a work by Rev. Isaac Robinson, A. M., upon some important doctrinal points. It is contained in one volume of two hundred pages, and adduces some of the strongest arguments in favor of impartial and universal grace that have ever been published, either by himself or others. This book was exceedingly popular at the time of its first appearance, and created not a little excitement among religious controversialists in New Hampshire, and, indeed, throughout the New England States.

He also wrote, while resident in Portsmouth, a series of letters addressed to the Rev. Joseph Buckminster, upon important doctrinal subjects, which was published in one volume. A Controversy with Rev. Mr. Walton was written and published here, besides one or two minor works, including a school catechism, for a long period of years in general use among the denomination. In addition to the labor necessary to produce these in connection with his regular professional duties, he was also associate editor of a religious quarterly, entitled the "Gospel Visitant," in which, however, he had no further interest than his editorial connection. His contributions to this work were copious, and marked by the same profound reasoning capacity and lucid style that have characterized every work he has produced. It was while engaged in editing this publication that he came to the full belief that there was no punishment after death, and ever after, he preached the doctrine of universal salvation in this spirit, and labored strenuously in its defence and support.

Relative to this subject Mr. Ballou has written: — "I

"cannot say that I was fully satisfied that the Bible "taught no punishment after death, until I obtained this "satisfaction by attending to the subject with Bro. "Edward Turner, respecting the doctrine of the Scrip- "tures upon this question. We agreed to do the best "we could, he in favor of future punishment, and I on "the contrary. Our investigations were published in a "periodical called the 'Gospel Visitant.' While attend- "ing to this correspondence, I became entirely satisfied "that the Scriptures begin and end the history of sin in "flesh and blood, and that beyond this mortal existence "the Bible teaches us no other sentient state but that "which is called by the blessed name of life and immor- "tality."

In another article relative to the same subject he says: — "The doctrine of punishment after death has, by many "able writers, been contended for; some of whom have "argued such punishment to be endless, and others lim- "ited. But it appears to me that they have taken wrong "ground who have endeavored to support the latter, as "well as those who have labored to prove the former. "They have both put great dependence upon certain "figurative and parabolical expressions, or passages of "Scripture, which they *explain* so as to cause them to "allude to such an event. It appears to me that they "have not sufficiently attended to the nature of sin, so as "to learn its punishment to be produced from a law of "*necessity*, and not a law of *penalty*. Had they seen "this, they would also have seen that a perpetuity of "punishment must be connected with an equal continu-"ance of sin, on the same principle that an effect is "dependent upon its cause."

This brief paragraph will show the reader how Mr. Ballou was accustomed to argue upon this subject, of such vital importance to all, and which is a question still in the minds of many of our Universalist brethren, both ministry and laity.

At the expiration of six years from the date of his settlement in Portsmouth, and during which time his association with the people of his charge, and others in that place, had been not only of the most pleasant and agreeable character, but also highly profitable as it regarded their mutual spiritual advancement, up to the period of the war with Great Britain, he made his arrangements to leave Portsmouth, having received an invitation from the Universalist Society in Salem, Mass., to settle in that town, and to devote his professional services to their especial good. Mr. Ballou says of his connection with the society in Portsmouth:—

"My connection with the people of Portsmouth was "very cordial and happy, until that gloomy war-cloud "which brought on a conflict with England came over "the land. The anti-war party was numerous, and very "influential; and, as I could not consent that my country "was in the wrong, a bitter spirit became manifested "towards me, which so operated towards the close of the "war, that I became satisfied it was my duty to stay in "that place no longer; and as the society in Salem was "without a pastor, I received an invitation, which I "accepted, to remove to that delightful place."

This was by no means a solitary instance or evidence of the warm patriotic fire that ever burned brightly in his bosom. He was ardently attached to the republican principles of our government, and never failed, on every suitable occasion, to evince the most earnest attachment for his country. Though a constant and untiring student of divinity, yet he was by no means a novice in political economy; the basis of our institutions, and their true spirit as set forth by the constitution, the influences and natural results of our style of government, and the political soundness of the nation, were themes on which he was more than well informed, but yet he always carefully avoided mingling in party politics.

He removed to Salem in the month of June, 1815, where he found many cordial and true friends, whose memory and companionship he cherished to the close of life. While resident here he wrote a pamphlet in reply to one by John Kelley, A. M., entitled "Solemn and Important Reasons against becoming a Universalist." This review was comprised in a pamphlet of eighty pages, and is a strong and powerful argument in favor of the principles which the author believed, and which he advocated with such successful zeal. These minor publications of Mr. Ballou's, when now referred to, convey but a faint idea of the interest which they then produced. Their extended and immediate influence was evident. Vast numbers were sold; some zealous people, rejoicing at the joy unspeakable to which they had themselves attained through the author's writings and public communications from the pulpit, purchased them by wholesale, and distributed them gratis, far and near. His hearers, too, largely increased in numbers, and he was rewarded for his labors by witnessing the rich harvest that he was reaping in his Master's vineyard, and the number of souls he was leading in the paths of truth.

While resident in Salem, he also wrote a series of letters in reply to a series addressed to him by Abner Kneeland, inquiring into the authenticity of the Scriptures. The book formed of the letters referred to makes a volume of two hundred and fifty pages. The first edition was published in Salem, in 1816, the second in Boston, in 1820. The origin of these letters, which created no small degree of attention, at that period especially, was as follows: Rev. Mr. Kneeland having at various times expressed serious doubts and fears relative to the genuineness of the holy Scriptures, and the system of Divine revelation therein contained, solicited Mr. Ballou to enter into a correspondence with him upon the subject, in which Mr. Kneeland agreed to do his utmost to disprove the truth and authenticity of the Bible, while Mr. Ballou should take the opposite ground, and as strenuously defend it.

It was thought that this mode of discussion would be of mutual benefit to them, and at the time of its commencement was designed solely for their private use. But they were finally published, at the solicitation of friends, and with the hope that they might be productive of more extended good. These letters, which are somewhat lengthy, and indeed necessarily so on the part of Mr. Ballou, who assumed the laboring oar, were always written, as he has told us, at a single sitting. They are highly valuable, and were more particularly so at that period, as forming a powerful chain of evidence in favor of Christianity, and are characterized, on Mr. Ballou's part, by a vigorous accuracy and earnest desire after truth, which prepossesses the reader in their favor.

Mr. Ballou knew very well the misgivings as to the truth of the Divine revelations by which Mr. Kneeland's mind was exercised, and, notwithstanding other pressing duties and regular engagements, he consented to a discussion which must needs cost him many hours of study and labor, hoping thereby to lead one soul, at least, to a full and clear belief in the gospel of Christ. These letters reached the number of ten on either side before the correspondence was brought to a close, when Mr. Kneeland was compelled by the force of evidence frankly to acknowledge his entire satisfaction and conversion; and having found such joy in believing, such relief at being released from the iron thraldom of doubt and fear, he was exceedingly anxious to publish the entire series of letters.

It should be remembered that at the present day, when we have so many excellent books to consult, and can avail ourselves of the experience and research of so many able minds,— men who have fought the good fight of faith,— it is a very easy matter to sit down and defend the gospel against the arguments of the sceptic, the ground being already thoroughly canvassed for us pro and con, and weapons keen and bright placed in our very hands. But Mr. Ballou enjoyed none of these advantages; his tools were wrought from the native ore, and skilled after the fashion of his own mind. Every line he wrote, every opinion he advanced, was the result of deep and careful study, without the assistance of any other book save the Bible itself.

"As 1815 was the year after the war closed," says Mr. Ballou, "all kinds of provisions were extremely "dear, and my salary was so poorly paid, that I could "not get money enough from my friends to meet my "expenses; and during the two years and four months "I tarried here, I was compelled to spend about three "hundred dollars more than I received, of money which "I had by me when I came to Salem."

While resident in Salem, he applied himself with unremitting industry and diligence to his studies, devoting his time wholly to writing upon the subject of his faith, and the exercise of his professional duties as a minister. His labors here were particularly blessed with success, and the converts to his church were many. The Salem society under his charge vastly increased in influence and numbers, and Mr. Ballou had reason to rejoice at the very evident success of his labors with this people. When he first came to Salem, his doctrine, even by professed Universalists, was thought to be too radical, too universal, in short *too good;* but ere he left them they had fallen almost unconsciously into his mode of belief, gradually, step by step, though the passage had been so easy that they had not realized the change until they found themselves already convinced.

It was not his practice to assail the unbeliever at once with blunt, open refutation of his principles, nor to stagger him by an array of unanswerable arguments, but realizing that a casual analogy often convinceth when the mind will not bear argument, he adopted an easy and soothing course of reasoning, and thus gradually and easily sought his object. Thus was many an otherwise hopeless spirit turned from the darkness of error to the light of truth. Endeared to all his acquaintances by his unostentatious character, and by his mild, patient, and prudent habits, the separation from his society in Salem was mutually a hard task.

As soon as it was understood that Mr. Ballou had been talked of as pastor of the Second Universalist Society in Boston, Rev. Paul Dean, of respectable and influential standing in the order, and settled in Boston, strove by every manner of means to defeat this purpose. He feared the bold, unflinching, and manly style of preaching, for which Mr. Ballou had already become widely celebrated. Himself a man who avoided all sectional controversy in his preaching, he foresaw that the advent of Mr. Ballou in Boston would compel him to come out openly and acknowledge either that he was a Universalist or that he was not. He was not willing to risk his popularity in the matter, and therefore strove, by letters and orally, to dissuade Mr. Ballou from coming to Boston, and finally he declared to him that if he came hither he should consider it a breach of fellowship, and should ever after treat him accordingly.

Mr. Ballou was not one to be intimidated by threats; personal fear was a quality that he never realized. He came to Boston, and the sequel shows a result that is perfectly satisfactory to his friends. Mr. Dean was not prepared to make any great sacrifice for the sake of truth; it was not at that time popular for him to preach downright Universalism. The opinions of most men are governed by circumstances, quite as much as by truthful evidence; but Mr. Ballou, with a single eye to truth, never catered for the popular taste, never asked whether the promulgation of this or that great principle of truth would be acceptable and popular; he had no such policy in his composition, but dealt only in wholesome truths, and such as his own heart had baptized in the clear, welling waters of conviction.

The editor of the *Christian Freeman*, Rev. Sylvanus Cobb, not long since published an account of his first interview with Mr. Ballou, which we subjoin in this connection, as being applicable in placing the subject of the controversy, which is well known to have existed, between Mr. Ballou and Mr. Dean, in a proper light. In speaking of his first visit to the city of Boston, from his home in Maine, the writer says: —

" At this time the scheme was in vogue with a few " brethren, among whom Brs. Turner and Dean were

" conspicuous, for a division of the denomination, and the " erection of a new order; which it was calculated would " be the leading order, nearly swallowing up the other, " to be entitled 'Restorationists.' We impute no evil " motive to any one; but those on whom we called before " reaching Bro. Ballou, felt it to be their privilege to make " the projected scheme the chief subject of conversation, " and to express much of the feeling of dissatisfaction " towards Bro. Ballou. We were made to feel quite un- " happy; and as we had heard of Bro. Ballou as a stern " and severe man, we expected to be even more harassed " with a talk of 'troubles and difficulties' when in com- " pany with him. At length we were introduced to his " presence, and took his friendly hand. He sat down by " us, and with much interest and affection he inquired " into our labors and prospects, and into the interests of " the cause in Maine. We waited to hear him introduce " the subject of the 'difficulties,' but we waited in vain. " At length we attempted to draw him out, by asking " him of the nature of the 'difficulties' among the breth- " ren here. 'I am ignorant,' said he, 'of any real diffi- " culties. Certain brethren are believers in a limited " future punishment; but I cannot see that that is any " occasion for difficulty. Certainly I know of no reason " why I should have any trouble with these brethren, or " esteem them any the less for their seeing cause to believe " as they do. But if they require me to believe it as " essential to the Christian faith, I feel that it is proper " for me to call on them for the proof of the doctrine.

"We cannot see with each other's eyes; we must be wil-
"ling to allow each other to judge for himself. I love
"those brethren, and wish them prosperity and happi-
"ness.' And tears started from his eyes when he spoke.
"We felt that he spoke from the heart. There was no
"envy, no scheming, no party spirit about him. He
"sought a knowledge of God's word, and would 'speak
"God's word faithfully,' and accord the same right to
"others.

"And such we have ever found him. We have lived
"in neighborhood with him twenty-four years, and have
"found him one of the most modest, unassuming, liberal-
"minded and true-hearted men we ever knew. He was
"always pained to see one crowding upon another. He
"would see all working and prospering, and rejoicing in
"each other's prosperity and happiness. May his spirit
"be with us all."

We might dilate upon the subject of this controversy, but it is not a congenial theme. Suffice it to say, then, that the shafts of envy and ambition launched forth against Mr. Ballou, were as innocent and harmless, as it regarded him, as the summer winds. It is true that they caused him anxiety of mind, and not a little annoyance, in disproving the malignant charges brought against him; but, in the end, these tests only caused his purity of character to shine out with more surpassing brilliancy.

CHAPTER VIII.

SETTLES IN BOSTON.

After a peaceful and happy residence in Salem, of a little more than two years, Mr. Ballou received a cordial invitation from the Second Universalist Society of Boston to become their pastor. The invitation was accepted and, in the forty-fifth year of his age, he removed to this city, and was installed December 15, 1817, in the church which was built with the avowed purpose of obtaining his ministerial services; and here he continued to preach to the people for over thirty-five years. His letter of acceptance, addressed to the society, is as follows: —

"Sir: The call of the Second Universalist Society, in "Boston, inviting me to the labors of the Christian min-"istry with them, together with the liberal terms which "accompany said invitation, have been duly considered; "and, after weighing all the circumstances relative to "the subject, so far as my limited mind could compre-"hend them, I have come to the conclusion that it is my "duty to accept their call on the conditions therein stated. "I largely participate in the 'peculiar pleasure' afforded "by the consideration of the unanimity of the society, "and entertain an humble hope that, with the continu-"ance of this harmony, we may long continue to enjoy "all spiritual blessings in Christ Jesus.

"The society's most humble servant in Christ,

"HOSEA BALLOU."

"To JOHN BRAZER, Esq."

Rev. Thomas Whittemore, a devoted, constant, and consistent friend of Mr. Ballou, and who was also regarded by the subject of these memoirs almost like one of his own family, thus speaks of this period: — "This society had just finished their house, the present "venerable structure, on School-street. They never for "a moment had a thought of seeking any other pastor "than the Rev. Hosea Ballou, if it were possible to "obtain his services; and, accordingly, two months "before the house was ready for dedication, a letter of "inquiry was dispatched to him, to draw out his senti-"ments in regard to a removal to Boston. In the mean "time the house was hurried on to completion. Rev. "Messrs. Jones, of Gloucester, Turner, of Charlestown, "Ballou, of Salem, and Dean, of Boston, were invited "to join in the dedicatory services; Father Jones being "invited to preach the sermon, and the others to arrange "the remaining services at their discretion. The dedica-"tion took place on Wednesday, October 16. Mr. Bal-

"lou was not present, as he was at the time in the "country. On the following Tuesday a meeting of the "proprietors was holden, and Mr. Ballou was invited to "take the pastoral charge by a *unanimous* vote. The "salary was fixed, at first, at thirteen hundred dollars "per annum, to which donations of fuel were occasionally "made. He was installed on December 25, 1817. Rev. "Paul Dean preached, on the occasion, from Acts 20: 24. "He also gave the fellowship of the churches. Rev. E. "Turner, of Charlestown, made the installing prayer, "and gave the charge. Rev. Joshua Flagg, who had "succeeded Mr. Ballou at Salem, offered the concluding "prayer.

"Thus was Mr. Ballou duly installed as pastor. The "congregations that attended on his ministry were exceed-"ingly large. He soon became widely known for his "eloquence and boldness, and the novel nature of the "subjects discussed by him. His preaching was of a "controversial and doctrinal character. He explained, "in his discourses, those texts which had been supposed "to teach the doctrine of a judgment in the future state, "and endless torment. He was repeatedly called on, by "letter, from inquirers after truth, to preach from par-"ticular texts of this character; and, as he gave public "notice of the time when he would explain such passages, "his audiences were immensely large. It was usual, "from Sabbath to Sabbath, to see the meeting-house "filled, in the forenoon, so that it was difficult to obtain "a seat. In the afternoon, many would be obliged to "stand, especially in tne galleries, and around the head "of the stairs; and in the evening the aisles would be "crowded, above and below.

"For the last six or eight years preceding the rise "of the Second Universalist Society, Universalism had "produced little or no excitement in Boston. The First "Society remained stationary. Mr. Dean, its pastor, "preached little on those subjects on which he differed "from other sects. In the vicinity of Boston there was "no movement in favor of Universalism. There were "scarcely ten Universalist pastors in Massachusetts. "The cause was evidently languid. The rise of the "Second Universalist Society in Boston, and the removal "of Mr. Ballou thither, produced a new state of things. "There arose a commotion among the elements; but the "effect was to purify the atmosphere, and give men a "clearer and more extended vision. New societies, hold- "ing Mr. Ballou's sentiments, soon began to arise around "Boston."

On settling in Boston, he at once found a host of true and solicitous friends, whose interest in his ministry, respect for his character, and attention to his general welfare, enlisted in their behalf his warmest feelings of regard; sentiments which were ever cherished by him to the last, and frequently recurred to at his own fireside, and in the quiet of his family circle. Exercised by a realizing sense of this fact, the more keenly when he remembers that his father can give oral form to these feelings no longer, the author of this humble biography has at its commencement dedicated it to the subject's cherished friends.

We have thus given a memoir of Mr. Ballou's life up to the period of his settlement in Boston, where he was destined to operate upon a more extended field of action, — where his mental and physical powers, thoroughly trained and tested as they had been, were to be taxed more heavily still; and where he was destined to build for himself a name that will live in the grateful memory of future generations, and to erect for himself a monument that points further heavenward than eastern pyramids,— the savor of a truly Christian life.

Immediately on his becoming settled in Boston, in addition to the duties of his pastoral charge, and that of writing for two or three religious periodicals, Mr. Ballou was obliged to answer the frequent demands that poured in upon him, from every quarter, to lecture and to preach in the numerous towns within ten, twenty, and often fifty miles of the city, at a time when the means of communication were, at best, but very indifferent,— rendering it necessary for him to drive his own vehicle, in order to reach the desired point without loss of time. So frequent and urgent were these demands for his services, in towns and villages of New England, that week-days, as well as Sundays, were occupied in holding forth to the people, who came from far and near to hear him. Not unfrequently were several consecutive days thus employed; portions of the night even being improved in travelling between the several places when at a great distance apart, and sleep, or rest of any sort, being but sparingly indulged in. But so zealous was he in the glorious cause that filled his whole soul,— so thoughtless of self, and so wedded to his Master's business,— that his own labors seemed to him as nothing; and neither his energies nor his spirits were wearied for a single moment. The bow of his mind and body both seemed ever strung and bent, yet never to lose their elasticity. The amount of actual physical labor which he thus performed can hardly be estimated; but certain it is that he must have been almost miraculously sustained, to have endured so much fatigue without most serious injury.

" Soon after coming to Boston," says Mr. Ballou, " opposition to my Unitarian views, and to the way in " which I explained many important passages of Scrip- " ture, put on a serious aspect. Most of this opposition " was exercised by professed Universalist preachers. " There was much hypocrisy and low cunning set to work " in order to check my success; but, though this was a " source of much grief to my heart, it was the means of " calling into action all my resources, which I found it " necessary to put in requisition for the defence of the " truth. All this resulted in good. My editorial duties, " my necessarily long sermons three times on every Sab- " bath, giving evening lectures at home and in the neigh- " boring towns, tried to the utmost my physical powers " of endurance. With all these engagements, I was " writing and publishing the two volumes of my Lecture " Sermons, and my Select Sermons, which proved too 'much for my strength, and I brought on a weakness " in my left side that has affected me for years."

The weakness here referred to was doubtless caused by sitting for hours together at his writing-table in his study, with only such brief intervals as were necessarily consumed in taking his frugal meals. At such times he partook very sparingly of any kind of nourishment, declaring, when solicited on this point, that his brain was clearer, his mind more vigorous, when he ate but little, than when he allowed himself fully to satisfy his appetite. During the hours devoted to writing he was never disturbed; his children never for one moment forgot that he was thus engaged; and though they might pass through his apartment, still it was with a careful step and noiseless way, that showed their constant consideration for one whom they so much venerated. When he was thus engaged, for the last thirty years, having become relieved of the immediate domestic cares of her family, his wife always sat with him, sewing, knitting, or reading, but never interrupting him. Thus they grew, year by year, when he was in the house, more and more inseparable, and the tender regard of each seemed to increase for the other as year after year whitened their venerable locks.

Concerning the period of his early settlement in Boston, Rev. Sylvanus Cobb says:—" When Mr. Ballou entered " upon his labors here, benignantly warring upon the " hurtful errors which enslaved and paralyzed the common " mind, and elucidating those prominent gospel truths " which are the bread of life to the soul, there was an "extensive movement of mind in the city, and in the "region round about, far and near. When the Twenty-"six Lectures, published by Henry Bowen, were in the "process of delivery, the church was usually filled an "hour before the set time of beginning, and multitudes "would be going away who could not find entrance. He "had done much before this, by his ministry in other "places, and the publication of his Notes on the Parables, "Treatise on Atonement, and controversy with Robinson, "to advance the cause of truth; but he was now provi-"dentially placed at a commanding stand-point, a central "position, the commercial emporium of New England, "whence his influence went out through all the land. "Business men, from different parts, who had occasion to "be in Boston over the Sabbath, would go in at School-"street church, become convinced by the able expound-"er's arguments, go home, taking with them some of his "publications, and commence a work in their respective "neighborhoods, which, in many cases, resulted in the "formation of societies."

As a sample of the spirit he was forced to encounter, and the animosity felt against Universalists generally, and their teachings, by the clergy of other persuasions, we relate the following anecdote. Being in the town of Mattapoisett, Mass., during one of his short journeys into the neighboring country to fulfil professional engagements, Mr. Ballou found that he must stop there for the night. It was soon known in the village that he was to remain for this period, and he was at once waited upon by a committee chosen for the purpose, and informed that the town's people were exceedingly anxious to hear him preach, and that permission had been obtained for him to hold forth in the Orthodox meeting-house, if agreeable to himself. Mr. Ballou cheerfully consented to their wishes, and the people were notified accordingly. It is proper to state, that several among those who invited Mr. Ballou to preach here, were themselves large share-holders in the meeting-house, and in two instances members of the church. Notwithstanding all this, when Mr. Ballou came to the meeting-house, not anticipating the least opposition to his purpose, he was met at the door by the Orthodox clergyman then officiating here, and who positively forbade his entrance. In vain did Mr. Ballou attempt calmly to reason with him; still the excited pastor insisted most vociferously that he should not enter, although fully informed of all the circumstances. Nor would he yield until at length he was absolutely dragged away forcibly by his own friends.

Erasmus, the reformer of the fifteenth century, "who stemmed the wild torrent of a barbarous age," was not more strongly opposed by the bigoted Catholics of his day, who charged him with having "laid the egg that Luther hatched," than was Hosea Ballou by the partialists of his times. Particularly was this the case during the early and middle period of his public labors. The reformation begun by Luther has been well termed "an "insurrection of the human mind against the absolute "power of spiritual order." Its earliest fruit was the vigorous but narrow belief of Puritanism; then followed the more liberal creeds of the subsequent period; but it seemed to be left for Mr. Ballou to strike out and illustrate the doctrine of perfect freedom through Christ, of entire impartiality and free grace, which the doctrine of universal salvation inculcates.

Relative to the bigotry and unreasonable spirit often evinced towards the subject of this biography, and the cause he advocated, we are reminded in this connection of another anecdote, which is authentic, and which the subject of these memoirs related to his family.

Not long after Mr. Ballou's settlement in Boston, he received a pressing invitation to visit the island of Nantucket. The inconvenience of communication between the island and the main land was considerable, but he consented, and passed some ten days there, preaching every successive day and evening to large and interested audiences, creating a very earnest movement in the matter of religion. On his return, arriving at New Bedford, he took the stage coach for Boston, and in it found but one other person. Scarcely had the journey commenced, when his fellow-passenger opened the conversation by saying,—

"You are just from the island, I suppose?"

"Yes, sir," was the reply.

"Well, they say old Ballou is over there, preaching his heresy. Did you see him?"

"Yes, I saw him," was the calm reply.

"Well, he 's a rough old fellow. I don't like him."

"Why not?" asked Mr. Ballou.

"Because he preaches that all men will be saved and "go to heaven in their sins, and no man in his senses can "believe that."

"But, sir, did you ever hear him preach?"

"No; I hope not," said the man.

"Then you may be misinformed as to what he does "preach," said Mr. Ballou, mildly. "Now I think he "would say, if he were here, that he did not believe nor "preach as you have represented."

"But what does he believe, then?" said the stranger, somewhat earnestly.

"I think he would say that sinners are to be saved "*from* their sins, not *in* their sins. Christ came to save "the world from sin, not in sin; and furthermore we are "told in the Scriptures that 'he that is dead is free from "sin,' and he that is freed from sin must surely be holy, "and consequently happy."

"Sir, if I may be so bold," said the stranger, after looking for a moment somewhat critically, "where do you "live when at home?"

"I live in Boston, sir."

"Whose church do you attend?"

"Mr. Ballou's church, sir."

"What is your name?"

"My name is Ballou," he replied, pleasantly.

The man was of course confounded. He stammered forth some excuse; but though he listened to Mr. Ballou's kindly-meant remarks with the utmost attention, yet he was evidently very ill at ease, and, watching his opportunity, left the stage at the next stopping-place.

By careful study, aided by his natural quickness of conception and vigorous powers of mind, he had, without other assistance than that of books, acquired a practical knowledge of the Greek and Hebrew languages, which greatly assisted him in his profession, by enabling him to translate the most important passages from the original Scriptures, and thus to throw light upon many points that had heretofore been in some degree shrouded in mystery, by the one-sided and partial translation given in our own version of the Bible. At the present day it is well known that our common translation of the Scriptures is deficient in several instances, and this too at the most important and most critical passages. This being the case, Mr. Ballou found the power of translating for himself to be of the utmost importance as an aid to repel false argument, as well as being a matter of much personal satisfaction and enjoyment.

"At different times, and for several years," says Mr. Ballou, in reference to this subject, "I have attempted to "solve peculiar passages of Scripture, which were so "difficult to understand as to lead me to question the "correctness of their reading from the original. In "order to do this, I have studied Greek, and have had "some aid from Greek scholars and Greek lexicons, and "have consulted various commentators; possessed myself "of the Septuagint, or Greek Testament, and other "Greek works. With all these helps and efforts, I have "been enabled to satisfy myself relative to any particu- "lar passage. I have found but little benefit from these "means in regard to the Old Testament; in respect "to the New, I have often been assisted, and found that "my little knowledge of Greek has been more useful. "For similar ends and purposes I obtained a Hebrew "Bible, lexicon, grammar, etc.; but, though I have "bestowed not a little labor on the Hebrew, my other "avocations and cares have prevented any great degree "of proficiency, though I have experienced much aid and "assistance in elucidating many points. I might say "about as much of my Latin Bible, lexicon, grammar, "and reader. I have made some considerable use of all "these books, and have given many of my leisure hours "to the Hebrew, Greek and Latin languages, but I pro- "fess to know so little of them that it is hardly worth "naming; though I must acknowledge I have found "them of considerable use when some arrogant disputant "should think to silence me by an appeal to the original. "But it is a fact that I have never met with many college- "learned ministers who appeared to have retained much "of their Greek, if indeed they ever had much. I think "it would require no little study and observation to "determine the question, which amounts to the most, the "benefit which the public gain by the extra learning of "their clergy, or the imposition they suffer by estimating "that learning above its value."

This last reference should not be misconstrued by the reader, as conveying the idea that the subject of this biography was opposed in any way to education, or educational movements. Those who knew him best will bear ready testimony to the contrary. Indeed, his own struggles in obtaining knowledge had given him a just estimate of the true value of such conveniences as should facilitate the dissemination of intelligence far and wide. "When I "look about me," he says, "and contrast the great im- "provements in the means for gaining knowledge, — when "I behold the youth of to-day and remember the youth "of my own boyhood, — I am struck with the contrast "that facts present relative to education. I am also ren- "dered thankful to a Divine Providence, which has been "pleased to advance the improvement in mental culture "and the facilities for learning, in an equal degree with the "surprising advancements which have been accomplished "in the arts and sciences. Few are so poor or lowly "now that they may not enjoy the advantages of schools "and able teachers, and I may add that few there are "who do not avail themselves of the rich opportunity "which is offered them for storing their minds with "knowledge, and thus preparing themselves for useful "members of society. Half a century since, the case was "very different; schools were little thought of among the "poor, and children in the country could seldom be "spared from home to attend those that were occasionally "opened. Yet I am satisfied that the advantages which "were offered at that time were even more assiduously im- "proved than they are at this period. This, however, was "but natural, under the circumstances." No man put a higher estimate upon knowledge than he did, but it was useful, practical knowledge that he valued. He had no respect for mere titles and college honors. He had seen the eclat of a college diploma go further with many simple people than a sound argument or the possession of sterling wisdom would have done, and it is not surprising that the observation of such weakness should have led him to speak out, as we have seen him do in this connection. He may have felt the remark, too, which his opponents sometimes sneeringly made of him, that he never enjoyed a classical or collegiate education.

We have a few words to say relative to this reflection. Now, we solemnly believe, and are prepared to argue, that a collegiate education would have materially detracted from his *usefulness*. A scholastic or classic course of study seems to unfit men in a great degree for active life. The practical too often becomes merged in the ideal, and the mind grows effeminate. A theoretical knowledge of human nature is imbibed, and we are led to contemplate our fellow-men through a false medium; for essayists write of men as they should be, but rarely as they are. Mr. Ballou was acknowledged by all who knew him, to possess a remarkable degree of knowledge concerning human nature, but it was gathered from men, not books, from experience, — Time's free school, — not from theory. No other kind of knowledge would have fitted him for the peculiar path he was born to pursue. A pioneer should be what he was; a follower, the roads once cleared, and the track made smooth, might, perhaps, without danger, be less practical and more imaginative. Education, to be truly useful, should be unequalled in its ability to instruct us in the things about us, and to strengthen us for the duties that lie in our path of life. The true being, end, and aim of all study should be, "to improve men in the best reason of living," while any learning that aims above the practical interests of life is comparatively unimportant. Even in the ministry,

> "Church ladders are not always mounted best
> By learned clerks and Latinists professed."

"That learning which makes us acquainted with our-"selves," says Mr. Ballou, "with the powers and faculties "of the human mind, with divine truth, which is plainly "revealed, with its power on the mind and heart, with "the concatenations of cause and effect, and to understand "our every-day duty, which grows out of our wants and "the wants of those about us, is learning of a better "quality than that which only enables us to call things "by different names, without giving us a knowledge of "their natural qualities either for good or evil."

The main characteristic of Mr. Ballou's habit of mind was that of looking at all things in a practical point of view. The importance and real value he attached to things were deduced from his estimate of their *use*. He regarded life as made up of constantly recurring duties, and his appreciation of principles, of religion or philosophy, was carefully regulated by this standard, as to the application they bore to every-day matters.

The great end of all acquirements should be the ability to discharge more effectually our duties as men and citizens. "He who is not a better neighbor, brother, "friend, and citizen," says an eminent writer, "because "of his superior knowledge, may very well doubt whether "his knowledge is really superior to the ignorance of the "unlettered many around him." Or, to state this great truth more in brief, a man knows no more to any purpose than he practises

CHAPTER IX.

COMMENCES THE UNIVERSALIST MAGAZINE.

On the third of July, 1819, Mr. Ballou commenced the publication of the Universalist Magazine, in connection with a practical printer, — Mr. Henry Bowen. As usual in every enterprise wherein he embarked, he entered into the purpose and plan of the paper with all his heart, its avowed object being the more extended dissemination of the gospel of truth, and the elucidation of Christ and his mission on earth. It will be observed that in whatever new position we find the subject of these memoirs, it is secondary to, or rather in furtherance of, his Master's business; he could have entered into no other pursuit, could have been contented and happy in no other occupation. It was meat and drink to him, it was the very breath he drew, and the only great object and purpose of his life-long career.

The object of the Magazine, as stated in the editor's salutatory article, was to discuss the principles of doctrine, religion, and morality, and all articles calculated to promote improvement in these essential matters would be freely admitted into its columns. "The Universalist "Magazine invites the sentiments of different denomina-"tions," says the editor, "to evince themselves to the "best advantage, clothed in their most simple light, and "shining in their purest lustre, that the mind of the "reader may be able to know where to bestow a justifia-"ble preference." Those persons laboring in their minds under difficulties and doubts concerning any passage of Scripture, were urged to communicate the same to the Magazine, where they would be publicly answered, and thus many might reap the advantage of the queries and the answer. "All articles calculated to elevate the mind "to the contemplation of divine things, to reduce haugh-"tiness, to humble pride, to exalt the Divine Being, to "endear the Saviour, to cultivate piety, to admonish, to "warn, or to justly rebuke, to administer comfort and "consolation, will be gratefully received, and as speedily "as convenient communicated to the public." These were the main objects, and this the plan of the paper, and to which the editor strictly adhered. Some of the strongest arguments in favor of universal salvation, which ever emanated from the pen of Mr. Ballou, were first printed in this paper, and the influence it exerted was too evident not to challenge the attention of both friends and foes at that period.

The Universalist Magazine was destined to attain to the most extended popularity, and proved to be of eminent service to the cause which was so ably treated upon in its columns, each number for a series of years containing an essay upon some important passage of the holy text, with the original construction as put upon it by Mr. Ballou, besides the elaborate reviewal of numerous discourses and articles which appeared in other religious magazines, opposed to Universalism. The paper was issued weekly, and drew very largely upon his time and pen. In his editorial capacity, even as early as this period, when a systematic effort in the cause of temperance had scarcely been thought of, and the subject was seldom if ever referred to in public, we find some forcible articles from him upon this subject.

This spirit was strictly in accordance with his private life and habits. Living at a period when it was universally customary to offer a guest or caller a glass of wine, let him come at what hour of the day he might, and when the decanters and glasses always stood invitingly upon the side-board, yet he never used ardent spirit as a beverage, never partook of it at all, even in after years, when perhaps a partial stimulant might have been of physical benefit to him, because of a fixed principle in his own mind concerning its pernicious effects. But, as we have before intimated, this temperate habit was by no means confined to ardent spirit alone; the same abstemiousness characterized his daily meal. He partook only of the simplest food, and of that sparingly. This excellent habit grew to be a second nature to him, and in all places and under all circumstances was always exercised.

In connection with essays, leading articles, reviews and

sermons, which he furnished for the Magazine, he also contributed many fugitive poems to fill the poet's corner. It should be remembered that they were generally written at a few moments' warning in his sanctum, and in answer to the printer's call. All of them are, however, indicative and characteristic of the spirit and state of mind which possessed his heart. The following piece, taken at random, is a sample.

IMMORTALITY.

"That orient beam which cheers the morn,
  And drives the murky gloom away,
Through trackless ether swiftly borne,
  To welcome in the infant day,
Reminds me of the heavenly light,
  Whose rays, dispersing error's gloom,
Open to man a glory bright,
  In a fair world beyond the tomb.

Those varying scenes of beauty fair,
  Which welcome in the youthful spring;
The blooming fields, the fragrant air,
  The leafy groves and birds that sing,
Remind me of that promised day,
  When from the dead mankind shall rise,
As pure as light, and wing their way
  To spring eternal in the skies."

For some years Mr. Ballou continued as sole editor of the Magazine, in addition to his other writings, and the ever pressing duties of his profession. After gaining a firm footing, this publication passed into the hands of Rev. Thomas Whittemore, an able and zealous man, who is still the editor and proprietor. Mr. Ballou continued to write for its columns regularly for more than thirty years. Mr. Whittemore has changed or added to its original title, so that it is now known as the Trumpet and Universalist Magazine, one of the most largely circulated and popular publications in the whole denomination.

During the year 1819 and the year preceding it, Mr. Ballou had occasion to make several replies, in pamphlet form, to reviews of his sermons which he was at that time delivering before the Second Universalist Society, and which he was induced to write out and publish, by their request. The reviews here referred to were written by the Rev. Timothy Merrit, a Methodist minister of this city. In the year 1820, Mr. Ballou published a pamphlet of some length, entitled "Strictures on a published Sermon, by Dr. Channing." During this year he also compiled a collection of hymns, for the use of the denomination generally, but more especially for the convenience of the School-street Society, with which he was connected. This collection contained about *fifty* original hymns from his own pen, and is the second book of the kind he published, the first being issued while he resided in Barnard, Vt.

It was about this period that the following incident occurred, and which we give herewith in Mr. Ballou's own words: —

"By the following anecdote it may be seen into what "inconsistencies men are liable to be drawn by an "intense desire to maintain favorite sentiments. I had "an appointment to preach a lecture in the town of Can-"ton, Mass., where Universalism was quite new, and "where there were but few who believed it. At the "time appointed I was there, and among the many who "were present as hearers, was a Methodist minister, "whom before I had never seen. After our introduc-"tion, he very civilly asked me if I was willing, after I "got through my discourse, that he should have the lib-"erty of offering some remarks in relation to it. I "replied that I should have no objections to his having "that liberty, reserving to myself the right to reply to "his remarks. To this he agreed. As I knew my hear-"ers had assembled with an expectation of hearing the "doctrine of Universalism held forth, I took for my text "a passage which seemed to me a strong one in favor of "the doctrine: First Tim. 2: 4,—'Who will have all "men to be saved, and to come unto the knowledge of "the truth.' In my discourse, I relied on the will of "God as the foundation of my belief in the final salva-"tion of all men. My sermon was lengthy, and I en-"deavored to strengthen my arguments, as well as I "could, by many scriptures and various illustrations, but "still relied on the will of God as the foundation on "which stood the superstructure I raised. When I had "got through, I signified to the congregation that our "worthy brother, the Methodist minister, desired to make "some remarks on my discourse, and that I hoped they "would candidly listen to what he had to say.

"He then rose and remarked on various points of

"my arguments, allowing their justness and propriety "'But,' said he, 'as the conclusions which have been "drawn in favor of the salvation of all men rest entirely "on the will of God, if we can prove that God's will is "not done, in many instances which may be named, it "follows necessarily that the doctrine contended for may "not be true.' This he then labored to make out. Now, "feeling confident that he had shaken my foundation in "the minds of our hearers, he proceeded to quote pas-"sages upon which he relied to prove the endless misery "of the wicked. When he had got through and sat "down, I arose and told the people that I knew no better "way to answer to what our brother had urged, than to "allow that he had refuted the doctrine of the salvation "of all men by proving the failure of God's will in "many instances; and this being granted, it also must "be granted that God's will in regard to the endless "misery of sinners might fail of being accomplished "also! This reply came so suddenly on the minds of "the congregation that it brought them on their feet, and "the aspect which they presented was so peculiar as to "abash our brother, and induce him to say something "more, which the people did not stop to hear. He then "turned to me, and said that he did not mean what I "had stated to the audience. I told him in reply that "what I had to do with, was what he had said."

This is but an example of the various incidents, controversies, and adventures that he was constantly encountering on his frequent missions into the country vicissitudes that taught him much of human nature, and rendered him ever prompt and ready in reply, familiarized him with various temperaments, dispositions, and phases of character, and thus enabling him to speak and act more understandingly when again assailed in a like manner, as well as to put his experience to other available use.

In the latter part of the year 1821 and the beginning of '22, Mr. Ballou passed a considerable period in the cities of New York and Philadelphia, which places he was induced to visit by the united invitation of the several societies in these two cities. While in the latter place, he delivered eleven sermons, which the societies procured a stenographer to transcribe in short-hand, as delivered extemporaneously from the pulpit. These sermons were published soon after in Philadelphia, making a book of two hundred pages, a second edition being published in Boston about ten years after. Mr. Ballou's manner of delivery was so distinct, his enunciation so clear, his language so impressive, that a practical short-hand writer could easily transcribe every word he uttered in a discourse. There was never any hurry, no impetuosity, no excitement that betrayed the speaker into undue haste, but, though all was tempered with warmth and zeal, still it was such admirably controlled earnestness as never to confuse the mind that followed his spontaneous utterance. We well remember when the book herein referred to was handed to him for the first time. "I am "surprised," said he, "for this seems almost miraculous;

"here are my own words and thoughts literally as I "uttered them, in living and indelible lines upon these "pages, while my pen has never transcribed one letter. "of the matter. I might have improved this by review- "ing it for the press, but, after all, *it is as God sent* "*it!*" Reading on, he would pause now and then to say, "I should not have remembered that I said that, "if it was not so literally recalled to me." These sermons being upon important doctrinal points and subjects, as indeed were nearly all his sermons, are of peculiar value. The book is also a very excellent sample of Mr. Ballou's extempore style of preaching, as these sermons were printed from the reporter's notes, unrevised by the author, who, indeed, did not see them until they were sent to him in Boston in book form. At the time these sermons were delivered, the churches were always crowded to their utmost capacity. The Sabbath was not only thus occupied, but also many days and evenings of each week, the simple announcement of a meeting being quite sufficient to ensure a large and attentive audience for the occasion. In the mean time, in private circles, Mr. Ballou was forming extensive personal acquaintance with the hospitable citizens, among whom he counted some of the warmest friends in the cherished host, who continued such with him to the closing hours of his earthly career.

"The largest audience I remember to have addressed," he says, "was in Washington Garden Saloon, Philadel- "phia, which my friends had procured for me, finding "the meeting-houses far too small to accommodate the "crowds that thronged to our meetings. This hall, "which will accommodate some six thousand people, was "crowded to excess. On no former occasion did I ever "feel more pressed with the weight of duty which lay "upon me, nor a more sensible need of divine assistance. "The attention of the audience, and the multitude of "friendly hands which were extended to receive my "adieu, seemed to speak a language which signified the "approbation of my divine Master, which, to me, is far "better than life."

One of the most marked peculiarities of Mr. Ballou's character was not only his almost inexpressible degree of simplicity, but his perfect self-possession, and unmoved and placid calmness, under any and all circumstances. When he arose to address an audience of thousands, as was the case above referred to, they awed him not; he would have spoken the same in a private dwelling of New Hampshire, before a few hastily assembled friends, or, with the same prophetic unction, in a barn; — the village school-house or the city church were all alike to him. When he arose to address an audience, whether of thousands or of scores, it was always with a heart so full of his theme, so lowly and humble before his Maker, that not a thought betrayed itself in action of a character to indicate that he considered *himself* in the slightest degree, or that there was such a being as self in existence. And then, when he spoke, it was not with the adornments of rhetorical elegance, nor with a striving after effect; not one useless or unnecessary word fell from his lips;

it was simplicity and impressiveness personified. Such preaching was *natural;* there was not an artificial element in it. No wonder that it produced such results; no wonder that he should witness the visible fruits of his labors ripening about him.

It was no spirit of fanaticism that created such a furore in the public to hear him, it was not *fear* for their own good hope of salvation that brought people together in such masses; it was not excitement, that grand agent of revival meetings generally. No; it was a far worthier influence than these; it was a desire to hear the good tidings that the preacher dispensed, as he alone could do. It was to partake of the bread of life that they came, and they were filled. He was emphatically the messenger of "peace and good will to men;" and the multitudes who came to hear the words of promise from his lips, received them as the shepherds did to whom the angels bore the glad tidings as they "watched their flocks by night."

After the departure of Christ, and the death of his immediate disciples, a darkness had crept upon the hearts and souls of mankind; faith in the boundless love of the Creator had been weakened, as belief in his vengeance strengthened, and nearly all Christian creeds were gloomy, disheartening, and repulsive. To dispel these erroneous views, — to withdraw the clouds that hid the brightness of the bow of promise, — to reveal all the priceless tenderness and love of the divine nature, — to radiate the light of hope upon a darkened world, was a task as glorious as ever fell to the lot of man. What more thrilling discoveries ever dawned upon the human intellect than those which revealed themselves to, and rewarded the prayerful search of, him of whom we write? We can easily understand how the greatness of this mission strengthened and sustained him in his arduous duties, in his daily gospel labors, in his long journeyings, in his voluminous exertions with the pen and in the pulpit. Verily the hour and the man had arrived. It mattered little that he did not spare himself, that he gave himself up wholly to his vocation; it was not destined, not designed, that he should succumb in the good fight; vigor and energy were given him to support him through all his trials, up to the very verge of a long and eventful life, when the chief end of his existence had been accomplished.

Not long subsequent to his return from this journey to New York and Philadelphia, he published a series of "*Lecture Sermons*," in one volume of four hundred pages. This book, like every one that ever emanated from his pen, had a very extensive sale, passing through several large editions, and still finds a ready market. These "Lecture Sermons" give, like the "Treatise on Atonement," an evidence of the fact that the author was always working in new veins of thought. He was not one contented to follow in the beaten track of others; his motto from the outset was *progress;* and each new work that emanated from his pen and comprehensive mind, gave fresh token of research and discovery. Not long after the issuing of the "Lecture Sermons," he published another book, entitled "*Select Sermons upon Important*

Passages," making a book of three hundred and fifty pages. Like the previous work, this book is peculiarly characteristic of its author, and treating, as it does, upon deeply interesting and doctrinal points, it has found a wide circulation. These books are distinguished alike for patient research, wise reflections, deep penetration, and the soundness of their moral influence. The last work has passed through seven editions.

Mr. Ballou was frequently heard to remark, that if we would reason in reference to the divine economy as we do concerning other matters, we should soon discard many of the false notions which do so much towards enshrouding our spirits in darkness, and thus preventing our progress towards the goal of gospel truth. In illustration of this, we subjoin the following anecdote, in his own words, as furnished for the Universalist Magazine at the time of its occurrence. It happened to him while on a journey from Boston to Watertown, New York, in the year 1824. While absent from his paper, Mr. Ballou was in the habit of supplying his editorial columns through the mail, partly made up of correspondence from the points he visited, and relating to such matters and themes as were calculated to interest a mind of his peculiar character. The following anecdote is taken from one of these letters.

"The day following, a widow belonging to Pittsfield, "Mass., entered the stage in that town to go to Den- "mark, New York, to visit her young son, whom she had "not seen for six years, and who is now about fifteen. "This lady I found to be quite orthodox in her views, "and disposed to question me concerning mine. At the "inn in Albany where the stage stops, we had some "serious conversation on the subject of the ignorance "and unbelief of man. Her queries concerning this "subject were directed in the usual way, and were "designed to prove that in consequence of unbelief in "the Saviour, the sinner is exposed to be cut off forever "without mercy. Having noticed in this lady an anxious "desire to find her son, and perceiving that her affections "were tender towards her fatherless child, I thought "proper to try to open her eyes by means of appealing "to her natural affection.

"'Madam, do you think your son will know you?' I "asked. She, with manifest emotion, replied, 'It is so "long since he saw me, that I do not think he will!' "'And should you find that he has forgotten you, so as "not to recognize your person and countenance, do you "think he would be in danger on that account of losing "your favor?' Tears started into her eyes, and the "weight of the question was sensibly manifest. She "replied in the softest accents in the negative. 'Well, "madam,' I continued, 'should you find that your son "has forgotten your countenance, and should you inform "him of the fact of which you find him ignorant, and "yet he should not believe you, should you then feel "unkindly towards your son?' She fully appreciated "the question, and answered in the negative. I then "called her attention to the remarkable passage in the "forty-ninth chapter of Isaiah, in which the divine "kindness is commended to exceed the compassion of a "mother to her tender offspring. She signified her sat- "isfaction, and gave me to understand that the argument "had reached its object."

This anecdote, striking and beautiful in its bearings, is also particularly interesting as being so perfect an illustration of Mr. Ballou's style of argument. He always brought the subject home to the feelings and affections of his hearers, illustrating his theme by the simplest facts. His examples by way of explaining his subject were ever so aptly chosen, as to seem to have occurred almost solely for his use; these illustrations were ever drawn from every-day life, and from the most familiar subjects about us. The family circle afforded an infinite variety of bearings and illustrations, exceedingly well fitted to delineate his belief; and those who have been accustomed to hear him preach, will remember how frequently he referred to the homes of his hearers for illustrations. In this respect his discourses were a close imitation of his Master's, who spoke as never man spoke.

There lies open before us at this moment the autobiography of Rev. Abel C. Thomas, where he speaks of Mr. Ballou on the occasion of his (Mr. Thomas's) first visit to Boston, and his meeting with the subject of this biography. "No one will deem me invidious in men- "tioning Hosea Ballou. There he stood in the simplic- "ity and maturity of a child-man. Was it marvellous "that his heart-speech should tingle within me as the "voice of a father? He stood up the taller in his man-

"hood for having bowed to brotherly fellowship with a "boy. There was no distinguishing grace in the act; it "was his way *alway*, and he was only the taller on that "account. He was preaching then (O! how luminously "and forcibly he was preaching!) at the age of three- "score."

It was ever thus that strangers were impressed on meeting with him. They had heard, of course, much of Hosea Ballou, they had read his books, or his essays through the newspaper press; by name and reputation they had long known him. Some had imagined him proud, austere, and distant. They approached a man, for the first time, who had reached to his extended span of life, to his experience and world-wide celebrity, with some degree of awe; but his warm pressure of the hand, the tender and soft expression of his eye, the soothing and melodious voice, (that gentle, soothing, yet impressive voice, how strongly our senses recall it now!) the kind word, — these instantly dispelled any feeling of distance that might have arisen in the breast of the new comer; and he found impressed on every word he uttered, on every lineament of his features, on every sentiment of his heart, a spirit of divine *simplicity*.

Arrogating nothing to himself, unassuming to the utmost degree, he counted his own services as nothing, and only aspired to be known as his Master's follower, and the servant of all men.

CHAPTER X.

COMMENCES THE UNIVERSALIST EXPOSITOR.

DURING the year 1831 Mr. Ballou commenced, with his nephew, Rev. Hosea Ballou 2d, the editorship of the "Universalist Expositor," a quarterly publication. He continued for one year as editor of the work, and afterwards as a regular contributor for a number of years.

In November, 1834, Mr. Ballou was again induced to make the cities of New York and Philadelphia a professional visit. He had, previous to this date, and repeatedly afterwards, been earnestly solicited to settle in New York, as well as in Philadelphia. Indeed, a systematic effort was made in the former city to obtain his services permanently, and he was offered the pecuniary consideration of several hundred dollars more per annum than he then or ever after received from the Second Universalist Society in Boston. Besides this increase in salary, there were several other important inducements offered in order to influence him to settle among them. But Mr. Ballou had, after so many years' residence and pastorship in this city and over a society he so much loved, become deeply and ardently attached to the associations of his charge, and had formed ties of friendship and love that were almost too strong to sever. He, however, returned an answer at last to these reiterated applications and proposals, that he would lay the subject before his society, and they should decide the matter for him. The society in New York signified their willingness to have the matter thus settled; and he accordingly represented the same to the Second Universalist Society, telling them exactly his own feelings, and bidding them to decide the matter for him. There was but one voice in the society; the feelings he had expressed were entirely reciprocated; the vote that he must remain with them, was unanimous; there was not one dissenting voice. He had been tried, and found faithful. Cheerfully acquiescing in this decision, the subject was dropped,— an understanding being had, and indeed a promise given on Mr. Ballou's part, that he would visit New York professionally as often and for as long a period at a time as he could make it convenient.

The following letter was written to his wife from New York, during his visit to that city in this year. It is one in his usual style, and will show the reader the tender relationship of his domestic associations, and also the reliance in Divine Providence which ever actuated him. He never wrote the briefest letter without expressing the same religious sentiment. The letter is dated New York, October 30, 1834.

"My Dear: It is with gratitude to the kind Pro-"tector of our lives, that I inform you of our comfortable "health. We had a very good passage from Boston to "this city, except that the sea was quite boisterous, which "caused our daughters to be quite sea-sick during the "night. We arrived in this city about nine o'clock, A. M., "and were kindly received by Col. Harsen and family, "where we are at home until to-morrow morning, "when we expect to leave for Philadelphia. Clementina "and Fiducia" (the two daughters with him) "rode about "the city yesterday, and had a view of nearly all its "beauties. We took tea with Mr. and Mrs. Sawyer last "evening, where we had the pleasure of meeting with "Bro. Fuller, who will supply my desk and bring you "this letter. I preached in Bro. Le Fevre's church on "Tuesday evening, and have an appointment in Bro. "Sawyer's church for this evening. I hope that your "cold has subsided, and that the family are in good "health. You will remember that Bro. Fuller is a "stranger in Boston, and that he will need those atten-"tions which will make him feel at home. Give our love "to all the inmates of our house, and, by the blessing of "Heaven, expect us at the time appointed.

"Affectionately yours,

"Hosea Ballou."

"Ruth Ballou."

We need hardly pause here to analyze this letter. The reader will at once recognize, in its composition, the affectionate husband and father, the devout Christian, and the thoughtful friend, all of which were innate qualities in the writer's heart. The address of the letter was the style he always adopted towards his wife. The commencement of the same is a perfect type of his constant acknowledgment of the Divine favor. The reference to the children who were with him, evinced the same thoughtfulness for their enjoyment and comfort that exercised his mind to his last days; his inquiry for his wife's health, hoping that her "cold" was better, was another evidence of his solicitous affection for his companion; and, finally, his recommending the bearer as he did,—"You will remember "that Bro. Fuller is a stranger in Boston, and that he "will need those attentions which will make him feel at "home,"—are all most significant of his mind and heart.

"Immediately after my first visit to Philadelphia," says Mr. Ballou, "a second society was formed, and a "large meeting-house was built in Callowhill. From "this society I received a very urgent invitation to "become their pastor; but, as my Boston friends felt "desirous to have me stay with them, I could not think "it my duty, for a few hundred dollars more remunera-"tion for my services annually, to leave them, as my sal-"ary was at that time sufficient for my wants. So late "as the year 1844, by invitation from the Callowhill "society, I visited and preached for them for four weeks. "While I was there, my friends proposed sending to Bos-"ton for Mrs. Ballou, with a desire that I would continue "with them for an indefinite period. But my age admon-"ished me not to undertake too much."

We may add here the following memorandum from notes which he gave the author of these pages relative to a subject before alluded to, concerning the matter of a larger pecuniary offer for his professional services:

"At one time, while I tarried in New York, the Pine-" street Society presented me with a pressing invitation " to settle with them, offering me some hundreds of dol-" lars more than I was then receiving for my professional " services, to induce me to remove to New York city. " This official invitation, together with a very brotherly " letter from the society in New York to my own in Bos-" ton, in which they endeavored to assign good reasons " for my removal, I took with me to the Second Uni-" versalist Society, in School-street. I had previously " given my friends in New York to understand that I " would not be persuaded to leave Boston, unless my soci-" ety would give their cordial consent to such a measure. " After submitting this letter to my society, I was given " to understand, in an official manner, that, by a unan-" imous vote, my society had resolved that I must remain " with them. This of course ended the matter, as their " wish was my guide."

We have related these circumstances more particularly to show the reader that Mr. Ballou was actuated by no mercenary motive in this matter, and indeed to prove that it was a principle altogether foreign to his character. We see that the offer of a greater pecuniary emolument (we believe the New York society offered him eight hundred dollars more than he was then receiving per annum, and also to bear the incidental expenses attendant upon his removal) had no influence upon his mind. If his society no longer desired his services, he was ready to leave them at once. If they were still attached to him, and preferred his ministration to that of any other individual, no pecuniary inducement should part them. We may use his own words, and say that the evidence of the unabated regard of the people of his charge, of their undiminished attachment to him and his services, rendered him far happier than any amount of silver and gold could possibly have done. Indeed, there was not one spark of mercenary feeling existing in his heart; it was contrary to his very nature.

Those who knew Mr. Ballou best were well aware of his punctilious notions as it concerned money affairs. He would not himself owe any man, and he liked "short settlements," believing in the old adage that they "make long friends." He was scrupulously exact in his dealings, and would be careful not to be overpaid or underpaid in a money transaction; and these peculiarities may have, with some, led to a belief that he was penurious in his disposition, though this was by no means the case. Could we with propriety refer to his numerous private deeds of charity, to the open-handed dealing that evinced the generous nature of his disposition and the liberality of his heart, we could exhibit a list of facts that would disabuse the mind of any one of such an unfavorable impression. We feel tenacious upon this point, realizing as we do the untruth of any such deduction; and for any one to make such a remark or inference, would be at once to expose his own personal ignorance of the man.

Mr. Ballou was not one to give injudiciously; he was not lavish in his bestowals; but what he gave to charitable purposes, more or less, he was careful to know would be productive of real benefit. Once satisfied of the worthiness of the purpose, he always gave in accordance with his means. His generosity was unostentatious, and sought such channels as run beneath the shades of domestic necessities, rather than those exhibited on hill-tops, or that advertise themselves in open places. The author of these pages has witnessed from childhood a most liberal and charitable spirit as exercised by the subject of this memoir.

When he was solicited for assistance, he always listened attentively to every appeal, and carefully examined the case and its merits, when, being satisfied of its claims for aid, he not only gave himself, but took pains to interest others for the same end. At times he would call on his society, either collectively or individually, and thus do a great good by affording timely pecuniary aid, in many cases. He never asked of a person his religion before he gave him in charity; all were considered as members of the same great family, and "where want resided, he knew the door." The needy found in him a firm and judicious friend; one who was careful not to do them a harm, in the spirit of kindness, by encouraging a slothful or idle spirit, but who sent them away wiser and happier than they came to his door.

"Among the many moral duties," says Mr. Ballou, "which contribute to the mitigation of the misfortunes "of human life, and to administer to the enjoyments of "social beings, that of charitably bestowing a part of "what a liberal Providence has put into our hands, on "those who have been unfortunate in the loss of prop-"erty, or by sickness, or other unavoidable visitations, "should claim our earnest attention. This virtue at "once combines many moral excellences, and seems to "call into action some of the best qualities of our social "nature. It is that, too, which seems to resemble the "bountiful conduct of the Giver of every good and per-"fect gift; and in some degree compares with the grace "of our Lord Jesus Christ, who, though he was rich, "for our sake became poor, that we through his poverty "might be made rich, and greatly ornaments the gospel "professions of brotherly love. This, too, is a virtue "which never loses sight of the good of its agent, who, "being blessed with the genuine spirit of heaven-born "charity, realizes that it is more blessed to give than to "receive. Nor is there anything more acceptable to the "Divine mind of universal goodness, than to see rational "beings exerting themselves to assist one another. 'To "do good and communicate, forget not, for with such "sacrifice God is well pleased.' "

While Mr. Ballou was in Philadelphia during the year 1834, he preached nine sermons, which, like those delivered in the same city at the close of 1821 and the commencement of '22, were taken down by a stenographer in short-hand, and published in a volume of two hundred pages. In the preface to this volume, which, having been, like its predecessor, obtained through the reporter, was never seen by the author until in print, Rev. Abel C. Thomas, the publisher, makes the following remarks; valuable as coming from a discriminating and intelligent mind, and one which would scorn flattery as it would falsehood.

"Mr. Ballou is in the sixty-fourth year of his age, yet "his eye is not dim, nor his natural force abated. His "public communications are distinguished by extraordi-"nary penetration, perfect knowledge of human nature, "aptness of illustration, and closeness of reasoning. In "private intercourse he manifests the feelings of a heart "baptized into the spirit of the living God. It is im-"possible to listen to his public exhibitions of love divine "without according to him the meed of sincerity and "intellectual power, and it is equally impossible to min-"gle with him in the walks of social life without loving "him from the heart."

Mr. Ballou was in the habit of making frequent use of the scriptural story of Joseph and his brethren, the parable of the Prodigal Son, the case of Saul of Tarsus, and other familiar parables, to illustrate the doctrinal points of his discourses upon the holy text. These illustrations, however, were always apt and appropriate, and any one who reads the Scriptures must very well know that these parables present almost innumerable bearings. Although he never did so without communicating some new point or bearing in the narrative, yet the frequency of these references was argued by some as an objection to his style of preaching. In reference to this subject, Rev. Abel C. Thomas, in an appendix to the book referred to, relates the following anecdote: —

"After the delivery of a certain discourse in one of our "cities, by Mr. Ballou, one Universalist minister said to "another, in a good-natured way, 'The old man is always "*harping* on Joseph and his brethren, the Prodigal "Son, and Saul of Tarsus.' 'Well,' said the other, 'it "is a good harp, nevertheless, and Mr. Ballou knows how "to play upon it. He always plays a new tune, and I "could listen to him all night.'"

His book of nine sermons embraces some of the most stirring and able arguments that the author ever produced, and it has been read by more persons probably than any book of the same character in the country. The first edition was a large one, but was rapidly followed by others.

Mr. Ballou ever delighted in promoting the innocent amusement of his children in every reasonable way. He never adopted that stern and unapproachable disguise that but too often estranges the affections of the child from the parent. He was fond at times of unbending, as it were, from the extreme tension of mental effort, and entering into the childish amusements of his family circle; it was only long enough, however, to endear himself to that circle, for his time was too precious to admit of much relaxation, however grateful this might be to his feelings.

It was not with the subject of this biography as with those who wear two faces, one when at home and another when abroad; there was no deceit in him; he carried forth from his home the same face he wore there, the same aspect of mind and body, evincing precisely the same characteristics in public as he did in private. He knew no change, but was always eminently natural everywhere.

His social character was such as ardently to endear him to every member of his large family. While he maintained the dignity and authority appropriate to his general character, still he ever evinced an exuberance of good nature, and was amiable, gentle, and even playful at times, in his domestic and public intercourse.

During the year 1834, Mr. Ballou wrote and published a work entitled, "An Examination of the Doctrine of Future Retribution," contained in one volume of two hundred pages. This is affectionately dedicated to the second Universalist Society of Boston, as a token of regard, by the author, who had so long presided over this brotherhood in the most happy fellowship.

In the following extract from the preface to this book, the reader will find not only the spirit of the work referred to, but will also observe that the author states, in plain and unmistakable terms, some important points of his faith, — points wherein he differed from some respected brethren of the order, but which, however, form almost the universal belief of the mass of Universalists. Our quotation from this preface commences as follows: —

"It has always remained the fixed resolution of the "writer of the following essay to keep a mind open to "conviction; always active in investigating religious "truth; constantly ready to profess and hold forth any "opinion, however unpopular, and however opposed by "divines, by the schools, or by his dearest friends, when "convinced of its truth. This course has led him to give "up many religious tenets which were taught him in "his youth, and not a few which were embraced by the "denomination to which he has from his youth belonged. "Travelling this course, he early renounced the doctrine "of endless punishment; the doctrine of the Trinity; "that of native depravity; that of the imputation of sin "and of righteousness; that of the vicarious sufferings of "Christ; and, nearly eighteen years ago, the doctrine of "punishment in the future state. It has been his lot to "meet with much opposition on most of these points, "from various denominations, and not the least strenuous "from those of the denomination with which he has been "happy to hold connection. For the painful travail "endured from all this opposition, he has been abun-"dantly compensated by seeing the rapid advance of the "doctrines which he has embraced and endeavored to "advocate.

"The object of the writer of the following pages is to "place his views, respecting the doctrine of a future state "of retribution, before the public, and to preserve his "arguments on that subject, that when the time shall "come, as he believes it will, when people in general will "number the tenet of future punishment among those "corruptions of Christianity which will then be aban- "doned, it may be known that the writer disbelieved it in "his day; and also that the arguments with which he "opposed it may then be known.

"Universalists now take a pleasure in looking back "and tracing, from Origen down to our time, the progress "of the doctrine which embraces the salvation of all men; "and so they will doubtless continue to do in future "ages.

"Some may query whether a proper regard to the "opinions and feelings of honest, faithful, and affectionate "brethren, who believe in the doctrine of future retribu- "tion, but yet earnestly contend for final restoration, "would not incline the writer to be silent on the subject, "and not to come out with this publication. To this "inquiry it is replied, that such brethren, with their "many commendable qualities, are warmly cherished in "the affections of the writer's heart, nor are they the "less regarded because they do not adopt his opinions. "And he feels confident that such brethren will entertain "no suspicions of his want of respect for them. They "will not fail to consider that the views of the writer, on "the subject of retribution, are not so wide from theirs "as theirs are from the views of those authors whom "they quote as authority in support of future retribution. "They would doubtless sooner embrace the opinion of no "future sin and misery, than defend the doctrine main- "tained by that good man, exemplary Christian, and "faithful minister, Elhanan Winchester, which supposed "that the wicked, in the world to come, would suffer, for "ages and ages, inconceivable torment in literal fire and "brimstone. Such torment is now denied by our doctors, "who maintain *endless* punishment, and rejected also by "those who believe in a state hereafter of discipline which "shall end in an entire reformation. Such brethren will "also cordially respond to the assurance that the writer "of the following work will never withhold a sincere fel-"lowship from a faithful brother, because he disagrees "with him on the doctrine of divine retribution.

"It is very possible that some, who have a strong "desire that nothing should be done which should tend, "in the least, to endanger the harmony and cordial fel-"lowship of Universalists, may think that prudence "would, at least, plead for a delay, and suggest the "propriety of deferring this publication to some future "time, when it might give less offence. Such may "be assured that their good wishes for the harmony and "fellowship of our order are duly respected; but they "cannot be ignorant of the fact that the doctrine of a "future state of punishment has been disbelieved, by "ministering brethren of our order, for many years, and "that much has been published with a view to disprove "that doctrine; and, moreover, that now that doctrine is "generally disbelieved by Universalists of our connec-"tion; and yet much harmony prevails, and our fellow-"ship remains, and is warmly cherished between brethren "whose opinions disagree on the subject of this doctrine.

"The writer would further remark, that both age and "infirmity admonish him that what he feels it his duty "to do, he ought not to delay; and he cannot believe "that any of his brethren can feel, in the least, wounded "because their aged brother should finish his labors in "accordance with the dictates of his own understanding. "It is a happy circumstance, that in the denomination of "Universalists, no one feels bound to defend and support "the particular opinions of another, any further than he "is himself convinced of their truth and importance. "Our platform of faith is general, and allows individu-"als an extensive latitude to think freely, investigate "minutely, and to adopt what particular views best com-"port with the honest convictions of the mind, and "fearlessly to avow and defend the same."

In perusing this book, or indeed any of Mr. Ballou's numerous works, the reader cannot fail to be struck with the complete simplicity and purity of the author's style, at the same time being deeply impressed with the magnitude of the subject treated upon: he finds the book to be more like a familiar friend with whom he is conversing, than the deep logical work it really is. This is caused by the peculiar clearness and force of the style, while all is so conceived and put down as to be within scope of the humblest understanding. All his comparisons and illustrations are drawn from the most familiar objects about us, bringing our every-day life and experience to bear upon the theme; and thus his arguments were doubly forcible and plain. It was the common remark that little children could understand his sermons, and remember the moral inculcated. "If I can only make my subject so "plain that children will understand me," he once said in relation to this subject, "my purpose will be gained, "and I shall not be preaching in vain." Probably there never was a public speaker who possessed more fully the power of making himself perfectly and clearly understood, in every bearing of his subject, than did Mr. Ballou. This was commonly remarked of him by all, and more especially by those in his own profession of the ministry, who had learned by experience what a difficult matter it sometimes is to impress an audience with the precise idea intended by the speaker.

About this date, in Mr. Ballou's manuscript memoranda he says: — "I well remember a conversation I had "with a learned doctor of divinity of this city, some "years ago. It happened that we were both going into "the country, and took the same stage. We had not "travelled far before the doctor very politely addressed "me, expressing a desire to know my opinion on a "certain passage of Scripture, as he did not know how it "was explained by those of my opinion in religious mat-"ters. The stage being quite full of gentlemen who were "strangers to me, but to whom I was doubtless well "known, I was somewhat surprised that the learned "divine should introduce a scriptural subject, and espe-"cially one concerning which he supposed we entertained "different views. However, I was well satisfied that he "expected to see me embarrassed in presence of the "passengers, whose curiosity was evidently excited. I "replied that I was not unwilling, on any proper occasion, "to give my views on any passage of Scripture when "desired to-do so, provided I was satisfied in my own "mind concerning its true meaning.

"There was the most profound attention evinced, and "the doctor introduced Gal. 6: 7 and 8. 'Be not "deceived; God is not mocked: for whatsoever a man "soweth, that shall he reap. For he that soweth to his "flesh shall of the flesh reap corruption; but he that "soweth to the spirit shall of the spirit reap life everlast-"ing:' the passage being one with which many occa-"sions had made me quite familiar. I replied imme-"diately, as follows: 'I presume, sir, you will under-"stand all you wish to know of my views of this text, if "you hear me repeat it, and duly observe where I lay "especial emphasis; — Be not deceived; God is not "mocked; for whatsoever a man soweth that shall he "also reap. For he that soweth to his *flesh* shall of the "*flesh* reap corruption; but he that soweth to the spirit "shall of the spirit reap life everlasting.' The moment "I pronounced the words of the text thus, there was a "smile on the countenances of all in the stage, and a "movement which signified satisfaction. I merely re-"marked, in conclusion, that no man who should sow in "one field, would think of going to another to reap. "The doctor made me no reply, nor did he ask any "more questions.

"The above is but a sample," continues Mr. Ballou,

"of the unnumbered cases in which I have seen how "utterly abortive is a liberal education, with the addition "of a theological school, in freeing the human mind from "religious errors. So far from effecting any such desir- "able end, these so highly esteemed advantages generally "serve to puff up the mind and heart with pride, and "close every avenue through which light might be "received."

The engrossing habits of a student, and the employment of a large portion of his time in writing, brought upon Mr. Ballou the weakness in his left side, before referred to, and which was still more augmented by his continued use of the pen. This trouble became at last a seated and irreparable one, and a source of much bodily suffering to him until the close of his life, though serious attacks of it were but transient, and usually lasting but a few hours at a time. This affection was of rather a peculiar character, so that when anything occurred, of an unpleasant nature, to trouble or distress his mind,— bad news of any sort, the sudden death of a relative or friend, or any matter of this character,— it would seem to affect the weak side, and there distress him.

Mr. Ballou was often solicited, by letters from a distance, for his autograph, with which he complied in a brief line, most generally; but personal applications for this object were very frequent during his journeyings from home. Being asked for his autograph by a young lady in one of the neighboring towns, who handed him her album for the purpose, he sat down and wrote the following verses impromptu, and which have been handed to us for insertion here. They will serve to show his ready power of versification; he never studied to be a poet, nor ever *labored* upon a piece of poetical composition. He found little time to plant and rear flowers along his pathway of life. At an early period the soil he tilled was of too bold and rugged a character to cultivate aught save the sterling literal seeds of truth, the sweetness of whose blossoms is fragrance to the soul. If subsequently he sometimes plucked a lily or watered a rose-bud, it has been at breathing-spells between the holding of the plough and the planting of seed in his Master's vineyard. He lacked not for refinement and delicacy of taste, or for the natural promptings of the poet, but there was more important business for him to perform, and he realized too fully his responsibility to allow himself to forget for a moment the great aim and business of his mission. The poem referred to above is entitled

THE MYRTLE.

" Come, take the wreath I 've twined for thee,
'T is wet with morning dew ;
And lessons rare of love and truth
These flowers shall bring to you.

The half-blown rose, whose spotless leaves
Speak of thy hopes as fair,
And spicy balm, with healing breath,
Are mingling odors there.

The sweet geranium so green
A fragrance doth impart,

True as the gentle breath of love,
That fills the youthful heart.

But most of all I 'd have thee mark
The modest myrtle bough;
It speaks of love that e'er will be
As pure and bright as now.

For though the rose may fade and die,
The balm may cease to cure,
Through summer's light and winter's shade
The MYRTLE will endure.

Then take the wreath I 've twined for thee,
'T is wet with morning dew;
And many a lesson true of love
These flowers shall bring to you."

We find a letter among our papers, written about the period of which we now speak. It is from his pen, and bears date New York, April 21st, 1839, on the occasion of a brief visit to that city, and was addressed to the author of these pages.

"MATURIN: A kind Providence brought me to this "city early yesterday morning. I had a very pleasant "passage hither, and the good company and kind atten- "tion of Capt. Parker. I am at the Walton House, "which was Washington's head quarters during the "Revolutionary war. It is now between nine and ten "o'clock, Sabbath morning. My health is good as when "I left home. My friends expect me to preach three "sermons this day and evening. Whether I shall return "on Monday to Boston, or remain another week here, I "have not now the means of determining. I pray God "to preserve the health of the family, and return me "soon to enjoy that circle from which it is painful to be "absent, though I have every attention and necessary "accommodation for my comfort. Take good care of "your health, and tell your mother that I shall endeavor "to be careful of mine.

"Affectionately,

"Hosea Ballou."

"M. M. Ballou."

This, and a private letter previously given in these pages, are not made public for any particular information they communicate, but simply to show the reader the feelings of the writer as expressed between himself and those whom he loved and in whom he confided. These letters might be greatly multiplied, but this would perhaps serve our object no better purpose. If a hundred were to be submitted to the reader, they would convey no other spirit than is evinced by the two already given. Mr. Ballou's private correspondence was never very extensive; his letters were nearly all of a domestic nature, or brief notes relating to exchanges with other brethren at a distance. The reason that his letters were so much of this nature, was, that when he transcribed his thoughts to paper it was for the press. Most men of strong and active minds are in the practice of relieving them, as it were, by writing down their thoughts, from time to time, to valued friends; it is a sort of necessary relief that some minds could not get along without. But Mr. Ballou's writings were so universally made public, and he was so constantly supplying the public press with matter, even to the very last week of his life, that his mind and pen were quite sufficiently worked in this vein, without seeking any other channel.

During the fall of 1843, Mr. Ballou, then at the age of seventy-two years, made a long journey to the West, to attend the national convention of Universalists, held at Akron, Ohio. On the route thither, in company with Rev. Thomas Whittemore and some other friends, he visited, for the first time, Niagara Falls. Mr. Whittemore, in writing home a description of their visit to his paper, the Trumpet, said: — "When we came to Table "Rock, Father Ballou stood in amazement, and when we "urged him to go back over the river before dark, 'Oh!' "said he, 'how can I go away?' He said his thoughts "were like those of Peter on one occasion: 'It is good to "be here; let us build tabernacles, and dwell upon the "spot.' A prism was handed to him, through which he "could see the rapids in colors ineffably glorious. 'Oh! "my soul! oh! glory to God!' were his exclamations."

No man had a more thorough appreciation of all that was grand and noble in nature, no one a keener eye for her myriads of charms that gladden our daily lives and illumine the pathway of life.

"We heard him, for the first time," says the editor of the American Phrenological Journal, "at a Universalist "general convention, Akron, Ohio, in September, 1843, "where he preached to a very large gathering, with the "ablest men in the denomination preceding and following "him. Many of them delivered more elaborate and "carefully studied discourses, but there was no other who "made the brown faces of the old farmers so fairly *shine* "with admiration and delight as 'Father Ballou.' Many "of them had heard him in New England thirty or forty "years previous, and now, hearing that he was to attend "the convention, had come thirty or forty miles to listen "to him once again, and for the last time on earth. "Though then past man's allotted period of 'three-score "years and ten,' his distinctness of utterance, clearness "of statement, aptness of illustration, and force of argu-"ment, might well have been taken as a model by a "young preacher; and, though he spoke more than an "hour, a very general regret was evident that he closed "so soon. In person Mr. Ballou was tall and slight, "with a bearing of unaffected meekness and humility."

In the summer of the succeeding year he made another visit to New York and Philadelphia, in accordance with the promise made some years before, to come as often and for as long a period as was convenient to him, and also in compliance with the earnest solicitations of the societies in both these cities at that time. As we have before remarked, he had formed many personal friends in both these cities, and it was, as we have heard him often declare, refreshing to his heart to meet them and enjoy their liberal and kind hospitality. He felt, too, an earnest solicitude for the spiritual welfare of those societies, before whom he had so often spoken with such satisfaction to himself and profit to them. During this journey southward, by the solicitations of the societies in Baltimore, Mr. Ballou extended his visit to that city, where he stopped for a short period, which time he improved by the delivery of sermons day and evening. On his return to Boston, he preached a sermon, we well remember, relative to the condition of the cause of Universalism, and was made glad at heart by the state in which he found it in these cities, and at being able to make such goodly report at home. It was like the husbandman going abroad in his master's vineyard, and counting the harvest of his lord, which he had himself planted.

The kind and hospitable treatment which Mr. Ballou always received, in the cities particularly of New York and Philadelphia, seems to have made a most indelible impression upon his heart. Often has he spoken of it in his family circle, until we have felt almost as though we had individually shared the delightful reunions which he described. True, it was thus wherever he visited, as it regarded making warm and lasting friends, but he has left memorandums that signify his remembrance more particularly of the societies of these cities. He says: — "In New York and Philadelphia, I have ever been made "by the brethren to feel that I was at *home;* kind "hearts and hands have ever greeted me in either place, "and some of the happiest and most profitable moments "of my life I think have been passed in ministering to "the beloved societies in these places. Had my Heavenly "Father seen fit to render my services less happy and "fortunate in their result in Boston, I should have "found a happy home in either New York or Philadel-"phia. As it is, my frequent visits to both have afforded "me undiminished satisfaction, and much social enjoy-"ment. My sincere prayers are constantly offered for "their happiness, well-being, and spiritual good." The great and moving cause of his exerting such an influence by his words and manners over the minds of people in his religious teachings, as well as his private intercourse, was the spirit of sincerity that imbued every motion, while the beauty and purity of his moral character seemed to sanctify every word and action, which emanated from him. With not the slightest stain upon his character from boyhood, he was such a being as people could afford to reverence, respect, and love.

Through the whole of his long and active career, Mr. Ballou never once turned aside from the one great object and purpose of his heart, that of promulgating God's fatherly and impartial love to all mankind, as evinced in the holy Scriptures and the dispensations of Providence.

In a poem, ending with the two following verses, he has himself expressed his devoted zeal better than we can do.

"Not all thy foes on earth can say
Can turn my heart from thee away;
And yet my heart is free;
These wounds and scars, that men despise,
Are jewels precious in thine eyes,
And this is all to me.

"Had I ten thousand years to live,
Had I ten thousand lives to give,
All these should be thine own;
And that foul scorn thy foes bestow
Still prove a laurel to my brow,
And their contempt a throne."

In this service he never wrote or uttered a single sentence that was not peculiar to himself for its plainness of purpose, yet depth of thought, and for strong logical reasoning to this grand end. He possessed for his purpose a large share of ready, manly eloquence, not nervous and startling, but cool and convincing; and this, coupled with a natural quickness in discovering the strength or weakness of an argument, ever insured him victory in religious controversy. No sarcasm, no reflection, no imputation could throw him off his guard for one moment. He was ever unruffled, yet forcible, evincing the spirit of the doctrine which he advocated at all times. It was perfectly impossible to so excite him in controversy as to lead him to say the least ungentlemanly, or even abrupt thing. He stood for years as a target for the poisoned arrows of malice, bigotry and envy, and bore all with a serene dignity of spirit, which a firm reliance in Heaven could alone have given.

In his public teachings he never indulged in abstractions, never ran away from his theme, upon abstruse and visionary ideas. He was in this respect, as in all others, eminently natural, eminently practical, eminently *original.* We do not find nature teaching us by adducing vague notions of facts, but rather by a display of the facts themselves. Abstractions and transcendentalisms are but thick fogs to cloud the mental vision, while plain matter-of-fact is the clear, bright view of truth, with the soft, rich perspective of wisdom. It is exceedingly questionable, when we hear a minister dilating upon the arts and sciences, or leading his hearers off in a vein of visionary philosophy, whether that man has a religion worth preaching, or that is congenial to his own heart.

"He was *a man of great originality and remark-* "*able power*," says Rev. Mr. Miner. "He walked not "in a beaten track. His method of interpretation was "all his own; it was evolved by the new faith which "inspired him, and maintained throughout a self-con- "sistency unknown to biblical writers fifty years ago. "Though his labor consisted in dealing with the most "familiar statements, yet he never failed to shed upon "his theme a new and diviner light, and to invest it with "rare and universal interest. It is no condemnation of "his method of interpretation to say that it seemed, to "the perverted understanding of that time, to be forced "and unnatural. The value of this circumstance may "be justly estimated by the fact, that the current meth- "ods of the world have been constantly assimilating to "his method, ever since it has been in conflict with "them.

"It was in his style of exposition and clearness of "illustration, rather than in his form of statement, that "his originality consisted. It was manifested not so "much by rhetorical aids, as by his vivid embodiment of "the principle he would inculcate. In the early part of "his ministry, he had too much hard work to do, too "many open and covert foes to contend with, too many "hurtful errors to overthrow, to permit him to loiter in "the fields of literature for the gathering of verbal and "rhetorical bouquets. He needed not these aids. His "thought was rare, and burned with the truths of God. "Howsoever expressed, it was sure to be remembered. "The hearer might have no recollection of the dress. "Whether clothed or unclothed, whether 'in the body or "out of the body,' he might not be able to say. One "thing, however, he could say; a new thought, glowing "like the sun in the heavens, with a light all its own, "had found a place in his heart. He who possesses such a "power need seek no other. The trappings of literature "can never do the work of truth. They may dazzle the "imagination; but truth alone can warm the heart. They "may lead to the admiration of man, but never to the "adoration of God."

This is so much in the spirit of what we have before remarked, that the quotation is most applicable.

Several short poems are introduced into these pages from Mr. Ballou's pen. They are generally taken at random from his published fugitive pieces, unless designed to illustrate some particular trait of character or frame of mind, some cherished principle of the writer's heart. Though we claim no fame for Mr. Ballou as a poet, yet his productions in this line of composition are numerous.

A volume of his poems has lately been collected and published, but these pieces were thrown off in the hurry of an editor's duty, and evince no care on the writer's part. He has left us scraps of verse, however, which show that the power was native in him, and the poet's genius a part of his natural endowment. The verses that will close the last of this volume, though written in old age, compare favorably with those of any production of the kind we have ever met with. As late as the year 1844, he was an occasional contributor of poems to the press, of a character calculated for the times. These verses were given to the public under the signature of "Spectator," and were designed to effect some prominent end, to reform some acknowledged impropriety, or to commend that which was good and useful. These, however, were never attributed to him, nor was it known out of his family circle that he had written them. Some of them were humorous, some pathetic, some patriotic. His poems were always easy and liquid in versification, full of point and meaning, expressing much in a few words, while the ideas are clothed in the sweetest garb of poesy. Witness the following, which is the only one at hand at this time:

HYMN FOR FOURTH OF JULY.

"Arise and hail the jubilee,
The day that set our nation free;
In song his honor chant who gave
Counsel and victory to the brave.

Ye daughters fair, fresh garlands weave,
With chaplets strew the warrior's grave;
Lo! from the mould'ring sod shall rise
Fame's sweetest incense to the skies.

Fifty bright summer suns have smiled,
And fifty harvest moons beguiled
Childhood and youth, since vernal showers
First moistened freedom's lovely flowers.

Let joy throughout our land inspire
Each manly heart with holy fire;
And freedom's song, by Miriam sung,
Be heard from every female tongue."

We well remember to have been present on one occasion, when a conversation took place between Mr. Ballou and a visitor who had come from a distance on purpose to see and talk with him on the matter of religion. He was vacillating in his faith, but was by no means persuaded of the truth of Universalism. He was a man of wealth, had retired from business, but having had his mind brought to a serious turn by a very critical illness, which had nearly proved fatal to him, he had resolved to make the Scriptures his study until he should be able to say that he had joy and peace in believing. This he told Mr. Ballou, who commended his resolution, promised to afford him any and all light within his own power to impart, and sitting down together, they conversed for some time.

"I cannot see," said the visitor at last, "why it is "that a religion which promises its believers and follow-"ers eternal life for obedience, and the woe of eter-

"nal misery for disobedience, does not make more truly "religious people than your doctrine, which holds forth "only temporary evil for disobedience, and temporary "reward for obedience. The matter seems very strange to "me."

"I will tell you the reason of this," said Mr. Ballou, "and in so doing I will give you an evidence also of the "truth of the doctrine I profess. The reason is found in "the very nature of man, his disposition, and natural "promptings. Give to him a task to perform, threaten "him with the most fearful sufferings and torment if he "fail to accomplish the duty you have prescribed for him, "and his calculation will naturally be to do just as little "of the hated work as it is possible for him to do and "avoid the punishment. Now, on the other hand, you "give him an occupation which he is satisfied will be "productive of his own happiness and good, that in the "very nature of things will produce him an ample and "abundant reward, and the selfishness natural to man "will lead him to be faithful."

"It would most certainly seem to be so," answered the visitor, thoughtfully.

"Certainly this is plain philosophy," was the answer.

"But I do not exactly understand your application," said the stranger.

"That is just what I am coming to. Present to man "a religion of which the services are calculated to pro-"mote his rational enjoyment, which takes nothing from "him without returning more than its value, and in the "spirit of which increase of duty is an increase of happi-"ness, and there is but little danger but that they will "eagerly accept it. This world is full of labor, toil, and "traffic, and the whole is carried on by the power of this "principle."

"I must acknowledge that religion has seemed to be "too much sustained by threats and promises," said the stranger.

"To be sure it has," said Mr. Ballou. "The idea that "we perform any service in order to escape punishment, "renders that service tedious and irksome to us; while, "on the contrary, duty is supreme delight when love is "the inducement and the labor." *

The individual above referred to was an Englishman, who came often to Mr. Ballou's house afterwards, and held similar conversations. This was no unusual case. Perfect strangers came and sat for hours sometimes, evidently seekers after truth, and anxious ones too. To such Mr. Ballou was ever condescending, patient, and took delight in answering all their queries upon certain doctrinal points, explaining each passage referred to, showing its bearing upon others, and challenging the visitor's respect by his urbanity and never-varying politeness in all things.

Mr. Ballou was ever ready and prompt at an answer, and his replies were frequently tempered with a quick

* The recollection of this conversation was recalled to the writer's mind by lately reading one of Mr. Ballou's published sermons, where a very similar argument may be found.

and pungent wit. He was on a certain occasion, on his way to deliver a lecture in the town of Reading, Vt., surrounded by a number of people, when an Orthodox deacon, confronting him suddenly, asked, with a taunting air and self-sufficient bearing, —

"Will you answer me one question, Mr. Ballou?"

"Certainly, if I can do so at such short notice," said Mr. Ballou, smiling at the man's impetuosity.

"Well, sir," said the deacon, "what will become of a "man who goes out of the world cursing and swearing, "and calling on God to damn his soul to hell?"

"Do you believe, my dear sir," said Mr. Ballou, "that a righteous God would answer the vile prayer of "such a wicked wretch?"

"Why no," said the deacon, "of course not."

"You have answered your own question then," said Mr. Ballou, quietly, while the deacon turned away much disconcerted.

It is so true that Folly's shallow lip can ask the deepest question, that it is well to remember sometimes, that a fool should be answered according to his folly.

"The frequency of his times of preaching, in the "former part of his ministry," says the editor of the Repository, "can be but ill imagined now, nor the "intense interest with which his message was listened to "by the multitude. At times he would preach between "two appointments, while his horse was feeding, — his "pulpit the base of a noble oak, and the congregation "reverently standing in its broad shadow. Taking "advantage of his haste in leaving, some question would "be asked him by some restive, dogmatic deacon, and the "undreamed of answer, that came as the lightning's flash, "would add new fuel to the fire of interest he had kindled "in the midst of the people."

In this connection we are reminded of an anecdote, for which we are indebted to Rev. Sylvanus Cobb, of the Christian Freeman. We introduce it here to show Mr. Ballou's power of argument without the least tincture of ostentation. It was often his way in debate to ask some apparently simple but natural question, which his opponent answering, as he obviously must do, would almost certainly refute his own fragile creed or position, and himself and others would be led to see where the truth really was. Mr. Cobb says: —

"The world at large have known much of the powers "and genius of Mr. Ballou's mind from his published "works, but he had most lovely traits of character which "a personal acquaintance only could discover. While an "intellectual giant in strength, he was unaffectedly mod- "est and unassuming, and never engaged in mere dis- "putations. He would never enter into a combat for "mere personal mastery, nor pursue a noisy contest with "one who showed himself to be insincere and trickish; "while his own meekness and simplicity of spirit, com- "bined with his clearness of perception, would generally "cut down the swaggering, cavilling spirit, if he came in "contact with it.

"An interesting incident, illustrative of this amiable

"trait of character, once occurred in a brief exchange of "words between him and Abner Kneeland. Mr. Knee-"land had become an atheist, and one day came into an "apartment where there was a little company of our min-"istering brethren, among whom was Mr. Ballou. Mr. "Kneeland was forward to communicate this supposed "new light to those with whom he was formerly asso-"ciated in the ministry of Christ. He could dispense "with the use of a creator of the world and of man, "regarding the physical universe and the human species "as eternal in their being without beginning. Yet he "got in the idea, in the course of the conversation, that "man is composed of the elements of nature.

"Mr. Ballou had been sitting in silence, with his "elbows resting upon his knees (an attitude he often "assumed when listening attentively to an argument). "At this point he raised his head, and assumed an erect "position of body, and said: —

"'Bro. Kneeland, you seem to have thought a great "deal on these subjects, and perhaps you can give me "some useful information. Now we see around us, in "the city and country, a great many wooden houses. "Of what are these houses made?'

"'They are made of timbers, boards, shingles, and the "like,' answered Mr. Kneeland.

"'And out of what,' said Mr. Ballou, 'are these "boards and shingles made?'

"'Out of trees,' replied Mr. K.

"'Then,' said Mr. Ballou, 'all wooden houses were

"made out of trees. If so, must there not have been "trees before there was a wooden house?'

"'Yes,' said the other, 'of course.'

"'Well, I thought so,' said Mr. Ballou; 'and now,' "continued he, 'here are many brick houses, — of what "are they made?'

"'They are made,' answered Mr. Kneeland, 'out of "bricks, which are composed of clay and sand.'

"'Well, then,' said Mr. Ballou, 'if all brick houses "are made of bricks, which are composed of clay and "sand, must there not have been bricks before there was "a brick house, and clay and sand before there was a "brick?'

"Mr. Kneeland now, perceiving what application Mr. "Ballou was about to make of his concessions, to explain "his philosophy of having men composed of the elements "of nature and yet having no elements of nature before "there were men, began to equivocate! He would not "admit the inference from the fact that all brick houses "were made of bricks, etc., and he even retraced his "steps, and took back what he had admitted in respect to "wooden houses.

"'What!' said Mr. Ballou, 'if all wooden houses "were made of trees, must there not have been trees "before there were wooden houses?'

"'No,' replied Mr. Kneeland, 'that need not fol- "low?'

"'Well, then,' said Mr. Ballou, '*how stupid I am!*'

"And as he uttered these words, he dropped his head

"again, and let himself back into a posture of quiet rest. "Mr. Kneeland at the same time choked and blushed; "and attempted to recover himself for renewed conversa- "tion, but he evidently could not, and so took his depar- "ture.

"This is but one of many incidents which might be "cited to illustrate Mr. Ballou's simplicity in the pur- "suit and love of truth, his readiness with argument for "its support and advancement, in connection with a "modest, unassuming habit, and a hatred of bluster and "noisy strife."

A volume might be filled with anecdotes equally characteristic of Mr. Ballou's manner and style of argument, had we the necessary time to collect them. But we trust that the few that are compiled and given to our readers herewith, may sufficiently familiarize them with the subject's character, both as a Christian and as a theologian. Since commencing this work, a vast number of anecdotes have suggested themselves to the writer's mind, and others, new to him, have been submitted by friends; but only such as have been considered valuable as illustrating his character, and which are known to be authentic, have been selected for publication in these pages.

CHAPTER XI.

DOMESTIC AND PERSONAL CHARACTERISTICS.

All who knew Mr. Ballou intimately, can bear witness that his home was a happy one. This, of course, was owing to the manner in which he had framed and modeled that home after his own heart and the dictates of the religion he professed. He was the master mind there; his word was law, his simplest wish strictly complied with. He was looked up to with a degree of respect and veneration by his children, that was an abiding evidence of his true character. In the government of his family, he *led*, but never *drove*, his children, endeavoring, to the utmost of his ability, to bring them up in the nurture and admonition of the Lord, and, taking his divine Master for his example, he governed them by love and kindness alone.

He was strongly characterized for his fondness of domestic enjoyment, and throughout his whole life, to the very end, evinced the most constant and tenderest solicitude for each and all of his children. Even after they had married and settled in life, with families about them, this solicitude continued as ardent as ever; nor was there one of those children who would undertake any matter of importance without first consulting his wishes in the premises, and seeking his advice upon the subject; so highly were both respected and esteemed. This is mentioned in this connection, not as an encomium upon the family, but simply to show the reader the universal love and respect that its head always commanded. We find this subject referred to by Rev. Henry Bacon, in his published remarks concerning the decease of the subject of this biography. He refers to the respect in which his advice was held upon secular matters, not only in his own family, but by others of his acquaintance.

"He was great," says Mr. Bacon, "in the clearness "with which he saw the essential truths of the gospel, "and in the power with which he communicated them to "others, by that spirit of calm earnestness, and that won-"drous faculty to make himself intelligible, which pecu-"liarly distinguished him. He was great as a logician; "great in wisdom that penetrates to the reality of char-"acter, and opens the real motives that sway the man; "*and his counsel in matters far removed from his* "*peculiar walk in life was weighed as the utterance* "*of an oracle that must not be slighted.* Simple in his "habits, he lost nothing of life in indulgences that rob "existence of its serenity; fixed in a few great princi-"ples, he made everything contribute thereto for the "enlargement of his views of men and things; and, rev-

" erencing the Scriptures with a depth of reliance that "was beautiful to behold, he brought forth the harmonies "of the divine Word in a manner that suggested more "than he ever expressed, though he expressed enough to "satisfy millions of souls."

May we add here, how grateful such words of appreciation are to the hearts of his family.

The following was furnished us by Rev. Thomas Whittemore, and would seem to come most properly under this chapter of Domestic and Personal Characteristics. Mr. Whittemore was solicited for something relative to the subject, being so old and valued a friend of the deceased, and he thus speaks: —

"The life of Hosea Ballou is, in almost every respect, "pleasing to contemplate. It was a very active life. "He travelled much, he preached often, he studied con-"tinually, and he wrote not a little. In the earlier part "of his life he joined teaching of the young in the com-"mon sciences to his other avocations. No small portion "of his leisure time he spent in reading; but he *thought* "more than he read. He was always digging for gold; "not, however, in books, but in the mine of his own in-"tellect. His mind was very active.

"The most pleasing part of his life was his serene old "age. The writer of this remembers him well when he "was forty years of age. Ten years afterwards, the writer "entered his family to pursue a course of studies for the "ministry. Mr. B.'s mind at fifty seemed never at rest. "If not reading, he was busily engaged in mental effort.

"Often, when he was walking in the streets, have we "seen his lips move, as if he were talking. At his home, "he would sit frequently with his eyes closed, his lips "moving, as if holding conversation with some invisible "person; and when he apparently came to some crisis in "his meditations, he showed some outward sign of his "feelings, sometimes by a smile, at others by suppressed "laughter, at others by a sigh.

"A mind thus active is in danger of disturbing, if too "much indulged, the proper action of the digestive pow- "ers, which, in their turn, react upon the mind, and "produce lowness of spirits and gloom. Mr. Ballou at "fifty was troubled in this way. His heart had an affec- "tion sympathetic with the stomach, and its action was "irregular and intermittent. At this point of his life, he "had lived but three or four years in Boston; and he had "had occasion to perform a large amount both of mental "and physical labor. He had preached three times "almost every Sabbath; had edited, for two years, the "'Universalist Magazine;' had visited many parts of the "country to preach the gospel, sometimes under very "animating circumstances; and these complicated labors "were too much for him. His most sagacious friends "then had fears either that he would not live to old age, "or, if he did, that his later years would be unquiet.

"We remember, with very great satisfaction, the ex- "ceeding gentleness and amiability of his wife, in the "days of which we speak. While this excellent lady "still survives, it is not proper for us to express all "that may be justly said of her. She presided over "her household with a fidelity, a blandness, a kindness, "steady as the current of a river, and unruffled as a lake "in the calmest day. This season of intermixture of "health and sickness, joy and sadness, light and shade, "continued for some half dozen years, when it was very "gratifying to Mr. B.'s friends to see that each change "denoted that his life might be protracted perhaps to old "age, and that, peradventure, his old age should be as "serene as his earlier days had been laborious and useful. "Such proved to be the fact. He died in his eighty-"second year, and his life grew more and more serene "unto its close; like the sun, obscured somewhat by "passing clouds at noon, but shining clearly during the "rest of the day, making its course through the western "sky, and passing away from the earth, as it were, into "the boundless heavens beyond.

"This quiet old age I attribute to several circum-"stances. Mr. Ballou was a man of sound sense. It "was his aim to make the best of everything. He was a "Christian philosopher. He sought to rule his own "spirit. He believed that humility and meekness were "the brightest jewels in the Christian's crown. He had "a firm trust in his Maker's goodness. He believed "that God was the Sovereign of the universe, a Father "of infinite goodness, as well as of infinite power, who "executed his will in the armies of heaven, and among "the inhabitants of the earth; and who, by everything "which he did, and by everything which he permitted to "be done, was seeking infallibly the good of his crea-"tures. What an influence would such a faith exert on "Mr. Ballou's life!

"Added to this, he had a wife whose constant effort "and highest joy was to make her husband happy. Few "such women have lived. It is my duty to declare, "that, during thirty years' acquaintance with her, I "never have heard the first unkind word from her lips, "respecting any human being. Towards her husband, "there was a devotion that never tired. It was her con-"stant desire and aim to make him useful and happy. "She appeared well in any society, but home was her "genial sphere. Much of the quiet of Father Ballou's "old age must be attributed to her. His children, also, "have been sources of great comfort to him. They dili-"gently aimed to make him happy. He loved them all "with surpassing tenderness, and they loved him in "consequence. Had anything unfavorable happened to "either of his children, it would have been like a dart "driven through his soul. We know that, even in that "case, his religion and his philosophy would have come "to his aid; he would have believed that God had a wise "purpose in it; but, even with that alleviation, it must "greatly have disturbed his life. No such affliction, "however, awaited him. Two of his sons became preach-"ers of the same gospel which he had defended, and by "their prudent lives gained the respect of all who knew "them. They have not, like many clergymen, moved "frequently from place to place, but, for about a quarter "of a century, have remained stationary pastors. In "respect to the goods of this world, they have been pru-"dent, and have prospered. * * * * The daugh-"ters have all been married to faithful, kind, and prudent "husbands, of whom two are preachers of the gospel, and "all, men of respectability, intelligence, and thrift.

"Such have been the circumstances of Father Ballou's "family. But we have yet to mention another source of "the happiness of his last days. He saw himself stand-"ing at the head of a large and prosperous body of "Christians, who loved and venerated him for his labors, "the purity of his character, and the good he had done. "He saw their regard for him manifested at such times, "and in such ways, that he had reason to believe it was "not done for effect, but was the outgushing of the real "feeling of their hearts. At the meetings of conven-"tions, associations, and other public bodies, all were "happy to greet the old soldier of the cross. His "strength was spared to him to such a degree, that he "was able to travel and preach up to the close of his life. "His last sermon was delivered within eight days of his "death. He used frequently to say that it seemed to "him no man had more to be thankful for than he. "Prudence in diet; prudence in labor; a kind heart; an "affectionate companion; loving children; ease in his "worldly circumstances; the homage of the class of "Christians to which he belonged; the respect of man-"kind at large; ability to pursue his favorite calling to "the end of life; a strong trust in God, whose commands "he sought diligently to obey; — these were the causes "of the serenity of his old age. 'Mark the perfect man, "and behold the upright: for the end of that man is "peace.' Psalm 37 : 37."

Especially was he fond of children and infants. This was a markedly prominent feature in his feelings; and children, too, never failed to make friends with him at once. In our own humble experience, we have made this a criterion of judgment in character. He who warmly and quickly interests a child,— whose temperament is such that infancy can easily assimilate with it,— whose sympathies are of a nature quickly to unite when brought in contact with childhood,— that man has at heart much of the real *purity* and *innocence* which are the main characteristics of those whom the Saviour blessed. We never saw a child shun or turn away from him; but we have seen scores of those who were strangers, put out their little hands and go willingly to him. In his own family circle his love of children found ample scope and a genial field for exercise.

More than forty of his own grandchildren might have been gathered together at one time during his life. But, as we have intimated, it was not with these alone that the spirit we refer to was evinced; it was the same with one as with another. All children he dearly loved, and particularly noticed. There seemed to be a magic power in his voice, and in the gentle beaming of his clear, expressive eyes, that carried assurance to their timid bosoms; and they would nestle happy and undismayed in his arms, or listen to his words, so cunningly adapted to the powers of their tender intellect.

The secret of Mr. Ballou's remarkable success in his family government, was, doubtless, his following those rules which he has so well expressed and laid down for others. It is a valuable excerpt that he has left, and we doubt not that the reader will thank us for introducing it here, and in his own words: — "When giving to your "children commands, be careful that you speak with a "becoming dignity, as if not only the right, but the wis-"dom also to command, was with you. Be careful not "to discover a jealousy that your injunctions may not be "attended to; for if the child sees that you have your "doubts, they will lead the child to doubt too. Be cau-"tious never to give your commands in a loud voice, nor "in haste. If you must speak loudly in order to be "obeyed, when it is not convenient to raise your voice "you must expect to be disobeyed; and if it be conve-"nient for you to speak loudly, you must remember it is "inconvenient for others to hear it.

"But, with regard to manner, be careful to speak in a "soft, tender, kind and loving way. Even when you "have occasion to rebuke, be careful to do it with mani-"fest kindness. The effects will be incalculably better. "When you are obliged to deny the request that your "child may make, do not allow yourself to do this with "severity. It is enough for our dear little ones to "be denied of what they may think they want, without "being nearly knocked down with a sharp voice ringing "in their tender ears.

"If you practise severity, speak harshly, frequently "punish in anger, you will find your children will imbibe "your spirit and manners. First you will find that they "will treat each other as you treat them; and after they "arrive to a little age, they will treat you with unkind "and unbecoming replies. But if you are wise, and "treat your little ones with tenderness, you will fix the "image of love in their minds, and they will love you and "each other, and in their conversation will imitate the "conversation which they have heard from the tenderest "friend which children have on earth."

In this connection we are reminded of a letter, lately published, from Mrs. C. A. Soule, relative to her impressions touching the death of the subject of this memoir. It will be remembered that her husband was a warm and cherished friend of Mr. Ballou's, and that he was associated with him as colleague over the Second Universalist Society, in School-street, Boston, as late as 1845.

"As vividly as though it were but yesterday, does "memory bring to me that sunny April day, in 1844, "when I first entered the sanctuary where he had min- "istered so many years. There was a dedication service, "and I thought then, and I think now, that I never gazed "upon a more impressive sight than was presented at "that moment, when the aged pastor took in his arms the "little helpless babe, and in touching words consecrated "it to Him who said 'Suffer little children to come "unto me.' That picture of infancy and age,—how I "longed for a pencil to sketch it! Thank Heaven, mem-"ory, with faithful touch, inscribed it on my heart, and "it will ever hang there, one of its most beautiful pic-"tures. And now I see him at my own threshold. I "meet him, and present him my own little one, my first-"born. How tenderly he caresses it! Long he looks "into her laughing eyes, and then exclaims, in a tone I "can never forget, 'How I wish I could read her "thoughts!' Then, sitting down, he tells me that he "never yet looked on a babe without longing to know the "workings, the thoughts, of the infant mind; and after-"wards gave me some excellent advice about so training "that little one that when age should enable her to reveal "her thoughts, they might all be pure and beautiful. "How lifelike is the portrait I have of him in my mind's "eye! It seems so palpable that I almost feel the light "as it streams from that thrilling eye, and hear the "eloquent words that tremble on that 'heaven-touched "tongue.'"

In illustration of the feelings which influenced him as it regarded intercourse with his children, and consideration for their enjoyment, and sympathy with them even in many seeming trifles, we relate the following anecdote, which, though perhaps trifling in itself, is by no means without value in point of application.

When Mr. Ballou engaged, in 1834, to go to New York and Philadelphia, it became known to one of his parishioners, who desired to send his child, a young lady, to the latter city, on a visit to some relations or friends His request to take charge of the young person was cheerfully acceded to by Mr. Ballou. It so happened that the person who was to accompany him was a classmate at school and a very intimate companion of one of his own daughters, the eldest then at home. When this daughter learned that her classmate was to accompany her father on his journey, she could not but express a wish that she were going also. There were no railroad conveniences then, nor were scarcely any of the present accommodations for travelling perfected. It was not only considerable of an undertaking to commence a journey of three hundred miles, but it necessarily involved not a trifling expense.

It came to the ears of Mr. Ballou that his child really desired to accompany him; and, when he understood the circumstances, he immediately gave his consent,—telling her, playfully, not to say anything to her young friend of this, but that he would manage an agreeable surprise for her. The stage came to the house very early on the morning appointed for starting,—long before daylight. Mr. Ballou and his daughter got in, and took their places on the back seat, the latter well wrapped up about the face. They then drove to the house of her schoolmate, who was to accompany them. She also took her place in the vehicle, exchanging a salutation with Mr. Ballou, and they drove off in the darkness. It was not long before the young lady took occasion to remark, casually, to Mr. Ballou, how agreeable it *would* have been could Elmina (the daughter) have accompanied them. "Very,— very indeed," said Mr. Ballou; and they still drove quietly on. At last, the city being now left far behind, and daylight having appeared, Mr. Ballou asked the young lady if she knew the person by her side. On hearing this inquiry, she turned to see her neighbor's face, and lo! it was her classmate and dearest friend with whom she had been thus seated so long without recognizing her! The daughter has since often declared that she knew not which enjoyed the ruse most on this occasion,— father or child.

During the year 1845, Mr. Ballou, being then seventy-four years of age, wrote and published two or three essays in the Universalist Quarterly, upon certain passages of scripture which had seemed to be a stumbling-block to many of his own denomination. One of these texts was that commencing, "In my Father's house are many mansions," etc. This, by some of the order of Universalists, was supposed to signify that in the future state there would be different degrees of blessedness, in proportion to the worthiness of the spirit, or to its moral character and mental cultivation. This idea was thoroughly exploded, as it regarded many minds, by the article referred to, which was thus the means of converting many doubtful minds, as they acknowledged, some of them orally, and some by letters addressed to him from at home and abroad. The clear, logical style of reasoning evinced in this essay, and in one published by him not long subsequent in the Quarterly, relative to the question as to what influence our present being may have on our future existence, showed conclusively that the full strength and vigor that originally rendered his writings so forcible were with him still, that his mental vision was as keen as ever, and that none of his powers of intellect had waned in their fire.

These articles were penned as correctly and distinctly, as it regarded the chirography, as was his early custom, and generally written, if not at one sitting, within the space of a few hours; for, when he had anything to do, he could not feel contented until it was done. The article completed, he would carefully fold it, and wend his way personally to the publishing-house in Cornhill, and deposit it there, never failing at the appointed time to read the proof, concerning which he was very sensitive, and very correct. It was but a few days prior to his decease that he read thus the proof-sheets of his last article, furnished for the Universalist Quarterly.

In the manuscript which Mr. Ballou furnished the author of this biography, there appears written about this period, the fall of 1845, the following interesting paragraph relative to the immense change that he had lived to see transpire in the religious world about him.

"Since I came to this city, I have enjoyed the happi-"ness of seeing the cause of religion prosper, and the "different denominations growing more liberal and more "charitable towards each other. I have seen, too, my "own peculiar views received very generally, and regarded "very favorably by the denomination to which I have "belonged from the commencement of my public labors. "Since I came here I have been rejoiced to see the won- "derful increase of Universalist societies in Boston and "the neighboring towns, as well as in the other States "of our Union. There are firmly established ones now "in Roxbury, Cambridgeport, East Cambridge, Medford, "Malden, etc., besides five or six in Boston, to the com- "mencement and building up of which I have had the "pleasure of adding my mite by way of labor."

It was very natural that he should then contrast the state and condition of the cause with its feebleness when he first came to Boston. A few scattered believers were all it numbered then; persecution and obloquy greeted its defenders at every step. To be called a Universalist was equivalent to being called anything vile and wicked, and the name was held as one of reproach by nearly all. But how vastly different was the prospect that presented itself to his view in the closing days of his life, and how grateful this must have been to him who had borne the burthen and the heat of the day! He saw the denomination vastly extended. He saw Universalists respected not only for numbers, but for the goodly influence they exerted far and wide.

He saw that there were now nineteen annual state conventions, eighty-two associations, eight missionary societies, ten hundred and seventy societies, professing the doctrine; seven hundred and ninety-nine meeting-houses devoted to this worship, and some seven hundred preachers in his Master's vineyard, who taught the doctrine of

God's impartial grace. These, and other facts equally illustrating the wonderful change he had witnessed, caused him, when toasted and called upon at the late festival of brethren in Boston, to speak to them, to say, that as he gazed on the crowd before him, and thought of the multitude they represented, he was reminded of the beginning of Universalism in New England, and to quote the words of the prophet: "There was a handful of corn in "the top of the mountain, but its fruit shall shake like "Lebanon!"

How apt and true the quotation.

We have seen that the vigor and keenness of Mr. Ballou's mind had in no way abated, that every mental faculty still shone brightly as at the prime of his manhood. Let us show the reader statistically what that mind had performed in its time. During his professional life he delivered *over ten thousand sermons.* This calculation, which at first appears to be so very large, is nevertheless strictly correct, and will not seem to be overrated, when we call to mind the fact that for more than thirty years of his ministration he not only preached three times every Sabbath, but *frequently* for several consecutive days of the week beside. Until within five or ten years past, three sermons on the Sabbath has been his usual performance, in the line of his professional duty. And after his sermons in country towns, the answering of questions, and the conversation he was obliged to hold in private with honest seekers after truth, were quite as laborious, in fact, as were his public services in the pulpit.

We have known him to occupy nearly half the night, not unfrequently, in this manner, patiently and zealously.

Including his essays and treatises upon doctrinal subjects, his fugitive sermons furnished for the different magazines and papers of which he was editor for a long period of time, and afterwards a constant contributor to the very end of his life, beside a large number which appeared in pamphlet form, and of which no particular mention is made in these pages, and the works herein referred to, Mr. Ballou has written and published enough to make one hundred volumes, containing the same amount of matter as the one now in the hands of the reader. The mere mechanical labor of writing such a mass of composition is in itself a Herculean task; but when we consider that each page is characterized by careful reasoning upon points that required much thought and study, and that the whole is largely original; that the author was unaided by any other books, save the Bible, in the formation of his arguments and opinions; and that he was a self-made man withal, we shall come to the conclusion, that, to say the least of it, the subject of these memoirs was particularly blessed and aided by Divine Providence.

One secret of his having accomplished so much, is the fact that he was never idle, never contented to sit down with folded arms in his chair and do nothing; a book or a pen was ever in his hands, except when he was taking the ordinary and necessary daily exercise. His life had been too stirring and active for him ever to relapse into dormancy, while his faculties were left to him. How well we can see him at this moment, in the mind's eye, as he used to appear at the centre-table, with his book close by the lamp, of an evening, and his wife opposite to him, listening to the work which he was reading aloud to her; such is almost the last evening scene we can recall in connection with him; his clear, distinct pronunciation, proper emphasis, and fine voice, even in old age, seeming to portray with singular accuracy the author's ideas, and to add a charm to the subject treated upon.

Mr. Ballou had always deprecated the idea of capital punishment, believing the law based on a wrong principle that would take the life of a human creature, while none but God could give it. During the winter of 1845, there was more than the usual interest evinced by the public on this subject, and numerous public meetings were held relative to the subject, and to endeavor to bring about a reform in the criminal code, so as to exclude the death penalty altogether. At several of these assemblies Mr. Ballou made eloquent addresses upon the subject, and wrote a number of articles, which were published, advocating the cause, in which he felt a very great interest. We subjoin the following poem, written by him at this time. It is peculiarly illustrative of his plain, straightforward style of composition.

THE CRIMINAL CODE.

If in the heart the virus dwell
Of murder, can we that expel
By dire revenge, or shall we find
We miss the law that governs mind?

To quench a flame should we engage,
And fuel add, behold the rage!
Now fiercer still the flame ascends,
And fear with consternation blends.

Man kills his neighbor. Why? Because
His passions rise against the laws,
Which God hath written on his soul,
Unmanned the man, and made a fool.

To cure the evil, now the law,
With tiger rage and open jaw,
Cries out for blood, for blood it cries,
Seizes the culprit, and he dies.

Two men are dead in room of one;
And now the work is but begun:
The virus spreads, and everywhere
The deadly taint infects the air.

And murder now becomes more rife;
Lighter esteemed is human life
And he who could not just before,
Now coolly looks on human gore

Revenge is wrong; cannot subdue
The vile affections, but renew
Their actions to a flame more dire,
To rage like a consuming fire.

When will our legislators learn,
That blessed, heavenly truth discern, —
When will it well be understood,
That evil is o'ercome with good?"

Mr. Ballou always had a purpose in view when he wrote, whether prose or poetry, and to this end, more than to the musical cadence of the verse, he exerted his ability at composition, and always successfully.

The subject of this biography was far from being loquacious, and seldom talked without some important and definite purpose in view. Yet, though he might be said to be somewhat reserved in speech, he was by no means secluded or abstracted in his habits, but, on the contrary, generally evinced the liveliest interest in the conversation of those about him. He was not one to break in upon the conversation of others, and if his opinion was given at all, it was almost always because it was solicited. There is such a thing as eloquent silence; and when we see a mind, much enriched by study and experience, offered as it were uninvited, at all times and on all occasions, we see very plainly that there is something wanting. Sidney Smith said of Macaulay, that he only wanted a few brilliant flashes of silence to make him perfect!

There are few old people, or such as have reached the advanced age of threescore and ten, who have not stored up in their memories a fund of stories and personal anecdotes, many, perhaps, of their own individual experience. These they are in the habit of relating frequently as they go on their way of life, and often do so over and over again to the same individuals, through mere forgetfulness. This is perhaps one of the earliest evidences of mental decay. Although, in the course of his long and chequered life, Mr. Ballou had experienced many interesting incidents, and learned many curious anecdotes, yet it was a very rare thing for him to relate one, unless when, in conversation or argument, some one peculiarly applicable to the subject in hand, suggested itself to his mind as illustrative of some feeling or passion of our natural dispositions. When he did speak, those about him always *listened.* It was on such occasions, that, like the sage of "Rasselas," he spoke, and attention watched his lips; he reasoned, and conviction closed his periods. This was particularly the case in his large family circle, where his opinion, as we have before observed, was sought and repeated, on all subjects and on all occasions. While there never was a parent more truly respected, there never was one more dearly beloved. This could not be brought about by an iron rule, and a stern, inflexible character. No. It was accomplished on his part by the exercise, in his domestic relations, of that holy fatherly love which formed the basis of his creed, and which he worshipped in his God.

For a number of years Mr. Ballou was in the habit of carrying a snuff-box in his pocket, and of using the article as freely as is generally the case with those who carry it about them. We all know, doubtless, how very easy a matter it is to contract a habit, and more particularly is this the case in advanced years. But if it is difficult for young people to abandon any bad habit, when the practice has once been fairly contracted, — if it is hard for them to conquer a pleasant but baleful appetite, with the many channels of amusement, occupation, and substitutes that youth and physical vigor present, — how much more difficult must it be for those who are aged and infirm, and who are thrown so much upon their own resources for amusement, and the means of agreeably passing their leisure moments. After having made habitual use of snuff for several years, Mr. Ballou found that it cloyed the nasal organs or passage, and thus slightly affected his voice as to distinctness in public speaking. Perceiving this, he laid by the article at once, without a murmur, and did not use it at all for three years, and never again habitually. This instance of resolution simply serves to show the natural firmness of his character, and the complete self-control which he exercised over himself.

There is still another illustration of this spirit, which we will give here.

About a year subsequent to the period of his discontinuing the use of snuff, a physician suggested to him the propriety of smoking tobacco after each meal, and being at that time slightly dyspeptic, it was thought that it might aid and stimulate the digestive organs. The suggestion was therefore adopted, and Mr. Ballou consequently soon acquired the habit of smoking regularly after each meal, three times a day, which practice he continued for a period of some two years. This habit is universally acknowledged to be one of the most seductive in its character, and one which will draw stronger upon the inclination and appetite than any other, except perhaps the use of ardent spirits. One day we observed that the old gentleman did not light his pipe as usual, after dinner, and we asked him if he had forgotten it. "No," said he. "I have been thinking that I am becoming a "slave to this habit, inasmuch as I find that I have to do "it *regularly* every day at certain periods. It is no "longer a medicine, but a pleasant habit, and I shall "leave it off until I find that I require it again for my "health's sake." His pipe was thenceforth laid aside, as his snuff-box had been, without a murmur, or any external advice to influence him; thus showing the strict self-denial he exercised.

The careful reader will follow out the application of this spirit, for it was adopted by Mr. Ballou in every bearing in which it was possible to affect himself, in accordance with the dictates of his better judgment, not only as it related to simple appetite and agreeable habit, but it was one of his fixed and fundamental principles of character, often evinced. Probably no person who possessed the means, ever desired more to travel over his own and foreign countries, than did the subject of this biography. Well read in ancient and modern history, and familiar with geography, frequent reference was made by him to this desire to visit more particularly Palestine and the East generally. But when urged to gratify what his children knew to be so strong a wish, and with every facility offered him, and one or more of his children to accompany him, his spirit of self-denial caused him to say:— "How much there is to do yet, "that I may accomplish in my Master's vineyard. To "gratify this desire would indeed be delightful to me, "but what benefit could it ever be to my fellow-men?"

He was assiduously kind and thoughtful in relation to animals. For many years, and until latterly, he kept a horse and vehicle for his own use, and he was always particular to see *personally* that the animal was properly fed and protected. He was accustomed daily to prepare from his own plate, after dinner, food for a large dog that belonged to a member of the family, as late as his seventy-eighth year. This kindly solicitude and thoughtfulness for the dumb animals about him was an evidence of the natural goodness of his heart. Animals soon learn to love those that are kind to them, and even the family cat purred more cheerfully when resting by his feet, while he often gave it a kind caress.

Mr. Ballou was very regular as to his personal habits, particularly during the last twenty years of his life. We refer to the taking of his meals, his sleep, exercise, and the like. In late years he was accustomed to retire early at night, and to rise very early in the morning. In former years, as we have shown, he borrowed much of the night for his hours of study. This was particularly the case when he was engaged in his earlier writings, and when acting as sole editor of the various papers with which he was at different times connected. He was indeed remarkably frugal in his diet, and to this may be attributed, in a large degree, the constant good health he enjoyed. He ever preferred the most homely and simple food, partaking of little meat, and more freely of milk and bread. Before the noon-day meal on the Sabbath, with his family assembled about the board, he always asked the divine blessing, in a most impressive manner, but on no other day was he accustomed to do so aloud.

His hand upon the door, or his footfall upon the sill, was a sweet sound to us all; for it was with him as Dr. Doddridge said of his venerable friend Dr. Clark, of St. Albans, — "He brought joy into *every* house which he entered, but most of all into his own house, when he returned to it."

We have once already referred in these pages to Mr. Ballou's wife. Our feelings would naturally prompt a much more elaborate allusion to her many virtues, both as a mother and as a wife. But as we design this biography to be strictly a memoir of Mr. Ballou, we only refer in these pages to such other matters as are deemed necessary to mention, in furtherance of the main object of the work. Mr. Ballou was fortunate in allying himself to a companion who was in every way worthy of him, one whom he loved with the most tender and undying affection through his whole life, and who was to him all that a wife should be. Her characteristics were remarkable industry, simplicity of heart, devotedness to him, and untiring domestic assiduity. With a naturally strong intellect and good judgment, she also coupled the agreeable attraction of personal beauty; but the outward comeliness of her person was far-eclipsed in his eyes by more enduring loveliness.

We have already given, in these pages, some remarks from the pen of the editor of the Trumpet, who, in a notice of Mr. Ballou's life, given on the occasion of a full-length portrait being completed of him, for the School-street Society, at the age of seventy-six, says of his companion: — "Sept. 15, 1796, he was married to "his present wife, a woman of unsurpassable goodness, "concerning whose praise it would be almost impossible "to speak too highly." Mr. Whittemore was, some years since, an inmate of the family for a considerable period of time, and his words must therefore have weight, as coming from one who spoke advisedly.

Many of us know from personal experience how great is the influence upon our lives and actions of her to whom we have been bound by the holy tie of matrimony. Characters are often made or marred by this association. The calm dignity of demeanor, the evenness of temper, the perfect contentment and general life of the subject of this biography, all manifested the true character of his home relations, influences, and associations. Had those relations been different from what they were, a sterner hue would have tinged his character, and a different spirit doubtless have imbued his whole career in life; at least the inference is but natural.

The following lines were written by Mr. Ballou, then at the age of seventy-four years, in an album which he had presented to his wife, and are introduced here to show the affectionate regard that existed between them at this advanced period of life. No comment is necessary, save that the lines were written by a husband to his wife after *fifty years'* companionship.

TO MY WIFE.

"Thou dearest of the dear to me,
Of the beloved the best,
Could'st thou but read this heart and see
The treasures of my breast,
Assurance surely would be thine
That undiminished love,
By age grown better, like to wine,
Can never faithless prove.

Not when the virgin rose of youth
Blushed on thy snowy breast;
Not when we pledged ourselves in truth,
And were by Hymen blessed,
Could strong affection boast as now
Of such resistless sway,
When age sits wrinkled on my brow,
And mortal powers decay."

The patient reader who has followed us thus far in this desultory memoir, must feel more than a passing interest in her who was the bosom companion of Mr. Ballou; and in this connection we therefore introduce the following extract from a communication to the Christian Freeman, dated Sept. 5, 1851, which refers to a visit to the house of Mr. Ballou, who had been indisposed for a few days. After a brief introduction, the writer says: —

"I wish to say a word through you respecting our "venerable and beloved father in Israel, H. Ballou. As "your report last week spoke of the indisposition of this "good brother, and knowing there would be a great "desire, both at home and abroad, to know how he might "be at this time, I did myself the pleasure, last Thursday,

"August 20, to call upon him at his own peaceful home. "Here I met this aged saint, with his faithful companion, "who have lived together over half a century, enjoying "that undisturbed domestic peace and felicity, which it "is to be feared that but few, comparatively speaking, "attain to. Indeed, Father Ballou's family may well be "called a '*model*' family, for love and attachment, fidel-"ity and trust; while the happiness of all is that of each, "and the happiness of each is that of all. They have "had eleven children, and eight are living to bless their "declining years.

"Mrs. Ballou has not been so extensively known to "the *world* as some; but as a *wife* and *mother*, none "can excel her, and her amiable and happy disposition "has enabled her to retain her former pleasant and affa-"ble manner, so that she is the same interesting and "agreeable company that she was when I first knew her, "thirty years ago. And hers is the privilege to have "her children rise up and call her blessed.

"And now, with regard to the present health of "Father Ballou. I was pleased to find him much more "comfortable than I had expected. He has been suffer-"ing very much from a severe cold which he took about "two weeks since, and which has been attended with a "bad cough. He was quite unwell last Sabbath, and "fears were entertained that he would be obliged to "relinquish some of his appointments, which his friends "are depending upon with such deep interest. But the "simple remedies which have been applied, finding such "a perfect and unimpaired constitution to work upon, "have wrought a very favorable and happy result; so "that, on Thursday, he seemed very comfortable, though "his cough was not wholly removed. He seemed to "have no apprehension but that he should yet, for some "time to come, be able 'to be about his Father's busi- "ness.' And many will be the fervent prayers that will "ascend from the altar of pure and devoted hearts, that "this faithful watchman on the walls of our spiritual "Zion may be yet spared to us, to teach us the blessed "truths of that glorious doctrine which, for sixty years, "he has most faithfully and perseveringly preached, "never shunning to declare the whole counsel of God.

'And when he dies, how many hearts will mourn.'"

This communication is from the pen of the sympathizing lady of Rev. Sylvanus Cobb. It is sufficient to show the opinion held by other people of Mrs. Ballou, and will also evince the general anxiety and interest realized at any symptoms of illness experienced by one whom so many loved and revered.

The only game that Mr. Ballou ever engaged in at all was the very simple one of chequers. This he would sometimes, though very seldom, sit down to on a long winter's evening, with one of his children, or perhaps some aged companion who was fond of the game. It is the most common thing for two persons, who are good players and thus engaged, to evince not a little feeling at the result of the game, either of pleasure at success, or of chagrin at being defeated. But as it regards this matter, we never saw him evince the least feeling either way, beyond one of his pleasant smiles, as often caused by defeat as by victory. He was what would be called an excellent player, but he evinced only a passing interest in the game.

At the age of seventy-eight Mr. Ballou was still as fluent and distinct a speaker as at the age of forty. His sermons were still characterized by the same powerful reasoning on every point, as well as bearing evidence of constant study, showing also most conspicuously one peculiarity of his, that of the practical as well as philosophical character of his investigations. One might think that, having preached for a term of nearly sixty years at the date of which we write, there would from necessity be a disagreeable sameness and repetition of ideas in his sermons; but this was far from being the case. We have heard old members of his society, who have listened to his public communications for more than thirty consecutive years, say that they have never heard him deliver a discourse without learning from his lips some fresh and beautiful evidence of the gospel truths,—some new and touching illustration of the ennobling sentiments he professed.

> "Age could not wither him, nor custom stale
> His infinite variety."

He has himself often remarked that each successive year of study made him happier than before, in the fresh truths and manifestations of divine goodness developed in that never-failing source of knowledge,— that flowing river of wisdom,— the Bible.

In his style of speaking, Mr. Ballou was very peculiar. There was none of the study and pomp of declamation in his delivery,— no attempt at effect; but he ever spoke to the people, before whom he raised his voice as that which he professed to be, an humble servant of all men. And yet he was eloquent, at times brilliantly so, and his oratory has been cited by competent judges as a rare example to follow. There are comparatively few men in these days, when the style of ranting, and tearing plain, straightforward sentiment to tatters, is so prevalent, who can so absorb an audience as he always did. When he commenced to speak, he would lay the subject before his hearers in a quiet but distinct tone, so as to place it within the capacity of a child, calmly and with judgment. Then as he proceeded he grew by degrees animated, and anon enthusiastic, yet ever to the purpose, while the expressive countenances of his hearers evinced how fully they entered into the spirit of the speaker. And when they retired from the place of meeting, the people were accustomed to feel that they had listened to profitable matter, and to follow out the theme which he had so distinctly and legibly marked for them.

In this connection, and as being illustrative of that which we have just remarked, we quote here from the sermon of Rev. Otis A. Skinner, of Boston (having been kindly permitted to do so), delivered before his society, relative to the decease of the subject of this biography. These remarks are as follows : —

"His sermons were all characterized by strength. "They were not pretty, not declamatory; but noble, "grand, strong. The hearer always felt as though his "arguments were unanswerable, his conclusions above "dispute. Who can gainsay that? That is unanswera- "ble! Such has been the feeling of thousands at the "close of his sermons. I question whether there was "ever a preacher who made so many converts by his pul- "pit labors, as Father Ballou. Thousands on thousands "have been convinced by him; and his converts were "always those most remarkable for ability to reason, and "for hearts of benevolence. He was ingenious as well as "strong. The moment he began to open his subject, you "began to be interested. You saw so much ingenuity in "his mode of reasoning, in exposing error, in illustrating "truth, that whatever you might think of his subject, you "could not refrain from listening with marked attention. "It was no uncommon thing for him to excite a smile, to "move his whole congregation; but usually that was "done by some ingenious argument that would electrify "every mind present. In his preaching he was never "light, never irreverent, but always grave, serious, "devout; but he was ingenious, and his ingenuity often "created a smile."

His discourses in the city generally averaged about thirty-five minutes; but in the country, where people came many miles to hear him speak, frequently crowding the place of worship to overflowing, and even standing at the windows on the outside, so thronged was the house within, he would sometimes speak from one to two hours. Inspired by the undeviating attention of the mass of honest seekers after truth who were before him, and incited by their eloquent countenances, in which he could read the influence of his words, it was difficult for him to know when to stop. At such times he was ever zealous, yet prudent, devout without ostentation, vigorous and unyielding in his opposition to error, but still always kind and conciliatory. He always complained that on such occasions he could not find one-half the time he wanted, while speaking upon the holy theme, and that minutes never flew more quickly than under such circumstances. The power of his eloquence upon the people at such times can be but poorly described; it must have been witnessed to be realized and understood. Honest countenances beamed with delight, calm and peaceful joy sat on the wrinkled brow and face of age, the eyes of the young sought each other in sympathy, full of a realizing sense of the riches of God's goodness. Even children were thoughtful, and forgot the restraint that the services had put upon them. As has been said in an extract herein, his converts were many. We do not mean that by one discourse he accomplished this reformation in their minds; but he removed the clouds from their mental vision, showed them the loveliness of the gospel as it is in Christ, and by hints shrewdly strown and arguments most potent to convince, with references beyond the point of his discourse, he led them to study and judge for themselves, when he had left them.

Rev. A. R. Abbott, in a discourse before his society, has expressed in brief, and very truthfully, some of the characteristics of his style of preaching. He says: —"His discourses were always simple, powerful, "clear, perfectly intelligible to all, yet made so, appar- "ently, without the least effort. You find there no "attempt to carry his points by any artifice of oratory. "Everything is plain and direct. Even the most intri- "cate and perplexing subjects, under his treatment, "gradually became clear. His thoughts were like clear "waters; — their perfect transparency disguised their "depth. When speaking upon any intricate topic, per- "haps no one ever listened to him attentively, under "favorable circumstances, without being astonished at the "apparent ease with which he removed the difficulties "from his subject, and at the felicity with which all his "illustrations were chosen. Often, when his hearers have "been wrought up to an intense and painful interest by "some apparently insuperable obstacle or unanswerable "objection to a point he was laboring to establish, they "have been both surprised and delighted, by the applica- "tion of some well-known truth or familiar text of Scrip- "ture, to see the light break in upon the dark point like "sunlight through a parting cloud. And when they saw "how clear the subject then appeared, they were vexed "with themselves to think that so obvious an explanation "had never occurred to them. His treatment of a sub-

"ject was like the prophet's healing the Syrian leper;—
"the method was so simple that its efficacy was doubted,
"till its success was manifest."

Rev. A. A. Miner has kindly furnished us with the following authentic anecdote, which is very appropriate in this connection, illustrating as it does the magic-like power of Mr. Ballou's eloquence, and the delight with which he was listened to by the masses, when his mission carried him into the country.

"He had an appointment to preach," says Mr. Miner, "some years ago, in the town of Berlin, Vt. There was "residing in that town a highly-respectable gentleman by "the name of James Perly, with whom I was person-"ally acquainted. Mr. Perly was exceedingly anxious "to hear Mr. Ballou preach; but, unfortunately, he was "so lame with the rheumatism that he could not get into "his carriage. The distance to the meeting by the trav-"elled way was some two miles; but a cross-way, through "a piece of wood, was much shorter. With crutches in "hand, he started at an early hour, determined, if possi-"ble, to reach the place of meeting by the cross-way. "He had not proceeded far, however,—having just "entered the wood,—when, to his great annoyance, he "found himself arrested in his progress by a large tree, "lying directly across his path. To go round it was "impracticable, from the obstruction of the underbrush; "to step over it was impossible, on account of his lame-"ness. What could he do? After studying the problem "for a time, he threw over his crutches, and, balancing

"himself on the body of the tree, managed to roll him-
"self to the other side, and to regain his feet. At length
"he reached the place of meeting, and listened with even
"more than his anticipated delight. The speaker was all
"that he had been led to expect, in person, voice, and
"power of reasoning. He was more than pleased,— he
"was charmed by his doctrine. The word of divine
"grace found a most welcome reception in his heart, and
"the very glories of the upper world seemed to possess
"his soul.

"The meeting over, he wended his way homeward
"again; 'but whether in the body, or out of the body,
"he could not tell.' As he entered his house, every
"hand was upraised in astonishment; and with one voice
"his family exclaimed, 'Why, Mr. Perly! where are
"your crutches?' Sure enough, where were they?
"The eloquence which had enraptured his soul had
"heated the body, and made the lame to leap for joy.
"He had quite forgotten his crutches, and returned home
"without them!

"I give this narration," says Mr. Miner, "on the
"authority of a sister of Mr. Perly, herself not a Uni-
"versalist. To many persons such a story may seem
"incredible; but those who are acquainted with the
"effects of an intense pleasurable excitement, will find
"little difficulty in believing it fully true. Few persons,
"sympathizing with him, could have heard Mr. Ballou,
"on the occasions of his visits to the country, without
"being able, from their own experience, to understand

"something of this wonderful influence. The writer of "this first listened to him at the New Hampshire State "Convention of Universalists, held at Walpole, in 1838; "and rarely, if ever, have I seen a man so deeply inter-"est an audience as he did on that occasion. Tears of "joy rolled down the cheeks of grey-haired fathers, as "the hopes of the gospel burned anew in their hearts. "Such scenes are remembered with gratitude by thou-"sands of believers throughout New England."

A certain brother in the ministry said to the writer of these pages, — "You are preparing a biography of your "father?" We replied in the affirmative. "Well," said he, "you have sat down at home and listened to his "preaching before his own society, and have doubtless a "true appreciation of his ability; but you should have "seen him before a body of ministering brethren, at a "state or national convention. You should have seen "him there, to write truly of him. When it was an-"nounced at such assemblies that Father Ballou would "preach, we all knew what to expect, and all reaped "a harvest of rich thoughts, pure doctrine, original argu-"ments, and available material for our own future use "in a more limited sphere. He was not only eloquent, "he was electrifying; and while we reverenced him, we "also loved him like a father." And this we feel positive is not merely the opinion of one man, but of the order generally.

"Would that I could renew the sights I have seen," says the Rev. Henry Bacon, "where thousands, in a

" crowded and heated assembly in New Hampshire, were " held in wondering and admiring attention, as the ven- " erated preacher set forth the 'exceeding great and " precious promises' as exhibitive of creating and pre- " serving Love. The riches of grace were poured upon " the souls of the people as a refreshing shower on the " earth; and hundreds of old men, who had been awak- " ened from the nightmare of traditional theology, or " the sleep of indifference to God and his service, listened, " while the tears coursed down their furrowed cheeks, as " he renewed in their souls the raptures of the past. O " never can I forget one sermon thus delivered, when " he spake to us of those who knew God's name and " would put their trust under the shadow of his wings, " which wings were stretched over time and eternity! " Eloquent, was he? Yes, if rapt attention, if profound " emotion, if lasting enthusiasm and tearful gratitude be " any test of the effects of eloquence. With no exer- " tion, that wondrously clear and silvery voice would " float over the congregation, and the auditor who was " the farthest removed from the speaker, caught the sim- " ple words, conveying the grandest thoughts most felic- " itously illustrated. There was no pretension in his " oratory; he spake right on, warming with his subject, " setting up the noblest claims for adoring obedience to " God, in all his requirements, exhorting the people to " religious duty by the mercies of God."

The effect of his words, in public delivery especially, was greatly heightened by the truly benevolent expression of his countenance, and by his remarkably venerable appearance. It has been beautifully said of President Kirkland, that his face was a benediction; and we have often heard similar comparisons made by those who have known and been familiar with Mr. Ballou. He wore his hair, white with age, parted smoothly in the centre of the forehead, and resting behind the ears, but not long in the neck. In a number of lithographs, engravings and miniatures, in the possession of his family and others, the hair is represented as short, and parted thus; but latterly he wore it long, as described above.

There was expressed in his countenance a serenity of disposition that was peculiar to him, a philanthropy of purpose which characterized all his dealings, and a wisdom and calm dignity that led even the stranger to feel a degree of respect for him at once. The blamelessness of his life and the gentleness of his disposition alone form a theme over which memory and friendship have poured their consecration. As to the matter of his personal manner and bearing, while he avoided the strict rules of forced etiquette, yet he was scrupulously attentive in society to the dictates of true politeness. His form was as straight and erect at the age of seventy-five as at twenty.

As he advanced in years, his style of delivery grew perhaps more subdued, but none the less distinct and impressive. He spoke perhaps with less of the fire of zeal, yet with none the less spirit and real effect. He could not treat of the divine love and sufferings of Christ, or of the deep and unbounded grace of God, without evincing the warmest feelings, and moving the audience to tears by his eloquence upon these touching subjects. He would not unfrequently be completely overcome himself, in dwelling upon this theme in public.

His was a noble example of a well-balanced mind, without any of that startling, comet-like splendor, which has usually been considered as the very light in which genius lives and moves. His faculties were all brought into admirable harmony, and thus operated with powerful and never-failing effect. There were no contending elements in his nature; no struggles of ambition; no strife of penuriousness; no battling of passion. Like the beautiful harmony of the elements of nature, his bosom was redolent of concord. And what a worshipper he was, too, of the forms of nature, and her mysteriously glorious works about him! There was no object in nature so minute or so apparently unimportant but had attractions for his scrutinizing eye. He was exceedingly fond of flowers,— those "illumined scriptures of the prairie,"— of the rural scenery, the lowing herds and various tenants of the grove. Often have we heard him praise and dilate upon these, when, a mere boy, we have travelled with him upon his various missions into the country. He was one to

> "Find tongues in trees, books in the running brooks,
> Sermons in stones, and good in everything."

"Stay for a moment," he said to us, on a certain occasion, as we were riding through the country, and had just surmounted a high elevation, commanding a beautiful view of the outspread plain below. It was the closing of a clear autumnal New England day. "What a mild and "holy religion is breathed by nature in such a scene as "this! How soft the influence that steals over the senses! "Though fresh from God's own hand, and quickened by "his presence, it teaches us no terror, no gloom; it rouses "no fierce passions within the heart; it is calm, meek, "forgiving; and equally for all breathing things. How "hallowed and God-like are the blissful teachings of "nature!"

He gazed so long, in silence, upon the silvery Connecticut, where it threads its course not far from Holyoke Mountain, following out the theme of his thoughts, that we marked well what he had just said, and remembered it. We had just risen a hill that overlooked the verdant plains of Hadley, and the scene is as fresh to us now as though but an hour had intervened. Such appreciations and realizations were most natural to him; and a vein of illustration, drawn from these lovely exhibitions of nature, will be found running through the broad meadows of his doctrinal arguments, like a purling stream, refreshing and vivifying the verdure of divine truth. A reference to nature in her rural dress and belongings, as illustrative of the great plan and purpose of God's goodness and impartiality, was a favorite custom with him. He would draw thence so many incentives for thankfulness, such unmistakable tokens of Omnipotent impartiality and universal love, such powerful reasons for disbelieving the unhappy creed that imputed to a Being, whose works are redolent of loveliness, attributes so repugnant to the heart of his children, that few could listen unmoved,—few refrain from outwardly evincing the realizing sense he produced in their pliant understandings. With a full appreciation of these divine evidences of God's goodness, we say it was most natural for him to pause thus; and, with eyes drinking in of the spirit of the scene before us, exclaim, as he did, that it "taught no terror, no gloom; "but that its influence was meek, forgiving, and equally "for all breathing things."

By strict frugality and industry, Mr. Ballou acquired for himself a competency, besides dividing a handsome sum of money between his children; and in this latter respect he was somewhat original in his mode of carrying out a disposition of his property. He chose to give to his children while he lived, preferring to witness the pecuniary assistance he might render to his family, and to participate in its enjoyments in his own life-time. His means were acquired solely through patient labor and frugality. He never enjoyed a farthing in the way of legacy, nor by any fortunate turn of business or speculation. These matters he never engaged in at all, and often said that he was perfectly satisfied with a return of six per cent. for his money; and that if others felt the same, much of misery and misfortune would be spared them and the world at large. Some idea may be formed of the careful manner in which he considered his responsibilities by the following facts, namely: he never placed his name to a note, or due bill, in the whole period of his life; never borrowed money; never kept an account at any place of business, but always paid for that which he bought at the time of purchasing, however large or trifling the amount; and, after his long experience of life, he endeavored to impress upon his children that an adherence to these rules, as far as was practicable, would be productive to them of much good, and prevent a vast deal of trouble, and needless anxiety of mind, in relation to secular matters.

By the different societies over which Mr. Ballou officiated as pastor, he lost, in all, a considerable amount of money, through want of good faith in the payment of his salary. This refers to his associations before he came to Boston. In one instance, the sum of money thus sacrificed by him exceeded one thousand dollars; yet he was never known to institute a suit against any individual or society, but left them to settle their unfaithfulness with their own consciences.

> "Some write their wrongs in marble; he, more just,
> Stooped down serene, and wrote them in the dust."

His greatly improved prospects, and increased pecuniary means, never in the least influenced his manner of living, his habits or demeanor. These ever continued to be characterized by the same simplicity and prudence that marked his course from earliest manhood. At his house there was ever the same open and free hospitality exercised; and every one, who knows anything about the life of a settled clergyman, is aware that he must, of necessity, have constantly about him a large number of visitors and partakers of his hospitality. Besides which, as we have before signified, his hands were ever open for the needy, whose wants he delighted to supply; enjoying in return that happiness that true charity alone can impart.

"It always appeared to me inconsistent," says Mr. Ballou, "with the profession of a minister of the gospel, "to live expensively; that is, far beyond what is required "for the necessities and comforts of life. As the minister "is supported by the people of his charge, the propriety "of his living beyond the income of his parishioners in "general, seems questionable. Moreover, it has best "suited my natural taste to avoid extravagances and "superfluities."

Tupper, the erudite and truthful author of Proverbial Philosophy, has very beautifully said,—"The choicest pleasures of life lie within the ring of moderation." Believing thus, Mr. Ballou wrote contentment on every dispensation of Providence that fell to his share.

The work we have in hand might be filled alone with the most sincere eulogiums from ministering brethren, who have referred in public to the life and character of the subject of this biography; but, in the few which we have selected and introduced here, we have been guided by the purpose of presenting only such as have seemed to us — knowing the facts from long experience — to be the most truthful in the delineation of the character and disposition of Mr. Ballou. Moreover, the reader will, perhaps, be too often led to remember that it is a son who writes this biography of a father; and when he can bring to bear the mind and evidence of older and abler writers than himself, as treating upon the subject before us, the work may be thus strengthened and enriched. In this spirit, and under this chapter of "Domestic Characteristics," the following extract from the discourse delivered upon this subject by Rev. Henry Bacon is given: —

"I am not now to speak of a stranger, known only by "reputation, but of one with whom I have been familiar "from my earliest childhood. The more I attained power "to judge his qualities, the more have I learned to esteem "the man, his character and ministry. He came to "Boston, as pastor of the Second Universalist Society, "when I was scarcely four years old, and though my "parents were members of the First Society, yet their "house was one of his homes. The impression made in "boyhood by the stately form of Mr. Ballou,— his meek-"ness, his speech of singular clearness, adaptedness and "wisdom, his singular temperance at the table, and his "kindness to childhood,— was never removed; and I use "no strained and forced language when I say Hosea Ballou "was a great man. I say this, not looking from a sec-"tarian point of view, but as guided by the principles "that ought to govern us in our judgment of men, com-"prehensively regarding their qualities, and what they "have been to their age.

"He is a great man who is impelled to bear the new "truth abroad, that, like its Great Source, he may be

" 'found of those who asked not after him;' to make the "hill-side and the grove, the river shore, the barn, the "humble farmer's room, or the shadow of a great tree, "his church, and there proclaim the gospel in its whole-"ness, with a readiness that shows the heart is full of the "matter, and with a willingness to answer any queries, "and respond to any voice that speaks a word against the "completeness of the redemption proposed in Christ. By "his keen insight into human nature, his rare powers of "logic, his unique use of words, his intelligibility to the "humblest capacity in treating of the greatest subjects, "and his profound wisdom in choosing means to reach "directly the ends desired, Hosea Ballou was a great "man. In an instant he stripped away all the show "and tinsel of learned ignorance, or drove the dart "between the joints of the harness of barbarian bigotry, "and laid low the pretender. By his unshaken and "majestic faith and trust; by the steadiness with which "he kept the honor of God, in the supremacy and "efficiency of the Scriptures, ever before him; and by "the willingness and capacity to receive any new appli-"cation of the great principles of the gospel, he was a "great man. All this was crowned and glorified by his "personal character, by the purity of his walk and con-"versation, his rare temperance amid the most solicitous "temptations, and the harmony he breathed into all his "children and the rule he swayed over them; he was a "great man, abiding the last, best test of greatness, " 'being such an one as Paul the aged.' "

As will be surmised by previous remarks in this work. Mr. Ballou, in the matter of politics, had of course his preferences of principles and of men, and he always voted for them, besides keeping himself well read in the most important political matters of the day, pro and con, and weighing well in his own mind their bearing upon the true principles of political economy; but here his interest ceased. He took no active part, even in conversation, upon the subject, though at times he would show by his remarks that the great principles of either party were familiar to him. Still he always avoided, as a topic of conversation, a subject which is so often the theme of bitter contention between those who in all other respects are excellent friends. He never changed his political sentiments, which, however, for very good reasons, were scarcely known, or, at least, not intimately so, out of the family circle.

His irreproachable life was in itself one of the strongest arguments in favor of his religion; his mild and dispassionate manner on all occasions, his unblemished integrity and unimpeachable character, through his whole life, rendered him universally beloved, as well as showing a living example of the divine principles he endeavored to inculcate in his public teachings. There is an energy of moral suasion in a good man's life, passing the highest efforts of the orator's genius. The visible but silent beauty of holiness speaks more eloquently of God and duty than do the tongues of men and angels. A minister's religious faith should be delivered to his people, not as a matter of theoretical knowledge,— something learned in the study,— but as something experienced. "Nothing," says Bishop Stillingfleet, "enlarges the gulf of "atheism more than the *wide passage* which lies "between the faith and lives of men pretending to teach "Christianity." Religion is not a didactic thing, that words can impart or even silence withhold: it is spiritual and contagious glory, a spontaneous union with the holy spirit evinced in our daily lives and example. Those who have true religion make it the garment worn next the heart, but, alas! too many make a cloak of it. The most learned divine, or philosopher that the earth has ever known, though he spoke with an eloquence and wisdom near akin to inspiration, must yet be powerless as to spiritual and godly influence, if, at the same time that he points to wisdom's way,

"Himself the primrose path of dalliance treads."

Hooker has very beautifully remarked, that "the life of a pious clergyman is visible rhetoric;" and some one else, with equal truth, that "to preach sound doctrine, and "lead a bad life, is building up with one hand and pulling "down with the other." Preaching, to be available, must be consistent.

Mr. Ballou may be said to have *lived* the doctrine he professed, in the strictest sense of the phrase, and to have followed the glorious example set him by his Divine Master. His ambition was to be an imitator of the meek and lowly Jesus.

"His preaching much, but more his practice wrought,
A living sermon of the truths he taught."

Touching this subject he was wont to say to his hearers:— "Brethren, I want a doctrine that I can prove by reduc-"ing it to practice; for we are enjoined to 'prove all "things, and hold fast that which is good.' People may "go to the house of devotion, they may hear learned "ministers hold forth the doctrine of future rewards and "punishments, they may admire the beautiful oratory and "flowery rhetoric in which such sentiments are dressed, "but they must leave them all behind them when they "go home to their beloved families. They can never "practise the domestic virtues and duties on these prin-"ciples of doctrine. The doctrine of Jesus is a practi-"cal one, and we can never do our duty in the family "circle unless we live and conduct according to it."

This is an example of Mr. Ballou's style of argument and of illustration. He brought everything *home*, where all could understand the analogy; he never went abroad to seek for illustrations, never indulged in deep philosophical dissertations, thus hoodwinking his hearers and marring his subject. The reader will at once be struck by the force and truth of the remark, that, however sincerely a person may believe the doctrine of future rewards and punishments, still, on leaving the house where these principles are taught, he must leave them behind him. No one, not even the most zealous supporter of such a creed, ever attempted to practise it in his family circle. Washington Allston has pithily said, "A "man cannot lie *all over;*" so it is a fact that he cannot be utterly wrong from top to toe; though his mind may be deceived, and his sentiments indicate partial delusion, yet his *heart*, ten to one, will be right. Some token of his nicely constructed nature will turn itself into "king's evidence" against his false theories. And thus we find men, sincere Christians at heart, who believe and promulgate the doctrine of partial grace, all the while evincing in their home influences and general lives, the truth of the gospel of Christ.

When Mr. Ballou was last in New York, some one of the brethren in that city induced him to visit the office of the American Phrenological Journal, where his head was examined after the rules of the science, and the following characteristics were written out by the examiner, as is customary in such cases. Since the decease of the subject of these memoirs, they have been made public through the journal referred to. To many this extract will possess more than ordinary interest, and we have therefore given it place here, under the head of personal characteristics.

PHRENOLOGICAL CHARACTER.

"His organization is very favorable to long life, good "general health, and uniformity of mind. The vital "temperament was originally decidedly strong. He has "an amply developed chest, lungs and digestive appara-"tus, which have imparted health and prolonged life; and "the muscular system is also fully represented. His "mind is active, but not so much so as to prematurely "exhaust his organization; nor is he particularly excit-"able. He has general harmony and evenness, rather "than eccentricity or want of balance. The tone of "his organization is such as to give him energy and "aim to carry through his purposes, without friction or "waste of strength. The size of brain is average, and "the vital functions are sufficient to supply the exhaus-"tion of mental action; hence he has been able to live "within his power of sustaining mental labor for so long "a time.

"He is remarkable, phrenologically, for evenness of 'development; none of the organs are extreme, and he "is not inclined to those excesses which cause eccen-"tricity.

"One of his leading traits arises from Adhesiveness, "which gives attachment to, and interest in, friends.

"He still clings to his youthful friends; and enjoys "their society. This quality of mind enters largely into "the whole tone of his feelings.

"He is also kind to children, and interested in them, "and quite successful in entertaining them, and adapting "himself to them.

"He is interested in woman, and capable of enjoying "the marriage relations highly, especially the social, "domestic relations. He is a strong lover of home, but "lacks continuity of mind; his thoughts and feelings are "easily diverted, although he may finish a subject that "he commences; yet he enjoys variety in the general "exercise of his mind.

"His Combativeness is of the higher order, connecting "with the reasoning and moral, rather than with the "animal nature; and it gives him the disposition to over- "come the obstacles in his way, and to argument rather "than the quarrelling propensity.

"He has fair energy, without any surplus, and a full "degree of appetite, without being excessive. He values "property for its uses, and is not selfish in money mat- "ters. He is remarkable for his candor, frankness, "open-heartedness, truthfulness, and disinclination to "deceive; he speaks the real sentiments of his mind, as "far as he speaks at all. He is not suspicious, but con- "fiding, and prefers to rely on the honesty of mankind "rather than to guard himself against the dishonesty of "others. He is not vain or showy; has merely ambition "enough to stimulate him to do what is his duty, without "any reference to publicity; but he is decidedly inde- "pendent and self-relying.

"He does not lean on the judgment of others, nor does "he feel that his character depends on their opinions; he "merely states his own opinion, and allows others to "judge for themselves.

"Firmness is another strong feature of his mind: he "is uniformly firm, each day successively; not stubborn "one day, and over-yielding the next, but consistently "steady and persevering.

"He is very anxious to do as he agrees, and is just as

"honest at one time as another; is consistent in his pro-"fessions and pretensions, and has always studied to "harmonize and balance his character, rather than to "encourage any extremes.

"He neither hopes nor fears to excess; enjoys what "good there is to be enjoyed, and makes the best of an "unfortunate occurrence. His mind is open to convic-"tion, is ready to look at new things, and to be in-"structed; but is slow to believe, and requires positive "evidence before he gives his assent. He has a marked "feeling of worship, deference, and respect, and regard "for superiority and sacred subjects. Few persons have "naturally more of the disposition to worship than he.

"His sympathies are also strong. His feelings are "tender towards objects of distress, either mental or "physical. Imagination and sense of beauty and perfec-"tion are decidedly strong. He is disposed to beautify "his ideas, and make as much of them as possible, espe-"cially by way of elevating the idea, and giving it a "refined direction.

"He is not inclined to mimic and imitate others; his "ways are peculiarly his own.

"He is mirthful, and enjoys fun as naturally as his "food, and it has been difficult for him to suppress the "disposition to joke. His intellectual faculties are well "balanced; the perceptive faculties are all large. He is "quick of observation, readily forms conclusions from "what he sees, and is very much interested in all "classes of experiments.

"He is disposed to make himself as much acquainted "with this world as possible before leaving it, and is "particularly inclined to study character and motives, "and the conditions of mind. He has a good perception "of forms, outlines, shapes and proportions, and has a "good memory of places, localities, and the whereabouts "of things.

"He is quite particular as to order and arrangement, and "must have everything done correctly: is precise in his "style of doing his work, or in arranging his ideas. His "memory by association is good; he is a very punctual "man in his engagements, and careful not to consume "the time of another. He is never in the way of others, "and does not go where he is not wanted; and, from "diffidence and fear that he may intrude himself, he does "not go where he is really desired. He is copious in the "use of language, yet is not wordy; his language is "direct and to the point. He has a clear mind, adapted "to analytical logic, and drives as straight to a conclusion "as the bee does to a flower; yet he reasons more by "association and analogy than from cause to effect.

"He readily sees the adaptation of one thing to "another; he seldom makes enemies, or fails to perceive "the character and motives of others; is more successful "than most persons in making friends, because he knows "how to adapt himself to others, and make himself agree- "able. He says and does things in a human-nature way.

"The six leading traits of his character are,—

"1st. His affection and friendship.

"2d. Independence and self-reliance.

"3d. Honesty, justice and circumspection.

"4th. His devotion and respectful disposition.

"5th. Sympathy and interest in the welfare of others, "and general philanthropy of spirit; and,

"Lastly, His practical common sense, and system, and "availability of intellect."

Mr. Ballou was once asked, in a most triumphant manner, by a religious opponent, in the presence of a large number of individuals, "If your doctrine be true, "sir, how is it that it has never been preached before? "Here in the nineteenth century it would seem to be a "new discovery." He replied, in his usual calm and effective manner, "Friend, it has been taught by two "eloquent witnesses at least, so long as the sun has "shone and the rain fallen on mankind. These faithful "agents of Almighty love have ever taught the doctrine "of impartial grace to all men; they dispense their "blessings on rich and poor, high and low, and thus bear "witness of the character of Him who sends them."

We well remember being present on a certain occasion when an intimate friend of Mr. Ballou's asked him,— "Do you not think that the life of a clergyman is far "from being a desirable one, when you consider all the "sorrow and grief that the discharge of the duty attend-"ant upon the profession necessarily makes one ac-"quainted with?" He replied, evincing the peculiar light that was ever emitted from his eyes when he spoke earnestly, "Were I to live my life over again, knowing "what I now so well know, by more than half a century "of experience, I would choose again the same profes- "sion I have followed so long. The humble and faithful "servant of Christ enjoys an inward happiness that none "but his Master may know. There is no employment "more fitting for the human heart, more ennobling to "the nature of man, than the study of God's word, and "none from which so great and reliable happiness may "be derived." These evidences of his experience were treasured by many who were accustomed to seek his society for the benefit and pleasure of his conversation. The brethren throughout the order, and indeed every one who knew him, seemed actuated towards him by a spirit which the universal title he bore served to indicate; they always called him *Father* Ballou. I do not think there was one minister in the numerous order of Universalists who did not acknowledge his preëminence in original talent, wonderful reasoning faculties, and unblemished moral excellence.

As illustrating this fact, we will let one of these brethren's remarks upon this subject speak for us here, by again quoting from the eulogy of Rev. Otis A. Skinner, delivered before his society in this city.

"But he was not merely our leader to the promised "land; he entered it with us, and for more than half a "century he continued with us, standing first in our "esteem and affection, honored and beloved, with no "effort to obtain authority, and no ambition to be a "leader. The place which he occupied was voluntarily "assigned to him; it was given in consequence of his "true heart, his profound judgment, his undeviating "attachment to principle, his entire freedom from art "and management. Envy hurled at him its arrows, "but they fell harmless at his feet; ambition sought to "rise above him, but it sought in vain. There he stood "like a father at the head of his family, content to exer-"cise the sway which he obtained by his superior judg-"ment, his commanding talents, and his devoted services. "He never dictated; he was never impatient when op-"posed; he was never unkind to those who differed from "him; he comprehended fully the true idea of religious "liberty, and in no instance exhibited a desire to act the "Pope. We doubt whether, in all the history of the "church, an instance can be found in which a minister "has had so high a rank in his sect, and yet manifested "a less desire to bear rule.

"Nothing is more natural than for old men to oppose "departures from their measures. All sects have had "those who bitterly denounced every step taken beyond "what they themselves had gone; but our honored father, "when he saw movements for progress, when he saw new "men proposing new plans of operation, placed himself on "a level with the humblest, freely discussed the plan, and "yielded with cheerfulness when convinced. Not only "did he yield, but held his mind open to conviction, and "on several points he came in and worked faithfully for "what at first he hesitated to sanction. He was not like "some advanced in years, ever looking to the past, and "talking as though all wisdom was concentrated in it; he "believed that new discoveries were yet to be made; that "progress was a law of the true church, and that meas- "ures must be suited to the times. Hence the most "radical, those most desirous for reform, never felt that "he stood in the way: for there was not a reform "which engaged the heart of the philanthropist that did "not have his sanction. He was a modern man, and "lived in the present time, as much, almost, as the "youngest in our ministry. *Let us go forward*, was "his motto."

Such was the universal meed of honor that was accorded to him by his brethren in the ministry.

CHAPTER XII.

MR. BALLOU AS A CONTROVERSIALIST.

As passage after passage of scripture, which had heretofore been misapplied, was satisfactorily explained by his clear and far-seeing mind, thousands, who had before believed in a partial faith, were brought to a knowledge of Christ and the gospel. Mysteries were made plain, and dark ways were lighted, and the veil was thus removed from the eyes of the prejudiced, or those upon whom the force of education and early association had exercised supreme sway in matters of religion. "I have often been led to wonder," says Mr. Ballou, "forcible as is my own realizing sense of the evidence of "impartial grace, that brethren, brought up and educated "in a religion so diametrically opposite, should yield so "readily, as they often do, to the arguments which we "present to them, and not unfrequently being won to "our belief and service with the least exertion on our "own part. The reason of this is, that there are some "independent minds, that boldly think for themselves;

"that acknowledge no blind obedience to the dogmas of "the church, when those tenets of faith desecrate the "rules of reason and justice. The very fact that it "seems to be a part of the faith of partialists to give "blind credence to the declarations of the church, and to "consider it an actual sin to question the assertions of "the minister relative to the signification of the Bible, "has done much to keep the minds of men in darkness. "My own youthful condition was an humble example of "this fact. It was only by thinking for myself,—by "receiving nothing without evidence,—that I at last "came to that knowledge of Christ and the gospel which "has since been to my life such a sustaining and precious "legacy."

But he was called upon to encounter much opposition in the advancements which he made, and in latter years, perhaps, quite as often from professed Universalists as from those who openly opposed the doctrine he taught. There are many, even at this day, who seem to avoid the subject of future punishment, and who will not speak out openly whether they believe or disbelieve it. Such talk vaguely of policy, and the propriety of preaching *moral* sermons instead of doctrinal ones, which argument is, in itself, a most inexcusable aspersion upon the gospel. What kind of a faith must that be which will not bear to be preached? This singular idea seems to have extended, in some degree, to the preachers themselves, who have, in many instances, acquiesced in the caprice of their hearers upon the subject, or, at least, that portion of them who reason in this way upon doctrinal matters.

The true reason that doctrinal sermons are decried by some of the ministers is, that they afford no opportunity for them to introduce, perhaps, some style or course of reading that inclination may have led them to adopt. True scriptural teaching calls for sound argument, and substantial treatises upon the word, and is a strong test of mental capacity; whereas such sermons as are too often delivered to the people run upon miscellaneous themes, that were more properly left for newspaper or magazine articles, and are of a school of composition that a shallow brain may become a proficient in. We are most forcibly reminded in this connection of the words of a certain English bishop, who was travelling in this country a few years since, and who made the remark, that ministers here take a text from the Bible and preach about railroads, astronomy, statuary and painting; but that in his country they not only select their texts from the Bible, but they make its doctrines and principles the subject of their discourses. That wise old divine, Jeremy Taylor, found it necessary in his day to chide these fashionable preachers. "They entertain their hearers," said he, "with gaudy tulips and useless daffodils, and not with "the bread of life and medicinal plants, growing on the "margin of the fountains of salvation."

The true doctrine of the Scriptures is the very fountain-head of all morality, and those who talk so much about preaching moral sermons and avoiding doctrinal ones, should pause and consider well their own inconsistency. Mr. Ballou's sermons were strictly doctrinal ones, ay, emphatically so; but they were none the less moral also. The principles are synonymous, as must be evident to any thoughtful mind. That was excellent advice given to a pious son by Rowland Hill, to preach nothing *down* but the devil, and nothing *up* but Jesus Christ.

The pulpit in these modern times has been sadly perverted by some in all denominations; its legitimate and holy purpose has been lost sight of by many; and any predominating hobby of its occupant is rode rough-shod over the heads of the congregation, to the almost entire detriment of his usefulness as a religious teacher. They dress up the tenets of faith in modern livery to please the popular taste, and, perhaps, their own vanity, forgetting that "religion helmeted is religion no more." The minister seems, too, often thoughtless of the fact, that while he preaches, Almighty God is one of his hearers; the various *isms* of the times are made to take the place of holy writ, and sermons are overcharged with abstruse questions and transcendental ideas; or perhaps so labored with rhetorical flourishes and ornaments, that the hearer, who seeks to be led by the straight and narrow way, finds himself losing sight of the grand purpose and end of wisdom, while he tarries by the wayside to admire the gaudy-colored flowers that line the road.

"Eloquence, to be profitable, must come from the "heart," says Mr. Ballou; "none other will prove effec-"tual. I have heard men speak in public, yea, in the "sacred pulpit, with an apparent effect that was evinced "in every hearer; but when I turned away from the "temple whither we had come up to worship the living "God, and was led to review the word as spoken to that "people, I could only recall the minister's excellent "oratory, his faultless gesticulation, his admirable *per-* "*formance.* Alas! what great truth had he illustrated, "whom had he glorified save himself, whom enlightened "as to the unbounded grace and goodness of God? And "then I have prayed that Heaven would turn the noble "endowments with which it had blessed that brother "to a more worthy use, and fill his heart with that "meekness and self-sacrificing spirit that is as a sweet "and acceptable incense before the throne of Jehovah."

Ministers who follow this style of rhetorical and flowery preaching are not unfrequently pronounced very eloquent, and indeed are able to fix the attention, and much to interest an audience. But it is unprofitable eloquence; like the cypress, which is great and tall, yet bears no fruit. Pope has truthfully said,—"Flowers of rhetoric in serious discourses are like the blue and red flowers in corn, pleasing to the eye, but prejudicial to the harvest!" Keeping at the greatest distance from such errors, Mr. Ballou looked upon man as an intellectual and responsible being; believing that truth is the food for that intellect to thrive upon, and keeping the whole range of man's natural duties before him, his discourses were weighty, not in decorations for the fancy, but in sound reasoning upon the holy text, and in impressive and useful practical sentiment. This was his principle of theology, and, moved by such feelings, he never wasted time

"In sorting flowers to suit a fickle taste."

Or, as the editor of the Christian Freeman says, relative to this trait of his character: — "It was not so much "his concern to be a man-pleaser, as to be a teacher and "benefactor of men. Hence he would grapple with the "errors of men, and take them out of the way; he would "explain and elucidate the Scriptures; he would appeal "to the reason and the moral sense of the people; and all "in the most kind and magnanimous spirit. Thus he "excited the active opposition of the conservative and "creed-bound, elicited the earnest inquiry of multitudes "of the people, and 'filled the world with his doctrine.'"

"He lived faithful to his own convictions of truth," says Rev. W. A. Drew, of the Gospel Banner, "never "sacrificed a principle to the love of popularity, stood by "his integrity as resolutely as ever martyr stood at the "stake, brought no reproach upon his cause, but lived in "the adornment of his profession, and died consistently "with his life."

We have felt disposed to dwell somewhat upon this point, and to speak the more feelingly upon it, for the reason that this was one of the most frequent objections brought against Mr. Ballou's style of preaching, by those who found fault at all; and here we are fortunate in being able to give his own words and views upon the subject. It is true, the extract which we give does not contemplate the subject in precisely the same phase as that in which we have considered it, yet it has its bearing. The objection was brought, of course, mainly by those who, although they believed, or partially believed, the doctrine of universal salvation, were yet too timid to acknowledge it. The argument is brought home at once to our understanding and earnest conviction by the simplicity and force of the illustration.

"We have often been asked why we preach the doc-"trine we profess, as this doctrine maintains that our "Creator has made the eternal state secure to all men, "and that the happiness of that state rests on the divine "favor, and not on any influence which we may exercise "in this life. No doubt it seems unaccountable to our "opposers that we should argue so much, preach so "much, and write and publish so much, when, after all, "we do not pretend that our eternal state of happiness "depends on these exertions. They do not see why, "allowing our doctrine true, it would not be good policy "to say nothing about it. Then we might enjoy the "esteem of the pious of all denominations, and be "regarded by the religious community, avoid all the "censure that is now put upon us, and still enjoy our "opinion in silence. Now that our conduct in this "respect is not so unaccountable as our opposers seem to "think, a few remarks will serve to show.

"Suppose my acquaintance with my earthly father to "be such as to give me the most favorable opinion of his "whole character, so that I view him as one of the best "husbands, one of the most provident and kind fathers, "and a man of uprightness in all his conduct, against "whom nothing in truth can be spoken. Suppose, under "these circumstances, being full of love and reverence "for my father, I hear him evilly spoken of, and that too "by those who profess to be acquainted with him,— yea, "by those to whom people in general look for informa- "tion, and in whose testimony the most of people are "disposed to place confidence. They go so far in this "evil speaking as to represent the parent, whom I love, "as guilty of acts of injustice and cruelty which deny "him the smallest share of humanity.

"What am I to do in this case? I have proof in my "hands to stop the mouths of these evil reporters, and I "can do it effectually. To be sure, I must exert myself "in the use of the means which are at my disposal, and I "shall no doubt incur the displeasure of my father's tra- "ducers. All this is, of course, to be expected. But "here I am told that almost all the people composing the "community at large, are really of the opinion of those "who thus speak evil of my father; and that, even if I "knew these reports to be false, I had better say nothing "about the matter, as it will only bring me into dis- "credit. Suppose I should be weak enough to hesitate, "and even shrink from the defence of my venerable "father's character, should I not feel justly ashamed of "myself? What could be more base in me than silence "and inaction?

"Look again, and see how such a case would be aggra-

"vated by circumstances. My father told me that these "traducers would speak evil of him, and on this very "account put into my possession every kind of evidence "which is necessary to refute all these evil reports, and "charged me, by the dear relation in which we stood to "each other, and the love which we have reciprocated, to "be faithful in the defence of his character. Shall I be "silent? Shall I be afraid that those who despise my "father will also despise me? Shall I purchase their "smiles at the expense of a character which is dearer to "me than my life? What would it avail to urge in this "case, that almost every one in the community would be "against me? Is not this circumstance my justification? "Surely; for, if people did not believe the false reports "before mentioned, there would be no use of disproving "them.

"But the subject admits of argument still more forci-"ble. Suppose those who speak evil of my father are my "brethren, and his own beloved children; and suppose, "furthermore, that all who are deceived by this evil "speaking are so likewise. We now have the whole "difficulty in our family. My brethren are deceived "concerning my father's character and conduct; he has "never done those base things which they think he has. "But they really believe these errors, and are tormented "day and night with fear that they and their children will "fall under the dreadful scourge of our father's wrath! "Now, as I know that all their notions are false, and "that it is a fact that the whole family are abundantly "provided for, day by day, by the kindness and love of "our father, can I, under these circumstances, be justi- "fied in not making even an effort to convince them of "their errors? Here we see the honor of our father, the "cause of truth and justice, all unite in calling upon me "to open the evidence which our father has put within "my hands for this purpose,— to give the knowledge of "the truth to those who need it. With all these matters "forcibly impressed upon my heart, which I have given "to you in this simple form, how can I justify myself in "doing otherwise than I do, humbly endeavoring at all "times to dispel the cloud of error that partialists have "contrived to throw about the received idea of our "Father in heaven,— how can I reconcile it to my own "heart to avoid doctrine, and preach aught else to the "people while they starve for truth?"

Mr. Ballou was declared to be aggressive, in his spiritual warfare, as well as defensive; and so he was. Every great reformer must be so; every one that has left a worthy title to that name has done likewise. With a great truth to promulgate, with new light to diffuse, with a subtle enemy to encounter, it would not have been enough for him to take a position and hold it; the war must be carried into the enemy's country, and the white cross of truth must be made to surmount the loftiest points in the castles of error, and to float over the banners of infidelity and partialism. And this was his mode of warfare against bigotry. He spared neither himself nor the common enemy; his standard was reared everywhere, even in the very citadel of his religious opponents; and, strong in the gospel truths he advocated and trusted in, their arrows of wrath, steeped in the poison of superstition, found no unguarded point in his armor of gospel mail, but fell harmless to the earth, or more frequently rebounded to the harm of those who had sent them. His warfare against error was indeed aggressive; he seized upon every weak point, and never failed to thrust home. "I "call God to witness," he says, "I feel no enmity towards "any name, denomination or sect, under heaven; but I "have a certain object in view which comes in contact "with their errors."

Again he says: —

"In all the statements which I have made of the doc-"trinal ideas of others, I have been careful to state no "more than what I have read in authors, or heard con-"tended for in preaching and conversation; and if I "have, in any instance, done those ideas any injustice, it "was not intended.

"The reason," he continues, "why I have not quoted "any author, or spoken of any denomination, is, I have "not felt it to be my duty nor inclination to write against "any name or denomination in the world; but my object "has been, what I pray it ever may be, to contend against "error, wherever I find it, and to receive truth and sup-"port it, let it come from what quarter it may. For the "sake of ease, however, in writing, I have reasoned with "my *opponent*, *opposer* or *objector*, meaning no one in "particular, but any one who uses the arguments and "states the objections which I have endeavored to "answer.

"It is very probable that some may think me too iron-"ical, and in many instances too severe on what I call "error. But I find it very difficult to expose error, sc "as to be understood by all, without carrying, in many "instances, my arguments in such a form as may not be "agreeable to those who believe in what I wish to cor-"rect. I confess I should have been glad to have written, "on all my inquiries, so as not to have displeased any, "but to have pleased all, could I have done it and accom-"plished my main design; but this, I was persuaded, "would be difficult. I have, therefore, paid particular "attention to nothing but my main object, depending on "the goodness of my reader to pardon what may be dis-"agreeable, in manner or form, as inadvertencies." But all he did and said was in the spirit of the true Christian. He fought against error,— not against those who walked in the ways of error; it was a creed he decried, not his fellow-men; — and the battles he won were far more glorious than the blood-stained fields that follow in the train of mortal warfare.

Let us add that the triumphs of truth are the more glorious for being bloodless, deriving their brightest lustre from the number of the saved, instead of the slain. Personally he could have no enemy,— he would not have recognized any human being as such; but against error he waged a most open and resolute warfare, throughout the entire course of his life.

In May, 1841, the society over which Mr. Ballou had so long held sole ministration voted to engage a colleague to assist him in the duties of pastor, and the Rev. T. C. Adam was engaged by them in this capacity. It was understood between Mr. Ballou and his assistant that each should preach on certain Sabbaths; so that when Mr. Ballou did not preach in his own desk, he might be able to answer some of the constant and increasing demands upon his services from the neighboring towns. Although at this time seventy-three years of age, he preached every Sabbath, frequently delivering three discourses during the day and evening. Mr. Adam was not long attached to the society; but other ministering brethren, at the desire of the society, assisted from time to time in the pulpit. From May, 1842, to May, 1844, Rev. H. B. Soule, a pure-minded and eloquent brother in the ministry, was the junior pastor, exercising a most godly influence by his teachings, and making in this period a host of sincere friends. In January, 1846, Rev. E. H. Chapin was installed as junior pastor, which situation he filled to universal satisfaction and continued usefulness for some two years; when, having resigned his connection with the society, Rev. A. A. Miner was unanimously invited to become the colleague of Mr. Ballou, and was duly installed May 31, 1848; retaining his situation until the decease of the pastor, Mr. Ballou, whose desk he now fills.

The connection of these several brethren with Mr. Ballou personally was of the most agreeable character, friendly, and profitable to their mutual spiritual interests. But, without appearing to reflect in the least upon the other associates in this connection, concerning this latter brother's union with the subject of this biography, we should be unfaithful did we not refer to it in the terms it merits, and should fail to do that which Mr. Ballou himself would have desired. For more than four years the most uninterrupted and delightful intercourse continued between them. No son could have been more considerate, kind, and assiduous, no father more affectionate and grateful, than in this case. Mr. Ballou has often declared, in our hearing and in his family circle, the earnest friendship he realized,— nay, the affection which entirely filled his heart towards one in whom he found no guile, and who seemed sent by a kind Providence to smooth the declining steps of his professional career. It is hardly necessary to add here, that this feeling was shared in by every member of Mr. Ballou's extensive family.

Rev. Henry Bacon says, relative to the period when associate pastors were connected with him: —"Mr. Ballou was out of his element in inactivity, and therefore "he travelled extensively in many of the states, especially the New England, 'preaching the glad tidings of "the kingdom of God. Many feared that he was thus "perilling his fame, going forth after the threescore years "and ten were passed; but he wisely used the labors "of his years of full strength, and seemed to renew "his youth as he entered into the expositions of the "Divine Word. I never heard more enthusiastic enco-

"miums on his preaching than within the few last years; "and there was power in the very aspect of the old man's "form, as he stood in the sacred desk, in an old age that "was indeed 'frosty but kindly,'— with a winning and "impressive venerableness, full of the raptures of early "years, and casting a beautiful shadow in the way of "those who needed such a guidance to the realms of "immortality and glory."

Not unfrequently, when some of his old friends were called home to their God in advance of him,— men who had perhaps been converted in their youth by his teachings, and felt thus strongly endeared to him by the ties of friendship and spiritual interest,— they would in their last moments express an earnest desire to have him perform the last ceremony over their mortal remains. When this was the case, notwithstanding his advanced age, and even at times in the depth of winter, he always complied with their desires.

When he had finally made up his mind to the performance of anything, and was satisfied that it was his duty to do it, nothing in the shape of ordinary impediments could possibly prevent him from carrying out his purpose. A case of this kind occurred, for instance, in the winter of 1845, during one of the most severe storms that had been experienced in this region for years. Mr. Ballou, with the snow of seventy-six winters upon his head, persevered in accomplishing and performing one of these Christian deeds of kindness on the occasion of the death of Col. Pierce, of Gloucester, Mass., a man widely known for his goodness of heart, and as a warm believer and advocate of universal salvation.

He seemed to have no dread or fear of the elements at all, or of personal exposure to them; and let the storm rage as severely as it might, he always kept his appointment, and to the very last was never in the habit of riding to the place of worship, but walked, in all weather, in sunshine or in rain. He retained his physical faculties in the same remarkable degree of preservation as was the case with his mental endowments. His hearing, up to the last week of his life, never perceptibly declined; and in his funeral discourse Mr. Miner says:—"Though "the weight of more than fourscore years was upon him, "his vigor was scarcely abated, and his unassisted sight "enabled him to read a Bible of fine print with ease." His step was firm, and his strength permitted him to walk from one extreme of the city to another, even to the last time he left his house. The simple deduction from these facts is, that he was never guilty of excess, or of the abuse of those faculties which a kind Providence had bestowed upon him in such perfection.

It was his practice to pray most earnestly with the sick, to whose bedside he was constantly being called. We would that every reader of these pages might once have seen him on such a mission of holy consolation. His step was so quiet and noiseless in the sick room, his expression of countenance so peaceful and hope-inspiring, his words so gentle and so redolent of heavenly assurance, that a spell of silence and peace seemed to surround all things. In prayer with him, "that key which opes the gates of heaven," did the sick and dying seek for confidence and consolation in their trying moments.

> "——— In his duty prompt at every call,
> He watched and wept, he prayed and felt, for all."

We have been present when, "beside the bed where parting life was laid," with his voice pitched to a low, soft cadence, and the sick one's hand held gently within his own, he has breathed such heaven-inspired language of peace, held forth the cherished promises of Christ, and shown the divine character of our Heavenly Father in its true light so clearly, yet so mildly and persuasively, that a smile of contentment would light up the pallid features of the sufferer, giving token of the same light of hope shining within his soul, and leaving an impression on the hearts of those who knelt with him in that presence never to be effaced. O! it is a glorious mission thus to be the herald of peace and good will to the struggling soul at its last moments,— thus to pass it over, as it were, in confidence to God who gave it!

Often have we heard it said, "I had rather hear "Father Ballou pray than any other person; it seems "almost impossible not to follow him in every thought "and expression." The truth is, his whole heart was in the prayer; he felt what he said; he humbled himself in sincerity before the throne of Jehovah; while the easy and spontaneous flow of devotional language that fell from his lips was calculated to charm the ear of the listener, and lead him to nearer communion with the omnipotent Being whom he heard so sincerely addressed. His prayers were void of that unpleasant hesitancy of speech which unfortunately too often, characterizes the delivery of ministers in this exercise. His effort proved one smooth and liquid flow of devotional thoughts, from a soul fully baptized in the love of God. On such occasions, the altar of his heart seemed lighted, and it burned pure and bright before the throne of his Father in heaven. The immense power of prayer can hardly be overrated, or its real influence upon our minds properly conceived of, when uttered in such a manner as we have described. It then becomes the peace of our struggling spirit, the rest of our care, the calm of our tempest.

It was thus with all his religious exercises. He never failed to impress the hearer with his own sincerity, and to imbue his spirit with a devotional feeling that brought with it refreshing influence and vivifying hope.

His devotedness to his profession, his untiring zeal in the cause which he advocated, his frequent self-sacrificing exertions in its behalf, were the constant theme of his brethren in the ministry. His never-varying and earnest pursuit of his grand object,— that of convincing the world of God's impartial love to all mankind,— his perfect reliance on an overruling Providence, his perfect faith in the omnipotence of truth and virtue, were all so ardently realized and manifested in his heart and dealings with his fellow-men, as to be the remark of all who knew him. His own experience had taught him to place the fullest reliance upon the Divine goodness, for it had strangely supported him through adversity, and had carried him through many dark trials, triumphantly supporting him amidst discouragements which must otherwise have inevitably overwhelmed a less confiding spirit.

It was a most extraordinary circumstance for him to miss a single Sabbath from church; and we do not think this occurred a score of times up to his seventy-ninth year. The weather, however violent, either in town or country, as we have before remarked, never prevented him from attending to his professional appointments. Even in physical illness he never faltered, and has more than once fainted in the desk from bodily weakness, caused by attending to his services at church when physically unable to do so. We are forcibly reminded here of a portion of a letter from Rev. H. B. Soule, then colleague with Mr. Ballou, to Rev. Stephen R. Smith. Both of these brethren, whose light burned so bright and lovely at that time, were called home by their Maker before this elder servant in their Master's vineyard.

"You will want to hear a word of our Father in Israel. "He continues in good health for a man seventy-three "years old; he preaches yet as strong as most men at "forty. Nothing but death will ever bring rest to his "labors. Most men, at his age, would sit down, and in "dreamy idleness or mere social converse wait their call. "Not so with him; his God-given mission will not be "finished till his lips are sealed forever. He will preach "as long as he can stand; and as long as he does preach "his preaching will be reverenced. Preach as long as he "can stand! yes, and longer! When that aged frame, "pangless and cold, sleeps in the grave; when that voice, "eloquent so long with 'good tidings of great joy,' shall "be hushed on earth, then will Father Ballou preach as "he never did before. His life, with its sainted virtues, "its noble toil, its Christian zeal, will be a sermon,— how "thrilling, how divine, they will know who read it. May "it be long ere it is written! God bless him in his old "days, and sanctify his example to the young servant "who stands beside him!"

The young brother who thus wrote spoke most truly. He studied well the character of him with whom he was associated; he realized the present effect of his words, and the future influence they must inevitably exercise. "His life," says the junior pastor, "when that voice "shall be hushed upon earth, will preach as he never did "before." That time has now come; we now realize this period referred to. "Though dead, he yet speaketh." Full of honors and of years, he has lain him down to sleep his last sleep; but he will still preach to us as eloquently as ever, perhaps with increased influence, through the memory of his pure and godly life, and the power of the works he has left behind. "By the world "he will be remembered as the apostle of Universalism," says T. A. Goddard, the superintendent of his Sabbath-school, in his address to the school, "the advocate of "the paternal character of God; and he will speak to "men as of old, when he charged them to cast away their "creeds and superstitions, and to search the Scriptures for "themselves. To his people he will speak whenever they "enter this temple, reminding them of the many years "he dwelt with them in peace, and of the glorious truths "that have dropped from his lips. To *us* he will speak, "with his benignant eye, as often as we enter this room, "telling us, in the language of the apostle, 'Beloved, let "us love one another; for love is of God.' This theme — "the love of God — was, indeed, one which he delighted "to dwell upon; and with what unction would he treat "it in all its length and breadth!" Yea, though his personal work be ended, yet the influence of his life-long labors will be perpetuated for centuries.

Mr. Ballou was particularly remarkable for his punctuality, and always took precaution that no matter, of whatever description, should be delayed by him. This was a point upon which he was always exceedingly tenacious. Often have we heard him say that punctuality is not merely a duty that we owe to others, but absolutely a duty to ourselves, and one of the most important principles that can be adopted and observed in every and all relations of life; and upon this belief he ever acted. If he had an engagement to proceed to any of the neighboring towns to preach, or was about to commence a journey of any considerable length, which was very often the case, he always allowed a reasonable period of time to *spare* at the place of starting, and took good precaution that he should never find it necessary to hurry in any emergency. In short, he made it a strict and abiding principle to be *punctual* in every case, important or comparatively otherwise. This was one reason why he was enabled to accomplish so much,—the proper division of time, and adherence to the appointed period for each specific purpose, giving him great command of his resources. Thus it has been said of him that he seemed completely independent of time and place, and so it would almost appear.

Burning with a constant desire to be about his Master's business, he could not remain idle for a moment when he realized that he might be profitably employed to the end of promulgating and enforcing the religion he taught. As we have before said, personal convenience or comfort were not taken into consideration at all; he was ever ready, ever willing, to respond promptly at each call; but so numerous were these, that he was obliged to adopt the principle of supplying the society first who came to him first, and those persons who read our denominational papers will have noticed that his appointments were frequently announced, up to the very last, for weeks in advance. The good that he undoubtedly accomplished in these itinerant missions must have been incalculable. Realizing that he could occupy but an hour or so in a place, he usually took up some prominent point of theology, and, by his masterly handling of the subject, cleared its questionable character entirely from the hearer's mind; and thus having gained one step before them which would impart a degree of confidence in his faith and general mode of explanation, he would then go over a most extensive field of faith, pointing out features here and there, and the props that should be raised to sustain this portion and that, and leaving the minds of the people, at last, strongly impressed with a system of theology that they might themselves understandingly pursue and reason upon, taking for a groundwork or platform that which he had clearly elucidated to their minds as the true fundamental basis of the gospel of Christ.

In reference to his frequent travels about the country, we would that it were possible to obtain more of the numerous incidents, so illustrative and characteristic, that used so constantly to occur to him. One anecdote strikes us at this moment, which is not without its bearing, as it relates to his power for repartee, or rather, we should say, his ability to turn the most familiar subjects into argumentative use and advantage.

When it is remembered that Mr. Ballou's belief was that salvation is *the process* of making people happy, the point of the following anecdote will be appreciated. It happened, on one of his short excursions in the neighboring country, that he stopped at a public house, where he had occasion to pass through a room which a woman was about to engage in cleaning. She had heard that he was at the house, and, being of a different faith, she determined to ask him, if an opportunity offered, just one single question, which, in her simplicity, she conceived to be perfectly unanswerable by those who believed in the doctrine Mr. Ballou advocated. As he came in, she began:—"Your name is Ballou, I believe, sir?"—"Yes, madam," said he, "my name is Ballou."—"I'm told "that you preach," said the woman, "that all mankind "are going to be saved."— "Yes," replied he, "I do." —"Well, Mr. Ballou," continued she, "do you believe "they will be saved without first becoming perfectly "holy? Do you believe they will be saved *just as they "are?*" He looked at her mop. "What are you "going to do with that mop?" he asked. —"Why, sir," replied she, "I'm going to mop up the floor."—"Are "you going to mop up the floor," he asked, "before it "becomes perfectly clean? Are you going to mop it up "*just as it is?*"

Could a more happily conceived answer have been given to the woman, if hours had been consumed in its preparation? We opine not; and herein the reader will observe the instantaneous and lightning-like operation of Mr. Ballou's mind.

His conversational powers were most remarkable,— remarkable because ever tempered with such a fund of logical clear-sightedness, such profound acumen, and such convincing argument upon the topic under discussion; then we have to add to this the effect of his speech, so distinct and impressive. Hazlitt's remark of Coleridge, that he was an "excellent talker,— very,— if you let him start from no premises and come to no conclusion," would in no way apply to the subject of these memoirs; for, at the outset of Mr. Ballou's conversation, you would at once divine the end he aimed at, and would only be surprised at the velocity with which you found him leading you to the desired result, always established in his own mind, though he addressed you with the calm and collected expression that was a second nature to him. No mountain of error seemed too lofty for him to surmount, with giant strides and unbroken strength; and you would find his white flag of truth waving from its summit, and yourself breathing freer and deeper at the consummation of the rough ascent, before you had fairly found time to realize the power of reason necessary to surmount the rugged obstacles of the path. And once elevated above the murky haze of error, his descent with you again to the lowlands and plains of every-day life was as easy and graceful as his ascent had been majestic and lofty.

Often, in private conversation with those who had come to his own fireside to meet him, he was most efficacious. In the grandeur of his conception, the glory of his theme, and the unequalled sincerity with which he advocated it, his soul would seem to expand, his eyes to kindle in the expression to a surprising brilliancy, his lips and countenance seemed like those of one inspired, while you would have been almost awed at the man, had not his theme so much more power over your heart. But, having uttered such language as few could frame, having challenged your admiration and wonder by the adaptedness of every word, and the conviction that he forced upon you, he relapsed again into the quiet, peaceable, domestic soul that he was, and you would seem to look around instinctively to behold the spirit which had so entranced your faculties but a moment before, it seeming impossible that it was he who sat so quietly beside you.

Mr. Ballou's reading was confined almost entirely to sacred history, and, comparatively speaking, he consulted little else, though he was well versed on all general subjects, and he carefully perused at least one daily newspaper regularly. We remember to have asked him, at a late period of his life, why he did not vary his reading somewhat from the great theme of divinity, arguing that it might afford some relief to his mind, and be of both mental and physical benefit to him, by somewhat relaxing the constant exercise of his brain. He answered us in the words of Milton,—"The end of learning is to know "God, and out of that knowledge to love him, and to "venerate him;" adding, that this was the great actuating purpose of his labors and study; in short, the being, end and aim, of his existence. "That which seems to you to "be labor," said he, "is to me as refreshing recreation. "No course of reading could afford me the pleasure and "delight that I find in that which has engaged me, heart "and soul, for more than half a century."

His whole library did not exceed three hundred volumes, but these were of a character that particularly indicated the nature of his mind and pursuits, being well worn by constant use, and relating to such subjects as might be supposed to occupy and interest him. His thorough acquaintance with the Scriptures was almost unprecedented, and he was never at fault as to any passage or quotation from its wealth of knowledge. It was the book he had studied more than all others put together; nor was there any passage, in the whole of the sacred record, which had been made the theme of controversy or misunderstanding, that he had not also made the subject of careful study and exposition.

Every unoccupied moment was given to mental exercise upon the subject nearest to his heart. We have seen him thus occupied often in the street, when all the turmoil and bustle of life passed him by unheeded. On this peculiarity, Mr. Bacon says, in the eulogy before referred to: —"He wasted no power in frivolity, but as he walked "the streets he seemed to be unaffected by the crowd "about him, meditating some new utterance of the truth. "I remember being amused, and yet impressed, by beholding him, in my youth, walking along with his head "bent, and his lips moving as in speech, heeding not the "passers-by or the shows in the street, appearing as "quiet amid the noise and bustle as in the solitude of his "own study. Yet should any one greet him by name, "he would instantly pause, fix his sharp, keen eye upon "the face before him, and, as he recognized the friend, "one of the sweetest smiles that ever illumined a human "face would spread over his countenance, deepening till "that countenance was youthful indeed; then, with ready "utterance of kind feeling and warm interest in the "happiness of others, he made his affectionate regards "known."

CHAPTER XIII.

SPIRIT OF HIS DOCTRINE.

MR. BALLOU ever strove to make the word and the principles which he taught appear attractive, by representing them in their appropriate dress, the livery of joy and peace, and from the principles of fatherly love and kindness he gathered the strongest motives for humility, gratitude and obedience. He would tell you that God has written upon the fragrant flowers of the field, on the breezes that rock them, and the refreshing sun that nurtures them, indelible tokens of his fatherly affection, and would refer you to the blooming clover, and the falling rain, as blessings not to be misconstrued, in God's own hand-writing, a "way-side sacrament," free to all. He would never tire of depicting the Almighty through the spirit of the most beautiful emblems in nature, and ever deducing from them the most amiable and glorious traits of Deity.

The employment he made of the familiar images of nature will remind the reader of what we have already said touching the influences of his birth-place. The blue skies, the green pastures, the gushing rivulets, the everlasting hills that rear their giant summits to the glorious effulgence of the noon-tide sun, or the cold kiss of the midnight moon, spoke to his heart a language that his intellect faithfully interpreted. The constant contemplation of beautiful natural scenery almost invariably inspires devotional feeling. In the wonderful solitudes of nature the sneer of the infidel is hushed upon his lips, and the worldly man forgets the passions, the jealousies, the intrigues, the heart-burnings and frivolities, of his daily artificial life. But the heart of the true, thoughtful, right-minded man does something more than mirror the images presented to his eye. It is not like

"——a sleeping lake,
That takes the hue of cloud and sky,
And only feels its surface break
As birds of passage wander by,
That dip their wing and upward soar,
Leaving it quiet as before."

Before the mind's eye of such a man, the beauties of nature do not glide away like the figures of a painted panorama, serving only to amuse, charming the eye for a moment with grace of form and beauty of manner, and then passing away like an idle dream, the "baseless fabric of a vision." In the true man, the child of God, the inner, the spiritual sense is awakened in sympathy with the material organs of vision. For him each lineament of nature is a revelation, each feature a symbol. The flowers are to him, as some one has beautifully remarked, the "alphabet of angels."

We have labored somewhat in these pages, even at the risk of repetition, to inculcate the idea that Mr. Ballou was one of these students of nature; and this was the case in a most eminent degree: the teachings that he received at her feet in youth he garnered up in his heart, to be repeated, to be illustrated, and illumined with new light from the brightness of his intellect, to be poured forth again to thousands who required so eloquent an interpreter. He had learned a lesson he could never forget, from the beautiful creations of God, of his fatherly affection. The fierce midnight storm, with its thunder-peals and lightning-flashes, had no terror for him; he knew better than to interpret it as a manifestation of the wrath and vengeful fury of the Deity; for he knew that it was to be followed by a purer and healthier atmosphere, by the glowing bow of promise, and by brighter smiles from the unshadowed sun.

In none of the varied phenomena of nature did he behold the God of wrath, the God of vengeance, the pitiless Deity of the dark theology, whose horrors he was destined to dissipate and overcome. Far from this. He deduced from every phase of nature the great truth of the all-prevailing and inexhaustible love of the Almighty for the children of his creation. Thus, by the simple symbols and tokens he had discovered, strewn like flowers along the pathway of life, he sought to awaken the torpid sense of those "who, having eyes, saw not, and having ears heard not," the wonders of the glad tidings the angel-messengers of the Deity were commissioned to communicate to man.

Mr. Ballou's examples and illustrations of God's unbounded grace and goodness, as drawn from visible nature, were very frequent. God's word first, and then God's works, were his strength and shield. Let the following show his mode of reasoning in this particular. He says:—"If our Creator has so bountifully provided for "our existence here, which is but momentary, and for "our temporal wants, which will all soon be forgotten, "what has he not done for the security of our immortal "state, and for our enjoyment in the everlasting world? "Pause, and behold what boundless scenes of riches and "glory are opening to our view in Jesus, by whom life "and immortality are brought to light! We have seen "the brightness of the morning sun, have known the renovating majesty of his noontide rays, have seen a fair "creation blest with his universal light and heat! But "this is only a symbol of the Sun of Righteousness; his "brightness is above that of the morning sun, his heat is "more renovating than the rays of the noon. In him "our Heavenly Father hath given unto us eternal life. "As the life of the natural is in the sun, so the life of "the moral creation is in Jesus, the light of the world, "the life of man. If the *earth* be full of the goodness "of the Lord, have we not in this a fair specimen of the "rest of his vast creation? Have we any reason to be-

"lieve that the *earth* is more favored with the divine "goodness than any other part or parts of creation? No, "surely we have not. All those worlds which sparkle "in the wide expanse of heaven are full of the goodness "of the Lord; and if time be all full of divine goodness, "so is eternity; and if God be universally good tempo- "rally speaking, so is he in relation to spiritual things. "What infinite reason have we to exercise our hearts in "gratitude to God, and our affections in love to him, who "giveth us all things richly to enjoy! With what pro- "priety may we say, 'Let everything that hath breath "praise the Lord!'"

Observe how vastly different was the effect produced by the tenets of faith preached by many around him! How far from lovable was the portraiture drawn of God and Heaven by those who held forth the creed of the old school!

How many preachers of this school have won their ephemeral reputations solely by awakening the terrors of their auditors, and have been esteemed great in proportion to their ability to produce fainting, convulsions, tears and groans, among women and children! The perverted vision of such men rests on no image of nature, except such as they can distort to symbolize some imaginary dreadful attribute in the God of their theology. He is clothed by them in storms and clouds, as the heathen Jove was depicted grasping in his hand a sheaf of thunderbolts. From their portraiture every gleam of light is excluded, — it is a murky and repulsive mass of shadows. The gentle and fragrant flowers, the sweet perfumes and rainbow colors with which the face of nature is so prodigally decked, claim no word or thought of theirs; they cannot employ these images in their illustrations, they cannot reconcile them with their gloomy theories, — their very existence is unaccountable to their perverse vision.

"That gloomy, heart-dejecting something," says Mr. Ballou, "which has been maintained in our world at an "incalculable expense of treasure, of comfort, peace and "joy,— at the expense, also, of the tender charities of the "heart, and the benevolent sentiments of the soul, — "though called religion, is all counterfeit. It has drawn "a sable curtain over the mildly radiant countenance of our "Father in heaven, and in room of leading the mind to "contemplate the Divine Being with pleasure and de- "light, it has attached a horror to the sacred name, "which gives a stupefying chill to the heart, repels the "mind, and forces it to seek relief in the contemplation "of visible and sensible objects; and after becoming the "author of this horror and disgust in the soul, it artfully "takes the advantage of the deception, to inculcate a "belief that the reason of these feelings is the natural "depravity of the human heart! Such are the views "which youth are led to entertain of religion, that they "contemplate it as something calculated to deprive them "of their present comforts, and only useful as it relates "to a state of existence hereafter, where, as a recompense "for sacrifices which they make of happiness in this "world, they are to receive extensive and lasting bless-

"ings. With such reflections, it is natural to delay the "concerns of religion as long as possible, with an inten-"tion to submit to its unpleasant requirements in season "to win the prize. This is evidently the reason why "youth are so little inclined to employ their thoughts on "divine things, and to prefer amusements and trifling "vanities to the acquisition of Christian knowledge.

"But true religion presents the Father of our spirits "as the most lovely character of which the mind can pos-"sibly conceive. It directs to the contemplation of that "almighty power which controls a universe, and to view "all its elements in harmony with the unchangeable love "of God to his creatures. In youth, while the heart "is tender, and sensibility quick and lively, what an "exquisite delight the mind is capable of enjoying, by "penetrating through visible objects and the beauty of "temporal things, to the contemplation of that wisdom, "power and goodness, which are manifest through the "medium of these outward forms! If the fragrance of "the rose can so gratefully delight the sense, how much "greater is the pleasure to the rational mind which flows "from the consideration of that wisdom and goodness "which gave this power to the rose, and this capacity to "sense! From this single item let the mind glance "through all creation, and freely indulge the reflection "that the universe is as full of the divine goodness as "the rose or the lily of the valley. Freed from super-"stition, what heart would not be charmed with the char-"acter which the Saviour gives of our Heavenly Father?

"'Behold the fowls of the air; for they sow not, neither "do they reap, nor gather into barns, yet your Heavenly "Father feedeth them. Are ye not much better than "they? Consider the lilies of the field, how they grow; "they toil not, neither do they spin; and yet I say unto "you that even Solomon, in all his glory, was not arrayed "like one of these.'"

These mute, but beautiful and eloquent testimonials of their Maker's love and gentleness, would rebuke the dogmatism of the schools; and hence they naturally avoid to mention the graceful, refined and touching features of nature. They prefer rather to revel in their own dark and unwarrantable conceptions of a future state, to gloat over the prospective agony of their brethren, to conjure up horrid pictures of future suffering and woe, and madly to pronounce all as being necessary to the full glory of God, and the exemplification of his almighty power. What wonder, then, that thousands, turning with loathing and shuddering from the image of a deity clothed with all the repugnant attributes of the most debased humanity, plunge into hopeless unbelief, refusing all credence in such a being, and in any future state whatever? Was it not a Herculean task to combat the immemorial and prescriptive dogmas of powerful and learned preachers, armed with all the rhetorical imagery of the schools for working terror and despair in the hearts of their listeners?

Again Mr. Ballou says:—

"The preacher of the old school exhorts his hearers, "above all things, to the practice of the most rigid self-

" denial; and assures them that God will be highly pleased " with their abstaining from those pleasures which he has " placed within their reach. The most innocent amuse- " ments, the most harmless recreations, he declaims " against with the utmost vehemence, as damning sins. " He considers religion essentially to consist in a perpet- " ual effort to suppress and eradicate that propensity to " acquire temporal happiness which the God of nature " has made to be the spring of our actions. But on no " subject does he delight to dwell so much as on the " future punishment of the wicked and impenitent. He " dresses up the Father of the universe in the awful " robes of eternal wrath and unbounded indignation, filled " with incessant anger at the crimes of the wicked, exert- " ing infinite wisdom in devising the modes and augment- " ing the severity of their punishment.

"The eternal din of future punishment soon loses all " effect in frightening the people, and has no influence but " to impress a melancholy gloom on their minds. Mankind " are to be animated to strive to enter the gates of heaven " by the love of God and of goodness. He who attempts " it through fear of damnation exhibits no evidence of " holiness of heart. As well may we call a man honest " who, having an inclination to steal, refrains for fear of " the whip, as we may a man religious, who, having " vicious inclinations, restrains them, and conforms to the " exteriors of religion, for the purpose of escaping the " flames of hell. It is matter of much regret that the " amiable religion of Christianity should be so disfigured "and misrepresented as to deprive many people of the "happiness of enjoying it. Jesus Christ has in the "clearest manner inculcated those duties which are pro-"ductive of the highest moral felicity, and consistent "with all the innocent enjoyments to which we are "impelled by the dictates of nature. Religion, when "fairly considered in its genuine simplicity and uncor-"rupted state, is the source of endless rapture and "delight. But, when corrupted with denials, mortifica-"tions, and a punctilious observance of external rites, it "assumes a form disgusting to men of taste, and a relish "for social happiness, and is productive of the most "destructive consequences. It drives one part of man-"kind into the practice of superstition, hypocrisy and "bigotry; and, by exciting a distaste and aversion in the "minds of the other part, it excludes them from the "rational pleasure arising from the practice of genuine "religion. The road to heaven is pleasant and delightful, "if mankind will go the right way; and certainly God "will bid the saint as sincere a welcome to the realms of "immortal felicity who has in the journey of life tasted "the temporal delights of innocence, as he will him who "has abstained from them. Why, then, should we leave "the path that is strewed with flowers and roses, for the "purpose of going in another through a wilderness beset "with thorns and briars, when both parts will terminate "in the same happy country?"

People listen to the dogmas of the schools, and are filled with awful forebodings; terror is the predominating principle in their bosoms, and sorrow takes possession of their hearts, speaking out from their faithful countenances in sadness. How far is the true influence of the gospel from inducing such results as this! Mr. Ballou believed, with Fenelon, that "true piety hath in it nothing "weak, nothing sad, nothing constrained. It enlarges "the heart; it is simple, free, and attractive." If this were not the true nature of the gospel, how could there be "peace and joy in believing"?

He held that the true way to cleanse the hardened and rebellious heart is to inundate it with a deluge of love, the only weapon of Omnipotence. Reason with the sinner, he will meet you with subtle argument; threaten him, and he will meet you blow for blow; against future interest he will adroitly balance present pleasure. The human heart rises against severity or oppression, while it is soothed by gentleness, as the waves of the ocean rise in proportion to the violence of the winds, and sink with the breeze, until it becomes a gentle zephyr, into mildness and serenity. Love, the warm sunshine of our existence, subdues the sinner at once; there is not one in a thousand whose heart is so hardened that its genial warmth will not melt it. True it is that force can subdue numbers, cunning conquers force, intellect can master cunning, but love conquers all. There is a vast difference between a wounded heart and a contrite spirit. You may break ice by force into a thousand pieces,—it is ice still; but expose it to the warm sun, and behold! how quickly it will melt!

We have enlarged somewhat upon this doctrine of divine love, and trust that our readers will bear with us in our desultory career, since this principle is the fundamental basis of Universalism,—the starting-point and the goal, the Alpha and the Omega, of Mr. Ballou's spiritual experience and teaching. By it he reconciled the impulses of his heart and the promptings of his intellect. The principle of God's perfect, unchanging and eternal love of man, was the great discovery of his earliest manhood, the object of his self-imposed mission, the inspiration and solace of his labors, the spirit and joy of his existence. His adamantine belief in this great idea, daily strengthening by the study of God's works and word, was his shield and spear. It touched his lips with living fire, as he stood in the pulpit, or beneath the blue canopy of heaven, where he often preached; in the solitude of his study, in the busy haunts of men, it fed the flickering lamp of life when it waned with severe exertion, and it shone like the brightest star of heaven on his dying bed. It was no solitary joy; the treasure he had found he journeyed through the land to share with others. From his lips the glad tidings rang through every nook and corner; and he lived, as we have seen, long enough to hear the accents caught up by the willing and faithful watchmen of the gospel, and the cry of "All's well!" echo from port to port, from battlement to battlement, on the castles of Zion, through the vast circumference of his native land. He saw his denominational congregation swollen from a little band of eager listeners to an auditory numbering hundreds of thousands. He saw the shadows of unbelief flying from the face of truth, as the mist of morning disappears before the rising sun. And he felt joyful, but not proud or elated, in the consciousness that his sacred mission had been crowned with such complete success, and that multitudes recognized the truth which he first enunciated, that *the law of God was the law of love.*

But let us give place here to his own words, beautifully expressed, and illustrating his belief, and the *spirit* of his doctrine, as appears in a poem he wrote upon this theme, some years since. It is entitled

GOD IS LOVE.

"When lovely Spring, with flowery wreaths,
Comes on young Zephyr's wing,
And every bird soft music breathes,
'T is love that makes them sing.

Love blossoms on the forest trees,
And paints each garden flower,
Gives honey to the laboring bees
In every sylvan bower.

Love breathes in every wind that blows,
And fragrance fills the air ;
Meanders in each stream that flows,
Inviting pleasures there.

Love brings the golden harvest in,
And fills her stores with food ;
It moves ten thousand tongues to sing
Of universal good."

"If we believe that God so loved us that he sent his Son to die for us, we ought to love one another," he says. "Shall I not love those objects whom my God "loves? Shall I not love all those for whose sins he "sent his Son to be a propitiation? Most assuredly. "This is a consequence naturally to be expected from our "belief. I do not say that all who profess the doctrine "do love one another as they ought; but I have the con- "fidence to say that no one who possesses the real senti- "ment, the real principle, in his heart, can do otherwise "than love all mankind. And here you will easily per- "ceive that all the commandments of the gospel are to "be obeyed. For when we love one another and love "God, what duty is there that will be neglected? If "this will not lead us to our duty, what will? Will ter- "ror make us do our duty? No; for, referring once "more to the similitude, what drove your children away? "It was believing the story they were told of your char- "acter. What *brought* them back? Knowing you "were good. And know you not that it is *the goodness* "*of God that leadeth to repentance?* Why, then, "should not his goodness be preached to sinners? Why "should we be told such awful stories with regard to "eternity? Why should we be told that there is an "everlasting state of burning, in order to induce us to "love our Father in heaven? O! incongruous doc- "trine! Let it be banished from the world, and let the "angel of the covenant proclaim the love of God to man- "kind; and may the world be converted. Man will then "love his fellow-man; we shall all see that we are the "children of God, that we are all the objects of God's "love, and all the objects of our Saviour's grace. Believe "this truth, treasure it up in your hearts, let your affec- "tions move with assent, love God and love one another, "and the God of love and peace shall be with you."

All his writings and all of his conversation, both public and private, were thoroughly imbued with this belief and principle of universal love; it ran like a golden stratum through all his life and conduct, imbuing every sentiment and every thought. His doctrine was such that a realizing sense of its character must invariably thus affect the firm and relying believer. He never held forth dark threats, nor adopted, like many preachers about him, the doleful tones of grief when he talked about religion. "If "good people," says Archbishop Usher, "would make "their goodness agreeable, and smile instead of frowning "in their virtue, how many would they win to the good "cause!" Mr. Ballou was affected, in his cheerful and happy belief of universal salvation, like Haydn, who, in answer to a query of the poet Carpani, how it happened that his church music was ever of an animating and cheerful character, answered, — "I cannot make it otherwise. "I write according to the thoughts which I feel; — when "I think upon God, my heart is so full of joy that the "notes dance and leap as it were from my pen."

How many there are among us who, the moment the subject of religion is mentioned, put on long faces, and talk as if they were mourning their own lot and that of all creation, "in hopes to merit heaven by making earth a hell!" Such people, by their example and bearing, would lead us to believe that churches are institutions reared for the purpose of encouraging long faces and dyspepsia, instead of pure altars from whence may ascend the glad incense of grateful hearts. How strongly it is impressed upon us that "God loves the *cheerful* giver!" and did not Christ reproach the Pharisees for disfiguring their faces with a sad countenance? To use the forcible language of another, they make of themselves "Hypo-"crites, who, to persuade men that angels lodge in their "hearts, hang out a devil for a sign in their counte-"nances." "It is quite deplorable," says Lady Morgan, "to see how many rational creatures, or at least who "are thought so, mistake suffering for sanctity, and think "a sad face and a gloomy habit of mind propitious offer-"ings to that Deity whose works are all light and lustre, "and harmony and loveliness."

Such was the philosophy of the subject of these memoirs, such his religion, such the doctrine which he taught. He found no cause for sorrow in his belief, but a never-failing fountain of joy ever welled up in his breast, pure and sparkling.

Mr. Ballou's religious belief, the faith which he promulgated with such zeal and wonderful effect, can be summed up in a few words. He held that God judges the human family in the earth; that every man must receive according to the sin he hath done, and that there is no respect of persons. That the "righteous shall be recompensed in the earth, much more the wicked and the sinner." That the future state of existence will be one of unalloyed happiness for the whole human family. That God is a being who governs the world with a parent's regard, and not with the wrath of a tyrant; that the world could be led to love him, but never driven to do it through fear. That love, not wrath, should be preached to the people. That all punishment is designed by the Divine Spirit for the reformation of the sinner, and consequently must take place where the sin is committed. That the reward of good deeds is to encourage well doing, and must come when and where the worthy acts are done. He believed in no more dreadful hell than is produced by the consequences of sin about us, with the still, bitter gnawings of conscience; and in no sweeter or more desirable reward than an approving conscience, and the natural consequences of doing good. He taught that man must be saved from his *sins*, not from the *punishment* of them,—*that* is impossible,—and that to be happy we must "do justly, love mercy, and walk humbly with God."

He believed that, in order to prove that misery will exist in the future or eternal state, it must first be made to appear that sin will exist in that state. But this he did not believe could be proved from any scriptural testimony; on the contrary, he was fully convinced that the Bible taught that "He that is dead is freed from sin." To quote his own words on this point: "We have "shown, in order for justice to require the endless mis-

"ery of any moral being, it must, of necessity, require "the endless continuance of sin, than which nothing can "be more absurd." Again he says: "We have suffi- "ciently argued that man cannot be miserable in conse- "quence of moral condemnation, any longer than he is, "in a moral sense, a sinner." And we have often heard him make the remark, in regard to limited future punishment, that if any one would produce but only one passage of scripture which proves, beyond a reasonable doubt, that sin or the sinner will exist, as such, in the eternal, immortal state, then I give up my doctrine of no future punishment; but until this is done, I shall hold to the doctrine that the Scriptures do not teach the principle even of a limited future punishment. Mr. Ballou would not allow analogy to take the place of scriptural proof on so important a subject as the destiny of man in the immortal state. He had nothing to do with mere assertions, which had not a "thus saith the Lord" for their support, on any doctrinal point.

This feature of his mind cannot be too strongly insisted upon. He was not content with relying on the *spirit* of the Scriptures, which would have fully sustained his doctrine, but he conciliated the spirit and the letter, and rested every proposition he advanced on this immutable and impregnable basis. If ever a man strictly obeyed the injunction to "search the Scriptures," it was Mr. Ballou. They were the armor from which he drew the shield that sheltered him in conflict, and all the shafts that garnished his quiver. He had the very words of Christ and his apostles for every item of his creed, and such creed alone would he accept as might be adapted to this standard. He was not one of those self-complacent and easy theorists, who readily support their favorite doctrine by a few ambiguous texts, or an arbitrary construction of a mooted passage. He was far too conscientious for this; the language of learned commentators, however elegant the phraseology and plausible the reason, never satisfied him. His standard was fixed in the Bible.

There was little of the enthusiast,— to use the term in its common acceptation,— nothing of the bigot and fanatic, in his nature. He first convinced himself of the truth of his ideas; he reflected and pondered them deeply by himself, in some of those abstracted moods peculiar to him, examining them in every light, trying them by every test, dispassionately and calmly; and then gave them to the world, armed at all points, and ready for defence against attack. And how prompt and ready he was to defend what he had satisfied himself was the truth, we need not reiterate here. The language in which he enforced his arguments was simple and clear, because his ideas were so. They needed not the tinsel garb of rhetoric, the flowers of a refined oratory, to make them presentable to the world; they needed no foreign or artificial aid; — no, they stood forth clear, simple, strong, arrayed in the garb and radiant with the light of truth and of nature. They stood the test of public scrutiny, because they had been refined in the alembic of his own severe and critical mind. This simplicity, which is fast becoming an old-fashioned virtue, commended the preacher to the earnest seekers after truth. It is a pretty fair inference to arrive at, when you hear a religion preached which requires disguise and ornament, that the truth is not in it. Where truth is there need be no such garbing; it is only error that requires to be gilded, like the covering to bitter pills, used to render them sweet. The gospel of Christ appeals to the judgment, not to the taste.

In relation to the argument of analogy, as used to prove the doctrine of punishment in a future state, we subjoin the following, in his own words: — "Another ground on "which the advocates of a future state of rewards and "punishments place much dependence for the support of "the doctrine, they denominate *analogy*. We think it too "hazardous to attempt anything like an accurate state-"ment of the particular arguments, which are made to "depend on this principle, in favor of this doctrine; for "we might be liable to some mistakes, which would repre-"sent the views of its advocates differently from their "mode of representing them. Our liability to misrepre-"sent in such an attempt seems unavoidable, on account "of the fact that there has been nothing like a system of "reasoning yet exhibited on the general subject. We feel "safe, however, in saying, that, as far as we have been "informed, those who rely on what they call analogy to "support the doctrine of future retribution, hold that, in "all respects which are necessary to carry sin and its "miseries into the future state, that state will be analo-"gous to this mode of being. So that, reasoning from "analogy, as moral agents sin, and thereby render them-"selves miserable in this world, the same moral agents "may continue to do the same in the world to come. In "connection with this argument it is urged, that, as it is "evident to our senses that sin often escapes a just retri-"bution in this world, it must be recompensed in another "state, or divine justice must forever be deprived of its "claims.

"On reasonings of such a character, we shall use the "freedom to say, that they appear to have no higher "authority than mere human speculations injudiciously "managed. That they are nothing more than simple "speculations, is evident from the fact that they are "not founded on any divine authority. We presume "that their own advocates never ventured to support "them by scripture authority. And that they are "managed injudiciously, is very apparent from the "circumstances, that while they profess to be justi-"fied by the principle of analogy, they are a direct "denial of the very analogy on which they depend. "Theologians who endeavor to exert an influence over "the minds of people by means of these speculations, are "constantly urging that in this world we see sin procur-"ing for its agents the riches and honors of the world, "while it escapes judicial detection, and goes unpunished. "Now, if they were consistent with their analogy and "with themselves, they would see at once that in the "next state of existence sin will procure for its agents "the riches and honors of that world, and there, as well "as here, escape judicial detection, and go unpunished. "They would likewise see that as divine justice can "quiet its own claims in this world, without administer- "ing a full and adequate retribution of human conduct, "it may do the same in the future state. In this way "we might proceed and make the future state precisely "like the present; for we have no more authority for "carrying sin and its miseries into a future world, than "we have for carrying all other things into that state "which we find in this. Reasoning from all that we "know, we must believe that, so long as men sin, they "will do so from the beguiling power of temptation. If, "then, we believe that sin will exist in the future state, "we must suppose that temptation will there act on the "mind with a deceiving influence. In this world the "wicked are allured with the hopes of temporal gain, and "these attractions are strengthened by the belief that "crime will not be detected, and that punishment will be "avoided. Were it not for these hopes and allurements, "no wrong-doing would be practised in this world; and "to suppose that we shall transgress the law of God in the "future world, without any temptation, is a speculation "altogether arbitrary and capricious, as well as contrary "to *analogy*."

"Of late, the writer of this," says Mr. Ballou, in one of his last published sermons, "has seen an inclination, "in some of the professed preachers of Universalism, to "adopt some of the peculiar opinions of our Unitarian "fraternity. Among other things, is the opinion that "men carry into the next world the imperfections of this; "so that their moral condition hereafter will depend on "the characters they form while here in the flesh; but "that they may and will improve and progress in virtue "and holiness in the spirit world. This opinion being "rather newly adopted, and as it seems to ingratiate "them into favor with Unitarians, it is quite natural for "such preachers to devote not a small share of public "labor to lead the minds of their hearers to the adoption "of such views of the future state. Whenever the writer "of this discourse comes in contact with these labors and "opinions, he feels it to be his duty, in a friendly, "brotherly, and candid manner, to endeavor to bring "them to the test of some acknowledged standard. It is "worthy of consideration, that the New Testament gives "us but little on the subject of man's future state. "There can be no doubt but Jesus was known to believe "and preach a doctrine embracing the fact of the resur- "rection, and an immortal state for the human family. "All this is clearly manifested by the question asked "him by the Sadducees respecting the resurrection. In "the answer which Jesus returned, we have all which "gives us any account respecting the state of man here- "after which was spoken by him. In this answer, we "are told the following facts: — 1st, That, in the future "world, they will neither marry nor be given in mar- "riage. 2d. That, in that state, men will be the chil- "dren of God, being the children of the resurrection. 3d. "That they will be equal unto the angels, and that they "can die no more. 4th. That the doctrine of the resur-"rection was shown by Moses, and that God is not the God "of the dead, but of the living, for we all live unto him. "St. Paul says more on the subject of the resurrection, and "of the future state, than did Jesus. He says, 'As in "Adam all die, even so in Christ shall all be made alive.' "He also distinguishes man's state and condition in the "future or resurrection state, from his condition here, as "follows:—'It is sown in corruption, it is raised in "incorruption: it is sown in dishonor, it is raised in "glory: it is sown in weakness, it is raised in power: it "is sown a natural body, it is raised a spiritual body.' "Thus we are taught that our future state will differ "from the present as incorruption differs from corrup-"tion; as glory differs from dishonor; as power differs "from weakness; as a spiritual body differs from a natural "body. Now, if we allow ourselves to carry our specula-"tions respecting our future state not only beyond all the "Scriptures say on the subject, but so as to adopt distinc-"tions in that state, which evidently conflict with the "divine Word, do we not say, by so doing, that divine "Revelation is not only incomplete, but also inaccurate?"

He believed that all those promises which give the assurance of the final *holiness* and *happiness* of the entire race of man depend solely on the will and power and goodness of God, and not on any conditions for the creature to perform. While dwelling upon this theme, which he delighted to do, he says:—"Let us pass "to the prophecies of Isaiah; see Chap. 25: 6, 7, 8.

"'And in this mountain shall the Lord of Hosts make "unto *all* people a feast of fat things. * * * And "he will destroy in this mountain the face of the cover-"ing cast over all people, and the vail that is spread over "all nations. He will swallow up death in victory; and "the Lord God will wipe away tears from off all faces; "and the rebuke of his people shall he take away from "off all the earth: for the Lord hath spoken it.' No "one will doubt that the provisions here spoken of are "those which are provided in the gospel of salvation,— "made for all people. The vail of darkness which is "over all people is to be taken away. Death is to be "swallowed up in victory, and tears wiped from off all "faces. The rebuke of God's people shall be taken from "off all the earth. And the proof is in the above pas-"sage, 'for the Lord hath spoken it.'"

Mr. Ballou says: — "I look with strong expectation for "that period when all sin, and every degree of unrecon-"ciliation, will be destroyed, by the divine power of that "love which is stronger than death, which many waters "cannot quench, nor the floods drown; in which alone I "put my trust, and in which my hope is anchored for all "mankind; earnestly praying that the desire of the "righteous may not be cut off. The fulness of times "will come, and the times of the restitution of all things "will be accomplished. Then shall truth be victorious, "and all error flee to eternal night. Then will univer-"sal songs of honor be sung to the praise of Him who "liveth for ever and ever."

In relation to the subject of his faith, Rev. A. A. Miner, in his funeral sermon delivered on the occasion, says:—

"Let me say, then, that he was *a man of unswerv-*
"*ing faith.* He believed in the Bible as the treasury
"of divine revelation. His ministry was based upon it.
"Few men have confined themselves so exclusively to its
"themes. None have treated those themes with greater
"clearness and power. He studied the sacred page with
"a spirit equally removed from the Germanic philosophy,
"on the one hand, and from Calvinistic bigotry on the
"other. In the fulness of its promises, the riches of its
"grace, and the blessedness of its hopes, his soul contin-
"ually delighted. It was to him the 'Book of books;'
"and, at the advanced age of more than fourscore years,
"its truths, still fresh in his memory, continually em-
"ployed his understanding, and its glories enraptured
"his heart.

"He believed also in God;—in God as the supreme
"good. He believed in him as sovereign,—not simply
"as a candidate for sovereignty, but as already sovereign;
"nor alone as sovereign to create, to uphold, to rule,
"to condemn, and to chasten or destroy. So far had the
"*world's* faith gone. He regarded him as sovereign,
"not to do evil, but to do good, and to do good only.
"He believed God limited by his very nature to the
"doing of good,—that he is no more able to do evil
"than he is to be untrue. And, since it is admitted, on
"all hands, that there are moral influences by which
"some will be saved in perfect harmony with the exercise

"of their own voluntary powers, he believed that a God "who is really sovereign in his moral domain can accom-"plish in all souls whatever is possible to be accomplished "in any. Thus, from the character of God he saw freely "flowing the blessed promises of his word.

"His faith, too, in Christ stood related to the affec-"tionate Father as the sovereign cause. Christ was "God's messenger to man. He came not to procure the "Father's love for the world, but as a testimony of that "love. He came not to open to man the door of mercy, "but to strengthen man to walk in the already open "door. His mission was not simply to explore the wide-"spread moral waste, but to possess and cultivate it; not "to make salvation possible, but actual; for God 'hath "appointed him *heir* of all things,' — 'hath given all "things into his hands, that he should give eternal life to "as many as God had given him.' Thus it was his mis-"sion to *accomplish* a work, rather than to *offer* to "accomplish it; and, by his ever-memorable prayer on "the cross, he perfected the power by which the world "will be saved; as he said, 'And I, if I be lifted up "from the earth, *will draw all men unto me.*' "

No one who has thus far followed this unpretending but truthful biography, can fail to admit the full justice of the foregoing analysis and eulogy of Mr. Ballou's moral and mental nature. The faith of which Mr. Miner speaks was the strongest characteristic of the man. It illumined his whole life. His intellect was not clouded by doubts. In the geniality and genuineness of his faith he proceeded to the study of the book of books; every leaf he turned in the sacred volume confirmed the steadfast belief of his soul. He read it not as a verbal critic, not as a worldly philosopher, ambitious to found some system on the hints he might discover, but as a Christian seeking, where he knew he should discover it, the eternal light of truth. It was, indeed, to him a source of unsullied, uncloying, constant delight. Daily and hourly he discovered new beauties and new truths in its pages. Its story rolled before him like a wave of unbroken harmony, until his mental vision became almost microscopic in its powers of detection. Thus filled with the word, thus made conversant with its glowing truths and beauties, he constantly renewed and multiplied the means of awakening and confirming faith in others.

As we have labored to show, his reverence and love for his Maker were boundless; they absorbed his whole being — not, however, to the exclusion of earthly objects of affection, for he well knew that a true love of our Father in heaven is totally incompatible with the neglect of his creatures. Therefore, he was as unlike as possible to those ascetics of the middle ages, or the recluses of our own day, who fancy that a strict seclusion from the world, and a complete abandonment to religious exercises, is the most acceptable offering that can be made at the foot of the altar. This was an idea that found no sympathy in his bosom; he knew that there was nothing inharmonious between religious and social duties, and that to love our fellow-creatures is a proof of love towards God. His devotion was filial, but of that transcendent nature which far surpasses all the affections of this world. His boundless love of God rested on his vivid conception of his nature, as all-powerful, all-merciful, and all-good, the enthroned sovereign of the universe, the Father and Benefactor of each and all of the human race.

In a recent letter to the "Star in the West," Rev. George H. Emerson says: —

"The theological mission of Hosea Ballou was this: "— *to assert the benevolent and perfect sovereignty* "*of Almighty God.* I once said to him, 'Suppose the "idea of God's sovereignty were taken out of you, how "much would there be left of you?' His answer was "significant, and comprised three words,—'*O my soul!*' "Of course, these three words, of themselves simply, "convey no answer; but the tone with which they were "uttered said, very distinctly, that, the idea of God's "sovereignty taken away, there would be no Hosea Bal-"lou. But this great man did not simply believe that "God is a sovereign, but, further, that God is a *benevo-*"*lent* sovereign; he not only believed that God ruled in "the armies of heaven and among the inhabitants of the "earth, but that he ruled them with the especial object "of bestowing happiness; he not only believed that God "worked all things after the counsels of his own will, but "that it was God's will that all should be saved and come "to a knowledge of the truth. Every one who has heard "or read him will recollect how frequently he would "illustrate his views of the divine government by the "beautiful story of Joseph and his ten brethren :—'But "as for you, *ye* thought evil against me; but *God* "meant it unto good, to bring to pass as it is this day, to "save much people alive.' This verse contained volumes "of meaning with Father Ballou."

Such was the sum and substance of his doctrine, his life-long mission, the creed he held forth to the people for more than sixty years.

Some of his religious opponents have frequently charged him with card-playing, an amusement which we conceive to be of no evil import in itself, but the charge was designed as a matter of reproach against him. Now, we happen to know, and can say for a certainty, that Mr. Ballou did not know one card from another, nor could he have named a dozen cards rightly, had his very life depended upon his doing so.

This may be thought, perhaps, a trifling matter to notice; but the truth is, his religious opponents, finding no evil in him that they might expose, invented this charge to prejudice the public mind, and one minister in New England more than once publicly declared it from his pulpit; though, when called upon by one who heard him, and who knew the subject of this biography, he was puzzled to produce the name of his informant. It is within our own recollection that these stories were rife, and that they were very generally talked of. It was also sneeringly said that he preached to the lowest classes of society, and that respectable or intelligent persons never attended his meetings; that some of the most wicked and sinful of the community were found listening to him, and that they were always welcome!

These declarations were often made as evidences, weighing not alone against him, but also against the truth and godly character of his doctrine; they were preferred by clergymen from their pulpits, and often in opposition religious papers; but, of course, this was more frequently the case during his early settlement in Boston than in subsequent years. The first part of the latter charge brought against him needs no refutation; an intelligent public can judge of its truth; but we cannot refrain from calling the attention of the reader to the spirit that prompted the last clause. How very like it is to that evinced by the Pharisees of old, who said reproachfully of their Divine Master, "This man receiveth sinners and eateth with them." And now mark the reply of Jesus to these grumblers:—"The whole," says he, "need not the physician, but they that are sick." "The most wicked and sinful of the community," said Mr. Ballou's revilers, "are found listening to him, and they are always welcome!"

The truth is, that Mr. Ballou made no distinction or selection among auditors; he as readily preached to the poor and humble, as to those "clad in purple and fine linen," who "fared sumptuously every day." He never withheld his services; it might be, perhaps, that he preached with more fervor to those who stood in the clearest need of consolation and good tidings, than to those who enjoyed every opportunity of mental and intellectual culture. But it is certain, that a preacher with the universality of Mr. Ballou's vocation neither can nor ought to draw distinctions; he is summoned to speak whenever and wherever his services are needed, and the preacher of the gospel who should refuse because the call came from the sinful would be as much to blame as he would be to disregard the call of the righteous.. The true soldier of Christ and the gospel recognizes no distinction of rank; his consolations are as warmly given to the nameless sufferer, as when beside the couch of the millionaire.

Still less is the minister of the true religion to refuse to afford words of encouragement and advice to the unfortunate being who is struggling in the toils of sin. To such an one his mission is absolutely imperative; he must wrestle with the perturbed and darkened spirit, he must aid the awakening conscience, struggling to throw off the burthen of evil passions, he must point to the undying love of God to man, and bid the tears of the sinner be dried up in the effulgent smile of Omnipotence. If, therefore, sinners crowded to hear the discourses of Mr. Ballou, it was a tribute of which a preacher of the gospel might well be proud. "To comfort and help the weak-hearted, and to raise up those who fall," is essentially the province of the conscientious preacher; and no one, however hardened his heart, could have listened to the sincere and earnest words of the subject of these pages, without deriving some hope, some consolation, and some strength, from the glorious doctrine he preached so eloquently; and that there were very many who were thus ransomed from the thraldom of sin and consequent misery, there can be no reasonable doubt.

Was it true that "sinners flocked to hear him," as has been said so often by his opponents in the way of reproach against his doctrine, as being conducive to the pleasure of such persons? Let us pause for one moment, and review what he used to say that was particularly pleasing to this class of hearers. The following, for instance, will suffice us,— it is from his own pen:—"The vile affections of "sin will burn to the destruction of the sweetest harmo-"nies of nature; the whitest robes of innocence are "stained with its indelible crimson; the soul is drowned "in the black waters of iniquity, and the whole mind, "with every faculty, is plunged into the hell of moral "death. Yet, listen to the worst of torments, in conse-"quence of sin. 'A wounded conscience who can "bear?' A fire that burns all the day long, a sword "that continually pierceth the soul, a sting that cannot "exhaust its poison, a fever that never turns till the "patient dies. 'A dart struck through his liver.' "What ails the sinner?—why his hand on his breast? "There gnaws the worm that never dies,—there burns "the fire that is never quenched. A consciousness of "guilt destroys all the expected comforts and pleasures "of sin. How strange it is that, after a thousand disap-"pointments in succession, men are not discouraged! O "sin! how you paint your face! how you flatter us, poor "mortals, on to death! You never appear to the sinner in "your true character; you make us fair promises, but "you never fulfilled one; your tongue is smoother than "oil, but the poison of asps is under your lips; you have "impregnated all our passions with the venom of your "poison; you have spread gloomy darkness over the "whole region of the soul; you have endeavored, with "your stupefactive poison, to blunt the sword in the "hands of the cherubim, which, for your sake, keeps "us from the tree of life. A mistaken idea has been "entertained of sin, even by professors. I have often "heard sincere ministers preach, in their reproofs to their "hearers, that it was the greatest folly in the world for "people to forego salvation, in a future state, for the "comforts and pleasures of sin in this. Such exhort-"ations really defeat their intentions. The wish of the "honest preacher is, that the wicked should repent of "their sins, and do better; but, at the same time, he "indicates that sin, at present, is more productive of hap-"piness than righteousness; but that the bad will come "in another world,—that, although doing well is a hard "way, yet its advantages will be great in another state. "Just as much as any person thinks sin to be more hap-"pifying than righteousness, he is sinful; his heart "esteems it; though in some possible cases, for fear of the "loss of salvation in the world to come, he may abstain "from some outward enormities, yet his heart is full of "the desire of doing them. It is as much the nature of "sin to torment the mind, as it is the nature of fire to "burn our flesh. Sin deprives us of every rational en-

"joyment, so far as it captivates the mind. It was never "able to furnish one drop of cordial for the soul; her "tender mercies are cruelty, and her breasts of consola-"tion are gall and wormwood."

Mr. Ballou's style of preaching was of a kind calculated to create regret in the hearer's heart at his own shortcoming, and to plant a contrite spirit there, rather than fear for the punishment of his sins. The object of his sermon was not to terrify the sinner, but rather to lead him into the ways of peace and pleasantness. His sermons were of the character referred to by Louis XIV., when he told that eminent preacher, Massillon, "Father, "I have heard many great pulpit orators, and I have "been much pleased with them, but every time I hear "you I am exceedingly displeased with myself;" alluding to the sorrow for sin which Massillon's sermons created in him. This is the true and effectual style of preaching, such as will convert sinners from the error of their ways, by inducing a correct feeling in their own bosoms, not by frightening them out of their senses. Representing before men's eyes such oceans of wrath that they feel as though they were sinking to perdition, will undoubtedly lead them sometimes to *profess* religion, as a drowning man would catch at a straw; but their profession is made by instinct, not conviction,— by an undefined consciousness of necessity, not by any incentive of love.

It might be said of Mr. Ballou's sermons as Thomas Fuller said of Perkins in his eulogy: "His sermons were "not so plain but that the piously learned did admire "them, nor so learned but that the plain did understand "them. Unshelling theological controversies of their "school terms, he made of them plain and wholesome "meat for the people." "Children can understand him," was the constant remark of the ministering brethren, in relation to Mr. Ballou's sermons; and he has said often, "If I can make children understand me, "then I am satisfied; for surely it must then be that "older minds will comprehend my words." In this connection we are forcibly reminded of the true incident of the minister and the child. Forcible, simple as it is!

"Mother," said a little girl, seven years old, "I could "not understand our minister to-day, he said so many "hard words. I wish he would preach so that little girls "could understand him; won't he, mother?"

"Yes, I think so, if we ask him."

It was not long after that the little girl's father saw her going over to the minister's, and calling her back to him, he asked: —

"Where are you going, Emma?"

"I am going over to Mr. ——'s, father," was her innocent reply, "to ask him to preach small!"

A hint this that many might improve by.

To the place of his birth Mr. Ballou was fondly attached, and often visited it during the latter years of his life, in company with his children. He seemed thrice happy among those well-remembered hills and dales, where "the dreams of youth came back again." Aside from the fact of its being the home of his childhood, which in itself will strew with roses the bleakest spot in Christendom, the valley of his nativity had many picturesque and glowing natural beauties, of a character to impress the lover of nature with admiration. Here he had set his snares at the skirts of yonder wood, and here made his morning ablutions in the clear running brook. Adown the crevices of this huge old rock, when a little boy, surfeited with the abundance of wild strawberries, he had pressed out their juice, and adown the green crevices in the mossy stone the red liquid had made its way. These old stumps, now decayed, and like himself passing away, once bore the orchard fruit that he had watched with anxious eye to its ripening. And this mass of rocks, this ruined cellar, is the only remnant left of the cot where he was born. Not a stone nor a tree was forgotten,—not one but brought back its peculiar legend to his quickened heart. And here was the old burial-ground, on the hill-side, where the dust of his father and kindred reposed. With what awe had he ever looked upon that place when a boy! How many times strolled thoughtfully among the rank grass and moss-grown slabs, whose gray old forms, now bending hither and thither with age, gave faint and feeble token of names long, long since passed away,—

"With uncouth rhymes and shapeless sculpture decked."

While on a visit to this spot, accompanied by his second son, Rev. Massena B. Ballou, in 1843, he lingered long and thoughtfully among the tomb-stones, and at last said: —"I believe I could sleep sweeter here, among the "hills of Cheshire, by the side of my early home and "kindred, than in the grounds of Mount Auburn." And this was in truth characteristic of him and of his feelings, as the reader will have gathered ere this. A retiring spirit governed him at all times, unmoved by one single prompting of ambition or a desire for fame, and only zealous in the service of his Lord and Master. His works he desired to leave behind him as perfect as might be, because he hoped that, even after he had himself ceased to live, they might be productive of good to his fellow-men; but it was the only memento he wished to leave behind. "I can hardly conceive of language," he says, "to express the flood of tender emotions that over-"flow my heart, when I look upon that valley and those "well-remembered hills. I seem as if touched by some "potent wand, and to be changed from age to youth "again. It becomes impossible to realize the crowd of "incidents and experiences that have thronged my path-"way for more than half a century. I am once more in "that frugal, happy home, where contentment ever "smiled upon us, and the kind words of my brothers "and the affection of my sisters, more than compensated "for what by some would have been considered not an "enviable lot. Though that cottage is now levelled by "Time's ruthless hands, yet how prominent it stands "before my mind's eye! That aged and beloved parent "now rests on yonder hill-side. Those brothers and sis-"ters,— how various the fortune of each! All, *all* have "now passed that portal to which my own footsteps are "steadily wending." He was often inspired to pour out his feelings in song, after visiting Richmond and the haunts of his youth, for his heart was full of the memories of those days that had endeared the spot to him. The following lines upon this subject were composed for his children to sing with instrumental accompaniment, and are written in the metre of one of his favorite songs, the air of "Dumbarton's Bonny Belle."

BALLOU'S DELL.

"There are no hills in Hampshire New,
No valleys half so fair,
As those which spread before the view
In merry Richmond, where
I first my mortal race began,
And passed my youthful days,
Where first I saw the golden sun,
And felt his warming rays.

There is no spot in Richmond where
Fond memory loves to dwell,
As on the glebe outspreading there
In Ballou's blithesome dell.
There are no birds that sing so sweet
As those upon the spray,
Where, from the brow of 'Grassy Hill,'
Comes forth the morning ray.

Unnumbered flowers, the pride of spring,
Are born to flourish there,
And round them mellow odors fling
Through all the ambient air.

There purling springs have charms for me
  That vulgar brooks ne'er give,
And winds breathe sweeter down the lea
  Than where magnolias live!"

This is but one of a large number of pieces composed by Mr. Ballou while inspired by the same theme. It will serve to show the reader the hallowed and inspiring feelings that lived in the writer's heart, as his memory went back in freshness to the days and associations of his boyhood, as in retrospection he shook away the snow of time from the evergreen of memory.

The attachment to one's birth-place, to the home of early youth, "be it ever so humble," is a beautiful trait of character, and is significant of a refined and noble spirit. It is in masses one of the first and most prolific fruits of civilization, distinguishing a stable community from a nomadic tribe; and, as another peculiarity of the trait, it is most touchingly exhibited in the least fortunate members of the human family. The Icelanders, dwelling in a hyperborean region, where for a large portion of the year they are deprived of the light of the sun, and depend upon the stars and the Aurora Borealis to guide their footsteps in the long, long winter midnight, are accustomed to say, with a spirit of unmistakable fondness and affection, Iceland is the fairest country of the globe! The poor Highlander regards the smoky hut where he was born with enthusiastic love. As life draws gradually towards its close, this feeling deepens in the human breast. Standing on the extreme verge of existence, and just about to leave the world forever, man, as he turns to survey the pathway he has travelled, overlooks its midway stations, and fixes his eyes upon the starting. The beginning and the end of the journey are then brought close together; from the earthly to the eternal home there is but one step; from the tenderest recollections of his earthly parent he passes into the presence of his Father in heaven. Love of home! what a theme for the essayist!

It would almost seem as if the deprivations and hardships of his youthful days must have thrown an unhappy spell about his early home, and as though the memories that came up to him from the long vista of years would be laden with recollections of want and severe trial, of personal endurance, of scanty food and more scanty clothing; in short, of all the stern realities of his childhood's home. But this was very far from being the case with him. He has often said to us, in relation to this subject, that he deemed his life at that time anything but unhappy, — that what now appeared to be so great hardships, by comparison, were then but trifling discomforts, and matters of course. He was never inclined to set up for a martyr, or to gather any credit for having endured patiently, and risen in time above the fortunes of his youth. He could only recall this period of his life with feelings of pleasure. Such feelings as these force upon us the conviction that there is ever about the place of one's birth a spell that hardship seems only the more closely to bind about the heart,— that deprivation and want but the more strongly cement. The cheerful allusion to the affectionate regard of his brothers and sisters, and the remark that contentment ever smiled upon his early home, show the true spirit of the man, and the natural trait which ever influenced him to make the best of everything.

"How I used to cherish a kind word from my father, "when I was a boy!" says Mr. Ballou. "He was in "some respects an austere man; and when I was born, "being the youngest of our large family, he had got to "be advanced in years, and looked with a more serious "and practical eye on the events of life and all things "about us. He was Puritanic, strictly religious, as he "interpreted the meaning of that word, and his mind was "ever engrossed upon serious matters. But when he put "his hand sometimes upon my head, and told me I had "done well, that the labor I had performed might have "been more poorly done by older hands, or that I was a "good and faithful boy, my heart was electrified beyond "measure; and I remember his words and smile, even "now, with delight."

How the simplicity and purity of the man shine forth in this little paragraph!

"It may be interesting to your readers to know how "Father Ballou was regarded in the town of his nativ- "ity," says the Rev. Joshua Britton, Jr., of Richmond, N. H., in a communication addressed to the Christian Freeman. "He was accustomed to visit this place once "in every few years, and always received a cordial and "hearty greeting. It was my privilege and happiness to "spend a few days with him on the occasion of his visit "here in October last. I removed to this town in October, 1850, and soon learned that there was a general "desire among our friends to see and hear their fellow-"townsman again. The approach of cold weather prevented our taking any immediate steps to accomplish "this object. In June, 1851, I saw him at the meeting "of the State Convention in Chicopee. He had many "affectionate inquiries to make respecting his friends in "Richmond, but then he could not name any time when "he would visit us. In July I wrote him, and he replied "August 5, and said:—'I want very much to visit Richmond, and will on one of the days you have named.' "He suggested that we could complete the arrangement at "the convention meeting in Boston. We did so, and fixed "upon Sunday, October 12th, as the day when he would "be with us. He was careful to have no appointment for "the following Sunday, in order that he might remain "in this vicinity. He was met at Fitzwilliam depot, by "one of our friends, on Friday, October 10th, and conveyed to his residence. Sunday was a favorable day for "meeting, and there was a large audience from this and "the adjacent towns in this state and in Massachusetts. "It was a happy day for us all; but I must not dwell here.

"Though I enjoyed the meeting very much, yet my "enjoyment was still greater on the following week, in "the society of our aged friend and father, at my own "home and the homes of our mutual friends in this town.

"It may be proper to state that Father Ballou had no

" very near relatives here. None, I believe, by the name " of Ballou. He was a cousin of Father Luke Harris, " and with him and his family he spent a portion of the " time quite pleasantly. He seemed happy in being once " more in his 'native Richmond.'

" Three days the writer accompanied Father Ballou " while he made calls upon various families in different " parts of the town. We were uniformly kindly received; " and those not acquainted with Father Ballou can hardly " conceive the ease and success with which he familiarly " approached all,— the young, the middle-aged, and the " aged. We had brief interviews, but they were agreeable " and profitable. Prayer was offered with and consolation " afforded to the sick. In one or two instances we met with " those whose minds were in doubt on doctrinal points: " these, of course, listened to a few words of explanation. " Then there was the going back to former days, and a " rehearsal of time's numerous changes. We visited the " old burying-ground, and stood by the graves of the " parents of my aged companion. We visited the old " homestead, the place where he was born, and spent his " boyhood. This was changed, and unchanged. The " buildings, fences, and some of the fields, presented a " new aspect, but the valleys and hills remained as before. " At the homestead we entered the orchard, where the " owner was engaged picking apples. We walked about " and found apples, of which my companion ate, though " he declined taking any, a short time previous, on an " adjoining farm. We also, by invitation, dined here, and "had a pleasant chat with the family. This farm is a "mile and a half east of our meeting-house. Grassy "Hill is on its eastern border, and overlooks the valley "in which it is situated. Some will recollect the poetry "of our friend, 'My native Richmond.' He repeated "this, at my suggestion, at a dwelling in full view of this "eminence; and as the words 'Grassy Hill' were spoken, "he gracefully waved his right hand in that direction, "his countenance expressing satisfaction and delight.

"Several times, during his stay, the inquiry was "agitated,—'Will you come to Richmond again?' His "reply was, ''T is uncertain,—I may; should life be "spared, and my health remain as good as it is at pres- "ent, I think I may.' But, as we had some reason to "expect, this proved to be his last visit. He was con- "veyed to Winchester on Friday, where he preached on "the following Sabbath. He returned on Tuesday, Oct. "21st. I made a few calls with him on the afternoon of "that day, and in the evening he spent an hour at our "singing-school, tarrying with us at night. On the fol- "lowing morning we bade him 'good-by,' and he pro- "ceeded homewards to visit a daughter, rejoined his wife, "and in due time reached their home in Boston."

In Mr. Ballou's letter to the Trumpet, describing this visit, he says: —

"When I arrived at the depot in Fitzwilliam, I was "met by a worthy and respected friend, from Richmond, "who came on purpose to convey me to his hospitable "dwelling in the neighborhood of the place of my birth.

"Our road passed through the farm on which I was born, "and on which my childhood and youth were spent. All "around lay the hills and the mountains, the valleys and "streams, which I always carry with me on the map of "fond memory. But where were the father, the mother, "the brothers and sisters, who watched over my infancy "and guided my youth? The hope of the gospel an-"swers, in HEAVEN! Before the Sabbath, I was con-"veyed by our worthy Brother Britton, the beloved pas-"tor of the Universalist society, to the dwellings of a "number of my kindred and friends, who received me "with a welcome corresponding with the esteem in which "they were held by me. But some bitter drops were "mingled with the sweet cordials of friendship and love. "Some deaths had recently removed the beloved and "respected, causing those sanctifying sorrows to which "love and friendship are heirs. When the Sabbath "came, I was conducted by Bro. Britton to the house "of devotion, and into the pulpit where he is wont to "break the bread of life to the flock of his charge. I "was agreeably surprised at beholding the crowded con-"gregation, which filled the house to its utmost capacity "with people, who came not only from all parts of Rich-"mond, but from all the adjoining towns. * * * * "When I beheld this large assembly, all of which seemed "to be moved with one spirit, every countenance present-"ing the same expression of desire and expectation, I "felt oppressed with a sense of my weakness, and lifted "my desires to Him who is able to strengthen the weak,

"and from what seems a scanty portion to feed the mul-
"titude.

"I could not avoid a comparison between what I then "saw with the condition of the cause of divine truth "sixty years ago, when I first attempted to speak in its "defence in a private dwelling in this Richmond. Then, "but a few could be collected to hear the impartial and "efficient grace of the Redeemer proclaimed and de- "fended.

"The Universalist meeting-house in Richmond is quite "respectable for size, conveniently constructed, and neat "in appearance. The society who worship here is not "very numerous, yet I believe more so than that of any "other denomination in town. As far as my acquaint- "ance enabled me to judge, I had reason to believe that "better disposed disciples of the Divine Master are sel- "dom found. Bro. Britton preaches here one-half of his "time. He is a sober, candid, well-educated and faith- "ful pastor, and highly esteemed by his society here, and "also in Winchester, where he labors successfully the "other half of his time. His family consists of an amia- "ble companion, who knows the importance of her station, "and is faithful in the discharge of its duties, and an "adopted daughter, who is justly held in high esteem both "by those whom she regards as her parents, and by all "her acquaintances.

"The Sabbath following my appointment in Richmond, "which appointment was on the second Sabbath in Octo- "ber, I preached in Winchester. The day was extremely "rainy and cold, and few comparatively attended meet-"ing. The society here has a very good and convenient "house, and its condition at present is said to be prom-"ising. The friends of truth here are firm and steadfast, "full of hope and confidence, promising perseverance unto "the end.

"After my labors on this rainy Sabbath, I found my-"self much exhausted, and was sensibly unwell. My "friends were kind and attentive to me, and the worn-out "servant was well provided for. On Wednesday a "respectable merchant of Richmond brought me in his "carriage to the depot in Fitzwilliam. By aid of Di-"vine Providence I arrived the same day at Lancaster, "where I found my wife and our family connections in "good health, and my own somewhat improved. Thanks "be to God for all his mercies!

"HOSEA BALLOU."

With other numerous calls upon his time and attention, and in addition to his never-ceasing professional and parochial labors, Mr. Ballou has had at various times over *twenty* ministerial students, who, for the time being, generally became residents of his family, and who studied the profession with him. To these young men he devoted his powers with the same untiring zeal that characterized his other professional labors. His mode of instruction with these students was peculiar; he went with them always, to use one of his favorite phrases, "to the root of the matter," and was never content until he had imbued their minds with at least a portion of the realizing sense he himself experienced relative to all the main points of the faith he advocated. His words of advice to them were few, but they were just what each one needed, and no more. He was never fulsome with them, but complimented when it was deserved, checked when it was necessary, and suggested when improvements might be made, but ever inculcating those Christian qualities which shone forth as a burning light in his own loveliness of character. Nearly all of those students are now teachers of the gospel of Christ, men honored for their Christian spirit, and as true disciples of the gospel. Most of these are settled in the New England States; and, as we write, we easily recall the names of numbers who are much respected and beloved by the denomination to which they belong.

In the instruction and guidance of so large a number of candidates for the sacred calling of the ministry, he assumed a very weighty addition to his constant labors. We have seen that his parochial, ministerial, scholastic and editorial duties, were exceedingly onerous, and many would have shrunk from the idea of adding to such an accumulation of labors. But it was a principle of Mr. Ballou's life never to neglect a single opportunity of serving the great and sacred cause in which he had embarked; he felt the full force of his mission, and to it he was constantly ready to devote every energy of his physical and mental nature, every moment of his time, looking to the source of all power for the strength and inspiration necessary to sustain him in his task. Among those who felt a vocation to preach the word of God, there was an earnest desire to pursue its study under the guidance of one who was the father and oracle of the creed they had espoused. They felt that, transmitted through other mediums, many of the rays of light that beamed from his original mind must necessarily be lost; they sought to derive directly from him the clear instructions, the vigorous reasoning, the straight-forward mode of investigation, which distinguished him. They wished to be near him, to follow his example in everything pertaining to a Christian's duty. As to himself, he was never so happy as when imparting instruction to those who really desired and sought it. His inquiring and intelligent spirit constantly sympathized with minds of kindred stamp, nor did he ever lose his warm sympathies for youth. With the motto *progress* inscribed upon his banner, he was at heart and in soul as much with the young as the hoary-headed. The child-like simplicity of his nature brought ardent youth very near to his vigorous and green old age, harmonizing the two extremes in a wonderful manner.

In biographical writing there is often an obvious and studied obscurity in regard to some certain portion of the subject's life. The reason for such a course, on the part of the author, is very plain; for there are few public men, who are deemed worthy the notice of a biographical record, who do not look back with regret, and often with deep mortification, to some heedless act of early life; — some deed wherein the laws of right and wrong have been disregarded, and honorable and upright principles trampled under foot; some thoughtless moment, when the tempter has found them with their armor off, and has led them into contact with evil that has pierced their defenceless bodies, and left there scars deep and rankling, as monuments of the frailty of their nature. In reference to this subject as it relates to Mr. Ballou, there is not one hour of his life which will not bear the scrutiny of strict justice. From his very boyhood he was remarkable for firmness of principle, and unwavering integrity of purpose. Had he a personal enemy in the world, that person could not point to a single act of his life that it would not give us pleasure to chronicle here!

We know that this is saying much, and that the reader will be apt to look back and re-read the last passage; but, while we write this strong language, we wish to be understood as doing so in all calmness and judgment; each word, as written, is duly set down and abided by. Now, we humbly ask, how many are there, among those to whom the world accords the meed of greatness, that can have this language applied to them and their characters in truth? I do not mean to signify that there are no such men; but to say — and the experience and personal knowledge of all will bear testimony to the fact — that such cases are very rarely found in this every-day world.

When we go back and consider Mr. Ballou's early life, the very limited means he enjoyed of mental cultivation, and all the vicissitudes through which he has passed, and contrast this view of his life with the station which he ultimately filled, and consider the works of his pen and mind, we are led to remember that it has ever been the fate of genius to climb the rugged steeps of fame and honor under the greatest disadvantages; that the brightest gems the exploring mind has brought from the caves of knowledge have been wrought, before they were given to the world, with the poorest means, and the least available tools. It is the circumstance of those very disadvantages that has elicited more mental diamonds than all the schools and richly-endowed institutions in the world.

Though the difficulties and impediments that thus environ the path of genius seem like a heavy stone about the neck, yet they are very often like the stones used by the hardy pearl-divers, which enable them to reach their prize, and to rise enriched. Adversity is to genius what the steel is to the flint,—the fire concealed in the one is brought out only by contact with the other. "Hard is the "task," says Coleridge, "to climb into the niches of Fame's "proud temple; rough and cold is the road; but rougher "and stronger than the rocks that strew it are the men "who toil over it. Up they climb from the cottages and "lowly homes of the world; over Alps and Alps do they "stride, heaving the millstone of persecution from their "towering heads, and bursting into the sunshine of glory, "despite of all that circumstances could do to keep them "down."

The experience of all mankind shows that nothing great can be accomplished without labor. The original difference between men who have achieved greatness, and those who have died in obscurity, is, perhaps, after all, very inconsiderable; but the same ideas which in the latter died in their birth for want of culture, in the former, fostered, sustained and developed, by assiduous labor, flourished, and produced both flower and fruit. Uncultivated genius is a melancholy spectacle; it is like the light of a shooting star, brilliant, flashing, but evanescent, dazzling the eye for a moment, and then sinking into outer darkness; while cultivated genius, blazing with a steady, constant and pure flame, dispenses a surer and vivifying warmth far around it, — its light is not that of the meteor, but the planet. All history and all experience go to show that the bane of genius is not adversity, but prosperity. It was not Alpine toils, but "Capuan delights," that decimated the ranks of Hannibal's army, and wasted them away; it is not the cold north wind, but the genial sunshine, that destroys the mighty avalanche. The soul of genius, like the iron of the mine, must undergo the ordeal of fire, ere it can become steel. We might quote many examples of history to prove that this is a universal law of our nature. It is true that some have achieved greatness when their worldly circumstances were easy and affluent; but in such cases the gift of genius has been accompanied by a mental organization which imposed internal struggles, and hence the rule may be said to be without exceptions.

Books, thoughts, deeds, imperishable memorials of their author, so laboriously accomplished, do not die with the body. No; a thought once expressed never dies; — it must exert its influence, and be the pioneer to many more. Like the gentle ripple upon a calm, placid lake, it starts upon the world a speck, but ceases not to expand its force until it reaches over all extent. Man does not die with the body; as the soul shall live forever, so does the influence he has exerted upon society live after him, and by that influence is he judged. Is not this thought in itself a strong incentive to virtue and well-doing? What man or woman is there, however humble be their sphere of action, but desires most earnestly to leave behind a good and honored name?

An ancient maxim avers that "spoken words fly away, but written ones are permanent." But modern science teaches us that no sound uttered by the lips of man is lost, — that the vibration of the air bears it onward and onward, through all time. How very few there are in this world whose words, written and spoken, are so considered that they are willing to have them consigned to immortality! How few whose utterance of a year old will bear the test of their own judgment! There are moments of existence, generally the closing ones, when all our words and deeds crowd back upon the memory with overwhelming force. There are records of men in seasons of extreme casualties, who have testified to the painful accuracy of memory under such imminent circumstances; and there are few, indeed, who so shape their lives as to be enabled to bear with equanimity a retrospective glance on the panorama of their existence. So to have lived that, in ceasing to live, they have no reason to blush for their existence, as it regards the daily duty of the Christian. — Alas! in seasons of trial and temptation this duty is often, very often, forgotten; the wayside of life is strewn thick with temptations and allurements to win us from the straight and narrow path. Fruits of golden promise tempt the hand to pluck them, and it is only after tasting that we discover them to be only dust and ashes, like those which grow on the fated shores of the Dead Sea. Happy, then, and worthy of all reverence, is he whose unwavering course through life has ever been onward and upward. The summit gained, whence both the promised land and that of his earthly pilgrimage are in view, he can turn back and say, as his vision embraces the line which his feet have trod so toilsomely, yet ever so cheerfully: — "I have held that path without variation; no temptation has seduced my footsteps to the right or to the left, nor have my lips uttered aught upon that journey which a wish, in this trying moment, would recall!"

There have been, at various times, and in different works, short biographical sketches of Mr. Ballou's life given, from various pens; — these, of course, contemplate only his public career, and are quite brief. In the third volume of the Universalist Miscellany, published in 1846, there appear the following remarks from the pen of the editor, which we subjoin. After giving a short account of his public career, the writer of the sketch referred to goes on to say: —

" We have not time, even if we had the ability, to give
" a just description of him as a man, a Christian, and a
" preacher. We will not, however, permit the occasion
" to pass without offering a word on each of these points.

" We presume no one was ever more highly beloved
" and truly respected by his acquaintances than Mr.
" Ballou. Pleasant in his disposition, and honest in his
" dealings, he has uniformly enjoyed their confidence and
" esteem. Though he always sustains a becoming dignity
" of character, and is never light or trifling, he has a
" pleasantry and shrewdness which render his company
" peculiarly agreeable.

" As a Christian, Mr. Ballou is firm in faith, and
" catholic in spirit. While he believes with undoubting
" confidence what he preaches, and has no respect for
" what he considers error in doctrine, he never manifests
" a want of kindness towards those of an opposite faith.
" We are aware that many entertain a different feeling;
" but they misjudge him. It is true that for the insincere
" and hypocritical he has no feeling; and, if he had, he
" would not be faithful to his ministry.

" As a preacher, Mr. Ballou, for clearness of concep-
" tion and power of argument, has few, if any, superiors.
" We have often heard him preach with an unction and
" power that we have never heard surpassed. But we do
" not design, in this article, to speak at length of his
" qualities as a preacher.

" No man ever enjoyed the respect of our denomination
" more than does Mr. Ballou. He is cordially loved and

"esteemed by all who believe in the salvation of the "world."

These remarks are valued the more highly as coming from one who was intimate with the subject of this biography for a long period, and also as a fair and unprejudiced tribute to his character and life by a brother-laborer in the vineyard of Christ. The number of the Miscellany which contains the remarks we have quoted is embellished by a mezzotint likeness of Mr. Ballou, from a painting by E. H. Conant, and engraved in the finest style of art by Sartain. This picture, however, is inferior, as to likeness, to many others which are preserved of him.

We conceive the following, from the pen of the venerable and beloved Father. Streeter, the oldest minister in the Universalist denomination now among us, to be of great interest; the work in hand would be quite incomplete without it. It is the impression of a faithful brother concerning the deceased, from the commencement to the close of his professional career.

"I first saw Father Ballou a short time before the "commencement of his public ministry. It was in the "town of Vernon, then called Hinsdale, in the State of "Vermont. At that time there was but one open and "decided Universalist in the place. This solitary cham- "pion of the common salvation had long been impressed "with a desire to have the gospel of the grace of God, in "the fulness of its universality, preached to those of his "neighbors who might feel disposed to give it a hearing.

"An arrangement was at length made with the Rev. "David Ballou, an elder brother, to deliver a lecture in "the place.

"The day was designated, and due notice of the meet- "ing given. At the appointed time the preacher came, "and Hosea came with him. He was then a tall, slim "young man, with an aspect, however, which indicated "profound thought, and a deep solemnity of feeling. In "his general appearance there was a marked peculiarity, "a certain something which arrested and fixed the atten- "tion, and which impressed the beholder with the con- "viction that no ordinary individual was before him,— "that the germs of eminence, the genuine elements of "intellectual greatness, were embodied within him.

"Such, at any rate, was the impression among the "more inquisitive and discriminating who attended that "meeting. At the close of the sermon, Hosea gave an "exhortation, and offered the concluding prayer; and "this effort was spoken of, especially by the less conserv- "ative and bigoted, as one of rare spirituality and power. "It became the topic of general remark, and of high "encomium.

"The next day, if I mistake not, he made his first "attempt as a preacher of the everlasting gospel, as a "public advocate of the sublime doctrine of the salvation "of all men 'by the blood of the cross.' It was, as I "have often heard him say, a partial failure. The exor- "dium went off very well; but, as he proceeded with the "discussion, he often hesitated, now and then came to a

" pause, and was finally obliged to sit down before he had " reached the original design of the discourse.

" He was deeply mortified. He was discouraged. He " resolved to abandon all thoughts of the ministry. He " felt himself utterly incompetent to the efficient dis- " charge of its high and momentous duties. His friends, " however, interfered in the premises. They succeeded " in changing his purpose. They persuaded him to per- " severe in the work of a Christian minister, and it was " not long before he made his second attempt at sermon- " izing. The effort succeeded. It was a complete tri- " umph. The manner in which he acquitted himself was " a matter of deep astonishment to his friends, and to all " who heard him. In that meeting his lofty and invalua- " ble career finds its legitimate date. It was followed by " no faltering, no irresolution, no shrinking from toil, " however laborious, or however wearing to the physical " frame or to the mental powers.

" He soon became immensely popular. His fame went " forth as on the wings of every wind. From all quar- " ters, far and near, the Macedonian cry, 'Come over and " help us,' poured in upon him. These calls, so far as it " was possibly practicable, were promptly and cheerfully " honored. His labors, of course, became exceedingly " abundant,—almost, indeed, without intermission. By " day and by night he was found at his post, and zeal- " ously doing his great work.

" He frequently held meetings in the town where he " was born and brought up, and in nearly all the towns "in that region. His circuits often embraced some hun-"dreds of miles, and in making them he preached almost "every day, and not unfrequently several times in a day; "and wherever it was generally known that he was to "hold forth, immense crowds rarely failed to be present, "that they might listen to his testimony. Though a "mere youngster, I myself once walked, or rather ran, "eight miles and back, to hear him. The news of the "meeting did not reach me till somewhat late on Sabbath "morning, and no mode of conveyance to the place could "be obtained. I was, of course, reduced to the necessity "of either losing that rare spiritual treat, or of making "my way to it on what Mr. Murray used to call 'apos-"tolical horses;' in other words, on foot. And so great "was my anxiety not to lose a word that might fall from "his lips, that I forgot to take with me a crumb of any-"thing for a lunch, and so I lost my dinner; or, rather, I "had to make it on the sermon and the prayers which I "had heard, and it was truly one of the most luscious "meals which it has ever been my good fortune to eat. "It was devoured with a high relish.

"The subject of these remarks was the youngest of "five brothers, three of whom were preachers; and I "once had the privilege of attending a meeting at which "four of them, with the venerable father, were present. "Hosea was the preacher. He seemed to have made "special preparation to meet the peculiarities of the "occasion. Contrary to his usual custom, the sermon "was written. At the proper time he commenced its "delivery. The old father—himself a Baptist clergyman "of considerable note—and the elder brothers, were seated "around him.

"He was not familiar with the use of a manuscript, "and, of course, to read from one he found to be a new "and somewhat awkward business. For a little time, "however, he persevered in the effort. The experiment "was far from being satisfactory either to himself or to "the congregation. In spite of him, the eye would quit "its hold upon the contents of the paper, and wander "about among the dense masses who filled the seats "below. These excursions caused him to lose his place. "He often found it again with no little difficulty, and "sometimes not without a most vexatious delay.

"At length his patience gave out. Its power of en- "durance was completely exhausted, and, taking up the "manuscript and rolling it between his hands, he deliber- "ately put it in his pocket. 'Brethren,' said he, 'I shall "weary your patience with these notes.' This was the "end of all hesitancy. He proceeded in the discussion "of his subject with his accustomed fluency, and every- "thing flowed onward with the smoothness of oil. It was "a season of deep and thrilling interest.

"The venerable father, though not a Universalist, and "with no disposition to become one, listened to the argu- "ments and illustrations of this youngest of his sons with "the profoundest attention. I carefully watched the "muscles of his face, and plainly saw that mighty emo- "tions were stirring within him. Every now and then a "large tear would start out from the eye, and course "down the furrows in his time-worn and manly cheek. "It is not strange that such should have been the case, "for the discourse was one of peculiar tenderness, and of "uncommon pathos and power. Probably it was rarely, "if ever surpassed, even by the speaker himself, in the "palmiest days of his ministry.

"Indeed, Father Ballou's pulpit powers were of an "exceedingly high order. Taken as a whole, my im-"pression is that I have never known his equal. Never "have I seen a man who could hold his hearers so per-"fectly under his own control. They were entirely at "his command. He clothed them in smiles, or melted "them to tears, and these things he seemed to do at "pleasure. This power embodies the chief component in "true eloquence. We often refer, and with profound "admiration, to the pulpit talents of Griffin and Beecher, "of Channing, and Dewey, and Chapin. And to these "men the meed of rare eloquence unquestionably belongs; "but still, taken all in all, they fall far below the stan-"dard of Father Ballou. Theirs is an eloquence of an-"other and a humbler type. They deal chiefly with the "intellect,—with the demands of a literary and refined "taste; he dealt more especially with the latent chords "of the heart,—moved and controlled the deeper sym-"pathies and more refined affections of the human soul. "Relying but little upon books, he went principally upon "the profundity and strength of his own resources. The "structure of his mind approached very near to an actual "intuition. He grasped the whole of a subject at a "glance. His powers of analysis were prodigious, and "singularly accurate. He stopped not to inquire what "others had thought or done. He examined every sub- "ject for himself. Like the diver for pearls, he plunged "to the depths of divine truth; and, when he had found "a precious gem, he rose with it to the surface, held it "up before the eyes of the people, and said to them, This "belongs to you, and there are more of the same sort "where I found it,—enough for you all, and for the mil- "lions of the race to which you belong.

"But it was not in the office of a Christian minister, "merely, that Father Ballou excelled. He was admira- "ble in every sphere of life. As a husband and a father, "the head of a numerous family, he was truly a model "man. He knew how to rule his own household. His "word was law, and obedience to it was prompt and "cheerful by all around him. There were no family jars "in that well-ordered and happy home. The idea, per- "haps, is an extravagant one, but I have often thought "that his house was the nearest fac-simile of the great "mansion of the Infinite Father on High of which I "could form a conception.

"And then as a brother and a friend he had no supe- "rior. With the exception, perhaps, of some members "of his own family, there is no one living who enjoyed so "long and so intimate an acquaintance with him as my- "self; and it is one of the happiest reflections of my life, "that, in all our intercourse, not a single unkind word or "emotion ever passed between us.

"Indeed, I never knew his kindly regards mastered "but once, and that was after the endurance of many "gross and most cruel provocations. But on one occa- "sion his philosophy and his religion failed him, and then "his brow was mantled with the very majesty of wrath, "the frowning aspect of a deep and withering indignation. "The roll of a moment or two, however, and it was all "over. The old saint was himself again, and never, from "that time to the day of his death, did I ever hear him "utter an unfriendly word in relation to the individual "by whom he had been so grossly and wickedly abused. "But I must not enlarge. I have no wish to deal in "flattery; but, in justice to my own feelings, and to the "memory of our departed father, I must say that he was "one of the very best men with whom it has been my "happiness to associate. Indeed, I doubt whether he had "a solitary failing,—so far, I mean, as the convictions "and purposes of his own mind were concerned.

"S. S."

CHAPTER XIV.

SENTIMENTS RELATIVE TO DEATH.

MR. BALLOU was ever governed by a calm resignation to the decrees of Providence, and as it regarded the subject of his own death,— that thought which is said to make cowards of us all, that theme upon which we are too much inclined to dwell with feelings of dread and fear.

Notwithstanding we are taught by Christian philosophers that life should be a preparation for death, there are very few of us who regard this inevitable event in its proper light. Dr. Young uttered a most profound truth when he said:—

"Each man thinks all men mortal but himself."

A man recognizes the certainty of this event's taking place with regard to his neighbor, his friend, and the members of his own family. He feels that the hour of separation from his aged and beloved parents must come; that the brother or sister, whose infant joys and sorrows are his own, whose sympathy has cheered his manhood, must one day be taken from him; that the wife of his bosom must close her eyes in death; that the stern messenger may at any time smite the darlings of their little flock, gathered around his knee in play or prayer; and while they are yet in life he prepares for them the last resting-place in some sheltered spot, some woodland cemetery, where the brightest smile of nature may gild the place of their repose. But he cannot realize that he himself, in the pride of his manhood, the blood coursing cheerily through his veins, a sense of vitality giving an elasticity to every movement, will be called upon to lay down this glorious panoply of life, to feel the bounding blood curdle and become as ice within his veins, and the bright vision of the world fade into nothingness before his glazing eyes. He himself, by some miracle, must be snatched from the universal doom. Thus death finds almost every man unprepared. The very criminal, upon whose ears fall the deep tones of the funeral knell, hopes for a reprieve even at the foot of the scaffold. The soldier cannot think of death as he mounts the "imminent deadly breach;"—his comrades may fall, but he must escape. Thus, in our strange, delusive sophistry, even if we think of death, we seek to alienate the idea from ourselves.

As it regarded the death of any member of his extensive family circle, what a tower of strength and consolation he ever was to the mourning hearts of his children! How calm and serene he would appear when called, in the providence of God, to sympathize with them at the loss of their little ones, near and dear to their parental hearts! However deep the distress of soul which exercised the breast of any member of his family by the solemn visitation of death, his venerable presence would always restore peace to the almost broken heart, and make the sunshine radiate once more in the mourner's bosom. He had several trials, and keen ones, too, through which he passed, of this character. His third daughter, Mrs. Whittemore, wife of Rev. Benjamin Whittemore, was called upon to lay one and another of her tender offspring in the grave, until, at last, when the third was placed there, she exclaimed, in the agony of her heart, that she could not leave the tomb where half her loved ones lay in death. But for his presence even reason might have deserted her throne; but his calm and sainted expression, his holy balm of religion, his simple words of hope, were as oil upon troubled waters. So again was he similarly exercised, through visitations of death, in the family of his eldest son, Rev. Hosea F. Ballou, and Rev. Massena B. Ballou; in the family circle of his third daughter, Cassendana, wife of Joseph Wing; and again in the home of his fourth daughter, Elmina, wife of Rev. J. C. Waldo; and also in the circle of the sixth daughter, Fiducia, wife of Abijah W. Farrar.

But more particularly was this power of consolation evinced as exercised in his own family, when the eldest daughter, Fanny, widow of Leonard Holmes, was taken from life. It was the first death that we had known in our immediate circle of brothers and sisters, and the stroke had all the power and force of a first great sorrow. Then his spirit shone forth in all the Christian beauty and loveliness of its influence. Then the majesty and holy power of his religion was evinced in letters of light. And while referring to this family,—for there were six orphan children left behind,—we might appropriately refer to the munificent bounty of his hand towards them; of a home purchased and given to them; and of much fatherly kindness and generosity towards those orphan children. This spirit of resignation he infused largely into his children, who in turn offered to his own spirit that strength of hope and divine reliance which in periods of trial he had imparted to them. This might be said to be particularly the case with Clementina, his fifth daughter, wife of Isaac H. Wright, who, without the domestic care of a family, was enabled to be much and often at home,—especially if any physical illness affected either father or mother,—and who, with others of the children, was with him night and day, constantly, during his last illness, and the closing hours of his life.

We have before referred to the grateful influence his presence exerted in the sick room, and when called upon to lift up his voice with the dying; but so prominent a trait of character, as evinced in his home relations, should not be omitted here. It may be interesting to remark, in these domestic notes, that Mr. Ballou resided, for over thirty years, with his second daughter, Cassendana, and her family, in Boston. A more cheerful and happy home it would be difficult for fancy to paint. There was no contention there,—no jealousies, no jarring of interests; everything seemed to take its hue from him; and calm domestic joy and serene contentment reigned over all. He seemed to exhale the atmosphere of peace, and no contending elements could withstand the soothing character of his presence.

Mr. Ballou's idea of death, as being but the portal to blissful immortality, may be gathered by the following, from his own pen:

"The idea of immortality makes everything in life "valuable. Here we may lay up all our treasures, "where neither moth nor rust can corrupt, nor thieves "break through and steal. Here God's bright favor will "never grow dim, nor will our love and gratitude ever "decay. Do you see Hope's celestial form, leaning on "her anchor, and, while the raging waves of a restless sea "dash against her, she remains unmoved? Do you "observe her aspect firm, and her eyes turned towards "heaven? And would you wish to cast her down, and "wreck her on the quicksands of dismal doubt? Go, "brother, to the chamber of sickness, where life's waning "embers can no longer warm the dying heart; there hear "from cold and quivering lips this hope expressed: 'I "long to be with Christ,—I long to be at rest!' Would "you blast this amaranthine flower? Would you plant "in its stead the nightshade of despair? Listen no longer "to the wild suggestions of fancy and wandering imagin- "ations, under the specious pretence of searching after "truth. For Jesus is the way, the truth and the life.

'Give me the light of this bright sun to see;
All other lights like meteors are to me.'"

"I think one thing is certain," says Mr. Ballou, in one of his last published articles, "and that is, that the opinion "that we immediately enter on that state into which "the resurrection introduces mankind is far more desir- "able, to all people, than the opinion that ages of uncon- "scious sleep succeed our brief existence here in the "flesh. * * * In conclusion, I will say that I am sensi- "ble that there are passages of scripture which seem to "favor the opinion of a general, simultaneous resurrection, "which appear difficult to reconcile with such as I have "above noticed; but that they outweigh them I have no "sufficient reason to allow. The supposition that all "who have died have until now remained in an uncon- "scious state, seems more like annihilation than well "accords with our glorious hope."

Mr. Ballou's mind was ever made up to meet death at any moment; and, with implicit reliance on the goodness and fatherly care of Him in whose hand we all are, and who does not permit even a sparrow to fall to the ground without his knowledge, he left all to the wise decree of Heaven, and loaded not his soul with fear of the result. He conversed but little upon the subject; but when he did so, it was with a cheerful spirit and contented mind.

His profession was such as to make him familiar with death in all its forms. It was no strange subject to him; but, on the contrary, one which had engaged much of his thought and earnest consideration. With so full and implicit a reliance in the complete sovereignty of the Almighty as his religious belief imparted, he could have no fear or doubt as to the perfectness of the decrees of Providence. He literally argued everything for good, and that nothing transpired without a purpose of the Director of all things; and in that purpose he recognized but one principle, which was the *good of the children of men.* These premises once established in his mind, what fear could he possibly entertain of death? It is a part of the Divine economy,— that was enough for him. Applied to any dispensation of Providence, or to tenets of faith, this same reliance will be found evinced in all his ministrations and life. He says: — "We have ever "this pleasing reflection,— this sublime, this instructive "lesson,— that the wisdom which constitutes the vast "frame of the universe, and which organized all nature, "— the power that raised this glorious superstructure "upon its basis,— has ever been directed, and ever will "be directed, towards the *good* and *benefit* of mankind. "That there can be no such thing as partiality, or any- "thing like cruelty, in all the system of God, as the "moral governor of the world, is as plain a proposition as "can possibly be stated. There is not in the bosom of "our Father in Heaven any principle but goodness to his "children. There is not in the bosom of our Heavenly "Father, nor can there be, anything like cruelty or par- "tiality; but his eternal wisdom is ever working for the "benefit of his creatures."

He held the grave to be a calm, safe anchorage for the shattered hulls of men,— the portal through which the spirit passes to God who gave it. Concerning this subject there are a few lines from his pen so applicable in this connection, that we cannot refrain from transcribing them here. In common with those pieces which we have already given the reader, there is no effort at grandeur in the piece; the beauty and propriety of the poem is undisguised by metaphor, being put down in the tender and persuasive language of a Christian heart, pleading for the good of man, and the honor of its Maker. Mr. Ballou's poetical productions are such an index of his soul, his real character, that we are induced again to refer to the fact. They are ever like himself, simple, yet forcible, and never without a purpose, and most incontrovertible argument, expressed or implied. The following poem was written in his seventy-third year, and is entitled

FEAR NOT DEATH.

"Why call we death to man a foe?
Why should we fear to die?
Does heavenly wisdom teach us so?
Let us the question try.

Is he of independent might?
Does he himself sustain?
These questions if we answer right,
Will make our subject plain.

See ye his scythe, his dart, his spear?
Who placed them in his hand?
Know this, and give the winds your fear;
Dauntless before him stand.

Death is a messenger of God,
And God is love, we know;
Nothing can come from him but good, —
No enmity can flow.

Death only comes when he is sent,
Commissioned from on high;
And all his weapons, too, are lent, —
Why fear we, then, to die?

Death comes, a friend to mortal man,
To set his spirit free;
Nor he, nor any creature, can
Reverse the blest decree.

Had death on us an evil eye,
Would he our pains remove,
And set our spirits free to fly
To peaceful realms above?

Teach not your children, parents dear,
To dread what God may send;
Nor fill their tender hearts with fear
Of Him who is their friend."

There is a lesson here that it would be well for us to remember, a principle that should be planted and nurtured in our breasts. Death has been too long looked upon as "the great enemy of our race," while it is in truth but the calling home of the spirit by the Great Shepherd. 'T is but the wedding of the soul with Paradise, the starting post for heaven. These were the sentiments entertained by Mr. Ballou, and which governed his mind even to the last.

He says, relative to this deeply interesting and important subject to us all: — "We are as pilgrims and "strangers on earth, as were all our fathers. The "places which now know us will shortly know us no "more. How reasonable, then, is it, that we should "often bring this great truth under serious consideration! "If duly considered, it will exert a favorable influence in 'relation to the estimates we may make of all temporal "things, and give a favorable direction to our purposes "and determinations. Our fleshly bodies, like the grass "of the earth, are composed of the elements of nature; "these elements support both the grass and our fleshly "bodies; and as the grass finally withers and returns "back from whence it came, is decomposed and joined "with the elements of which it was composed, so do our "bodies return to the earth from whence they came. "Dust we are, and unto dust we must return. The cer-"tainty of our mortality is as apparent to us all as it can "possibly be made. However seldom we may think on "the subject, however we may endeavor to put it out of "our minds and thoughts, however we may endeavor to "drown the subject by devoting our attention to worldly "objects and worldly pursuits, we know that in a short "time we must be called to leave all this bustle of life, "close our eyes on all earthly things, and return to the "bosom of our common mother, the earth, from whence "we came.

"As the question whether man should exist or not was "not submitted to him, no more is it left to him to say "whether he will continue in this state forever, or depart "out of it. 'All flesh is as grass, and all the glory of "man as the flower of grass; the grass withereth, and "the flower thereof falleth away.' So hath the Creator "appointed and ordained; and it is not in the power of "man to prevent this withering of the grass, and this fall- "ing of the flower of grass. However endearing are the "ties of consanguinity, however tender and affectionate "are kindred hearts towards each other, with whatever "longings and fond desires fathers and mothers may look "on their sons and daughters, and with whatever devo- "tion they may nourish these flowers and watch over "them, they are altogether like the grass and the flower "of grass. They are perishable. It is not in the power "of children, however affectionately they may love their "fathers and mothers, and however they may desire the "continuance of such kind friends, to prevent that waste "of constitution and strength which time and disease are "sure to bring. The whitened locks, the wrinkled face, "the tottering frame, the palsied limbs and faltering "voice, are sure indications that the time of departure is "at hand.

"How wonderfully beautiful is the full-grown grass, "with its blushing and fragrant flowers! We cast our "eyes over the luxuriant meadow; with pleasure we "behold its beautiful flowers, seeming to vie with each "other in glory; and though we may fancy a preference "for this or for that, no person ever beheld a blossom "that was not beautiful to the eye. So we behold the "society of man in health and in the prime of strength;

"and how pleasing is the sight! Look at these sweet "babes! we may fancy a preference for the beauty of "this or that, but no one can help admiring every such "endearing object. Look around and behold the spark-"ling eye and blushing cheek of youth and beauty; but "remember these are flowers gathered for the tomb! "Whether we see them or not, Time has wings; whether "we realize it or not, his flight is rapid. What is time "when it is past? Nothing!"

> "He taught us how to live, and O! too high
> The price for knowledge! taught us how to die!"

Touching the matter of death-bed scenes as they refer to religious belief, and the influence that such scenes and circumstances exerted over his own mind, he says:

"It has often been said, by the enemies of the doctrine "for which I have contended, that it would do to live by, "but not to die by; meaning that it would not give the "mind satisfaction when sensible it was about to leave a "mortal for an immortal state. As to the truth of the "assertion I cannot positively say; that moment has not "yet been experienced by me: and as those who make "the remark have never believed the doctrine, I cannot "see how they should know any better than I do. Thus "much I can say: I believe I have seen, and often heard, "of persons rejoicing in the doctrine in the last hours "of their lives; but I do not build my faith on such "grounds.

"The sorrows or the joys of persons, in their last

"moments, prove nothing to me of the truth of their "general belief. A Jew, who despises the name of Christ "from the force of his education, may be filled with com- "fortable hopes, in his last moments, from the force of "the same education. I have no doubt but a person may "believe, or pretend to believe, in the doctrine of universal "salvation, when he knows of no solid reason for his "belief, but has rather rested the matter on the judgment "of those in whom he has placed more confidence than he "has, in reality, on the Saviour of the world; and I think "it very possible that such Universalists may have "strange and unexpected fears, when the near approach "of death, or any other circumstance, should cause them "to think more seriously on so weighty a subject.

"What my feelings might be concerning the doctrine "which I believe, was I called to contemplate on a *death-* "*bed*, I am as unable to say, as I am what I may think "of it a year hence, should I *live* and be in *health*. But "I am satisfied, beyond a doubt, that if I live a year "longer, and then find cause to give up my present "belief, I shall not feel a consciousness of having pro- "fessed what I did not *sincerely believe;* and was I "called to leave the world and my *writings* in it, and at "the *last hour* of my *life* should find I had *erred*, yet I "am satisfied that I should *possess* the *approbation* of "a *good conscience* in *all* I have *written*."

That Mr. Ballou felt fully prepared to die, there can be not the least doubt, though he did not say so in the exact words that would express this state of mind. He frequently, during the last two or three months of his life, made use of expressions, as relating to current events, in a way that led those about him to see that he was striving, particularly, to have every matter of business, or family arrangement, so completed as not in any way to be contingent upon himself. Then his frequent observations relative to the idea that he was nearly worn out; and in his sermons, too, his often repeating at this time how near he was to the brink of the grave, and that those who heard him might realize the honesty of his reasoning and the sincerity of his doctrine, since, with so short a span of existence left to him, he could not in any instance bring himself to support what he did not most solemnly and religiously believe to be the gospel of Christ, and in full accordance with the word of God; the caution already referred to as given to his wife, and various other simple but expressive tokens that he evinced during the few weeks previous to his decease,—all go fully to show that his mind was made up to die, and that he foresaw, as it were, the approach of his demise, with almost prophetic vision. The philosophy, or sophistry, therefore, as to looking upon death as the inevitable visitant to others, but as something which must miraculously pass him by, did not exist in his mind. He looked upon death as "the messenger of God, commissioned from on high;" and he held himself calmly ready to answer the blessed decree of Heaven.

Though almost constantly engaged at his study of the holy text, or in other reading and writing, still, so domestic was Mr. Ballou in his disposition and feelings, that he always took a lively interest in all the arrangements of the family, and in each one's well-being, seeking to cause as little unnecessary labor as possible on his own account. No motives other than those of the kindest character could possibly have induced this thoughtfulness, on his part; for all those about him, even the servants, always deemed it a pleasure to serve him in his slightest expressed desire, while his children ever sought to anticipate his wishes. In his directions to those called upon to attend him, there was none of the austerity or sternness of a master evinced in his manner of speech. The order direct we never heard from his lips, but, in giving directions, it was ever in the form of permission,—"You *may* do this, or you *may* hand me that;" and the appropriateness of this mode of speech was most apparent, since it was a privilege to us all to fulfil his desires.

With profane history, ancient and modern, he was well acquainted; and at the age of seventy-four, five and six, he devoted some considerable time to the reviewal of both, and particularly to the history of our own country. With Rollin, Plutarch, Smollet, Hume, Prescott, Bancroft, etc., he was perfectly familiar. At this period he was engaged, as we have said, in re-perusing the works of his library, treating mainly upon profane history. As may be supposed, to one of his disposition, home was very dear, and he was always happiest with his family.

> "To them his heart, his love, his griefs, were given;
> But all his serious thoughts had rest in heaven."

During the whole of his public ministrations and professional career, he never labored with more evident effect and general influence than at this time. The ripened harvest of his experience was poured forth in the most simple and touching truthfulness, and his discourses were redolent of holy manna to the souls of his hearers; the sober arguments of conviction obtained even more fully than in former years, when the vigor of ripened manhood added its physical powers to the balance. Persons who had sat under his preaching for many years would listen with the most absorbed attention, as well as with surprise, to hear the easy flow of eloquence that seemed to come from an inspired heart, bearing witness to his quick, sure discernment, and boundless fertility of invention,—the truth and exemplifications of divine goodness were ever so fresh and abundant in the feast he spread, the arguments so logical and convincing. He was endowed in many respects with the great requisites for a lawyer, possessing a mind exceedingly active, capable of constantly commanding its own resources, and a faculty of tenaciously pursuing his argument with exceeding force and power.

It really seemed, latterly, that, realizing how brief must be his labors, and how near he was to the end of his earthly mission, he labored with increased zeal, and consequent success. His eyes, when in the desk, seemed to kindle with superhuman fire, his thoughts to flow with inspired eloquence; and those who heard him must have entered most thoroughly into his own spirit, for we have heard, from all directions where he preached, very earnest remarks of the striking effect produced by his discourses. And this effect was by no means confined to the laity; many of his ministering brethren have told us that they had never heard him discourse with more power, nor ever with such decided effect, as was the case within the last two years of his life. It was impossible for him to answer all of the demands upon him, but neither ordinary inconveniences nor distance ever caused him to decline to respond to those who, at this late period of his life, sought his counsel. In vain did we beseech him to consider his bodily comfort, and not risk his health and try his strength so much, at his advanced age, by these constant travels. "I am vain enough," he said, "to believe that "I still do some good, and I am never so happy as when "exercised by such a realizing sense; but, whether at "home or abroad, I am still in my Maker's hands, and "he will do with me as to him seemeth good."

Mr. Ballou's manuscript was always remarkably plain and correct, being, in many respects, very characteristic of himself. It was regular, exceedingly neat, and well executed, yet unostentatious, and in no degree ornamental. For our own part, we would give more for a scrap of the hand-writing of one whom we had never met, or even of him whom we had casually seen, to enable us to judge of the general characteristics of the individual's disposition, than for the testimony of many an intimate friend. It is, of necessity, in a very great degree, a sample of the man; and when we look upon it, and think that it was the work of his hand, the emanation of his brain, mechanically and mentally his, it possesses peculiar interest.

Mr. Ballou was sometimes addressed, by letter, from a distance, from those who were strangers to him, and sometimes by brethren in the ministry, who would request him to reply to certain queries which they proposed, that they might reap the advantage of his wisdom. These letters were various in their character; some related to religious questions, some to his own history, and some as to its bearing upon his belief in the tenets of faith. One who professed to have read his numerous works, and who was also an ardent believer in the doctrine of universal salvation, converted through his writings, sent the following queries to him in a letter some time in 1847, during his seventy-sixth year. Having the letter and reply, we subjoin the spirit of the former, and give the latter to the reader entire.

"*Queries.*— With what feelings do you look back upon "your past life, its influence and results, its commencement and its end? As it regards your published "works and writings, has experience strengthened the "opinions and points laid down in them, or have your "after years of study and reflection found cause for "change? What is the present end and aim of your "life, and how does it differ from the morning of your "existence?

"*Reply to Query 1st.*—When I survey the course of "my past life, as I often do, I am filled with wonder; and "a clear conviction that, as a whole, it has been appointed "and directed by Infinite Wisdom, all but reduces me to "nothing. True, I can simply realize that I exist; and "can compare myself to a drop of water in the midst of "the ocean, dependent, as I always have been, on that "Being who holds the unmeasured deep in the hollow of "his hand. I am fully satisfied that none of the event-"ful incidents of my life would have been what they "were, had not an overruling Providence disappointed "my own plans and purposes in many instances. Pur-"suant to these considerations, in viewing the apparent "'influences and results' of my labors, I should be quite "at variance with the conviction of my own under-"standing, should I indulge a feeling to credit them to "myself. With such views of the past and present, I "feel satisfied, and even thankful.

"My childhood and youth were, like most of others, "full of vanity. My public life commenced with no "extensive prospects. I do not know that the thought "ever entered my mind that my public labors would ever "procure me a livelihood. . . . . . My main desire now "is that it may please Him whose I am and whom I "serve, so to direct that what remains of my fleeting "days may in no way dishonor, but promote, the cause "of his truth, to which I have so long been devoted.

"*Reply to Query 2nd.*— All the *important* doctrinal "points contained in the several works which I have "published are still my honest convictions; and as they "were widely different from the views generally enter-"tained by theologians, I examined them with all "possible care, and have never seen cause to rescind "them. And I can add, that I have never, in my public "labors, allowed myself to present to my hearers any "sentiment, or to expound any portion of scripture, but "in accordance with the sober convictions of my under-"standing.

"*Reply to Query 3d.*—The main object by which I "was actuated at the commencement of my public labors "was to understand the true doctrine of the Scriptures, "and by all possible means to convey conviction of its "truth to the understanding of all who had ears to hear; "and my present aim is to finish, in the best manner I "can, these labors, by persuading people, not only to "understand the true nature of the gospel, but to cherish "its blessed hopes, and to faithfully practise its pre-"cepts."

During a visit of the author of this biography to the Southern and Western States of the Union, in the summer of 1846, he had an opportunity to witness the most evident token of the popularity of Mr. Ballou in these sections, and the high esteem in which his writings are held. This was particularly the case in the State of Ohio, the most distant point from his home that Mr. Ballou ever visited. Here, in passing through the state, we had frequent occasion to register our name and place of residence, which often led to our being asked whether we were a connection of Hosea Ballou's; and when the existing relationship was made known, there were no bounds to the hospitality that was urged upon us. In

Cincinnati, it so happened that an original lithographic print of Mr. Ballou was being struck off just as we left the city, and we were kindly furnished with the first dozen impressions taken from the stone. This lithograph is from a crayon drawing taken from life, at Akron, Ohio, during the visit of Mr. Ballou to that town in 1844, by an artist sent up from Cincinnati for the purpose. The likeness is a good one in many respects, but much inferior to several taken in Boston, both as it regards likeness and as a work of art.

During the summer of 1847, Mr. Ballou visited his eldest son, Rev. Hosea F. Ballou, at his residence and farm in Whitingham, Vt., where for several days he applied himself to labor on the land; reaping, mowing, and the various departments of farming, during the week, and to public services in that and the neighboring towns on the Sabbath. These few weeks of healthy toil invigorated him to a most surprising degree, and, though more than seventy-five years of age, I was assured by those who were on the spot that he did the work of a day-laborer with ease, and that his hand wielded the scythe with the steadiness and effect of early years. He told us afterwards himself how sweet his food tasted, how refreshing his bed felt, and how clear and invigorated his brain was, by this homely labor, and the sweat of the brow. He would sometimes sigh at the constraint of his town life, and eulogize the green fields and verdant hill-sides. He says: "All of us have our prescribed duties, "and the economy of nature requires certain tastes and "temperaments that will apply themselves to the various "concerns of life. We find the mechanic, the farmer, "the minister, the artisan, the lawyer, all endowed with "some prominent qualities, which particularly fit them "for the proper discharge of their peculiar calling; and "this is necessary, that all things may be done well and "harmoniously. But, of all the business occupations of "life, it has always seemed to me that the farmer's em-"ployment must be the most agreeable. The country is "real, the city is artificial; one is nature, the other is "art. In the earlier portions of my life, I gathered some "experience in tilling the soil; in boyhood and early "youth, it was almost my sole occupation. Even as late "as my residence in Salem, I was accustomed to plant "and cultivate a portion of ground. The great charm of "the farmer's element is that it brings him in such close "contact with nature; his labor, so healthful and invig-"orating, being performed to the soft hymns and sacred "melodies that creation ever chants in open fields and "woodlands."

During this season Mr. Ballou travelled considerably in the New England States and New York, in accordance with letters of invitation sent to him from every direction. During the month of August he preached at numerous places in the vicinity of Montpelier, Vt., and the route thither from Boston. This journey was peculiarly gratifying to his feelings; everywhere he was received with that warmth of heart and real sincerity that invigorate the soul. Meeting-houses were abandoned as too small, and temporary pulpits were erected in the open air, from whence he addressed the thousands who came from far and near to listen to his words. His name was so well known, and his character so beloved, throughout the order, that the simple announcement of his presence drew multitudes together, who listened with the utmost avidity to his words, which carried with them the "clear running wine of conviction."

Here let us pause for a moment, and ask the reader to consider what a powerful and godly influence the life of such a man must have exerted upon community, and those persons with whom he was brought into frequent contact. There was such perfect harmony, such a beautiful consistency, between his pure Christian life and the religion he taught, that the most thoughtless could not but observe and note it. We heard an old man say, but a few days ago,—"Before I knew your father I heard that "he was one of the vilest of men; that he was intem-"perate, profane, vulgar, and, in short, everything that "was bad. But when I saw him, meek, unostentatious, "gentle, reverential, and preaching such glorious truths, "I said to myself, so was his Divine Master reviled and "persecuted!" This was the false report that was raised against him thirty and forty years since. The subject of this biography did not answer these calumnies; he *lived* them down, and manifested as strong an argument in favor of his doctrine by his every-day life, as by his oral communications from the pulpit. His writings, too, evincing the same spirit as his personal career, manifesting so much sincerity, and logical force of argument, garbed in such simple language, and yet conveying such sublime truths, and these so largely enforced by a personal knowledge of their author,— at least throughout a large portion of the eastern states,— must have exerted, and will continue to exert, an influence of almost incalculable extent.

It is in perfect unison with the analogy of nature that the sunset of life should be more cheerful and joyous than the meridian. The sweetest notes of the nightingale are heard at evening, the woods put on their most cheerful aspect in the autumn of the year, and the sun is the brightest when about to sink beneath the horizon. It was at this period of life that Mr. Ballou seemed to have arrived at the goal of his ambition, actuated only by

"Those calm desires that ask but little room."

The principles which he had so long and so strenuously advocated prevailing beyond all precedence, his family happily settled in life about him, and himself respected and beloved by an entire denomination as a faithful disciple of Christ and a true Christian. In a conversation with him upon the comforts and troubles of old age, we asked him, one day, about this period, what was his greatest trouble. He facetiously referred us to the reply of Fontenelle, who was asked, in extreme old age, what inconvenience he experienced, when he replied, "None, but that of existence," signifying by this answer how really happy and contented he was.

For the last twenty years of Mr. Ballou's life, it was not an uncommon occurrence for strangers from a distance to call on him and introduce themselves, as desirous of looking upon him and making his acquaintance. "I "have read your works, and it has seemed as though I "knew you well already, for they are like familiar con-"versations." This would be the purport of their language. "Your books," they would say, "have made me "a Universalist; and I could not feel satisfied until I had "seen personally one to whom I am so much indebted, "and whom I so highly respect." This was the case in more than one instance, at different periods, when Englishmen declared that it was the great purpose that had influenced them in visiting the Union. In such cases they met with a cordial and hospitable welcome at his house and table, and hours of pleasant discussion would ensue upon the doctrines of the Scriptures, and congenial themes. Many were the visitors from various parts of the country with the same avowed purpose, and similarly influenced.

In the latter part of 1848, owing to some unfortunate exposure to the weather, he was most violently attacked with ague in the face, so severe as to cause the whole face to swell so much as to close one of the eyes entirely. The attack lasted in its effects for several days, and was exceedingly painful. Though moved with the keenest regret at the pain we knew he must suffer, still we could not but admire the strength of mind and calm philosophy with which he endured it. Not a murmur escaped his lips, and intervals occurring between the most severe moments of his suffering were devoted to writing or study, while the constant kind offices of those about him, and more particularly those of his dearly-beloved partner and children, were ever received with grateful words, and tokens of a full appreciation of the warm love that prompted them.

In the summer of 1847, the School-street Society requested of Mr. Ballou, through its standing committee, that he would sit for a full-length portrait, to be the property of the society, and to be hung in Murray Hall, adjoining the church. Mr. Ballou agreed to their proposition, and granted the requisite sittings, and a magnificent portrait was produced. The picture is as large as life. The preacher is represented standing in the pulpit of the School-street church, the fingers of the right hand inserted in the Bible, the left slightly extended. The likeness and expression are perfectly life-like, and true to the original. From this excellent painting several copies have been taken for his family and friends.

This painting was the source of a great degree of satisfaction to the society and Mr. Ballou's friends generally, for, in common with many others left of him, it is excellent as a likeness, and therefore is a pregnant page in his history; for, of the three principal channels of judging and arriving at the knowledge of character, namely, looks, words and actions, the former is the most faithful. Professions pass for nothing, actions may be counterfeited, but a man's *looks* he cannot hide. A modern writer, in language perhaps too forcible, says: — "A man's whole "life may be a lie to himself and others, and yet a picture "painted of him by a great artist would probably stamp "his true character on the canvas, and betray the secret "to posterity." Subscribing in a large degree to this principle, we consider that the paintings, busts, medallions, and likenesses generally, of Mr. Ballou, may be highly valued as speaking his true character in the expression, and telling a faithful story of the original.

As it regards the likeness which the publisher has placed in the commencement of this biography, to those who have not seen the subject of the picture within the last few years, it may look perhaps a little too aged; but in this respect it is the most truthful of any likeness of him extant. He has been often represented, as the reader is aware, at almost every period of his life since his thirtieth year; and with more or less correctness, in each instance, as it regarded his expression and formation of features at that time; but it strikes us that those who have been familiar with Mr. Ballou's face to the last of his career will esteem this engraving, aside from its superior artistic excellence, as transcribing for us the *last* looks of his dearly-loved face.

In a notice of the large painting now hanging in Murray Hall, which appeared in the Trumpet of Sept. 4th, 1847, the editor says: —

"He (Mr. Ballou) is now in excellent health, firm, "erect, and preaches vigorously; his mind is unimpaired; "he is strong in the faith to which the labors of his life "have been given, and we do not see why he will not be "able to preach for ten years to come, should his life be "spared. He can preach three sermons with but little "fatigue, while some of the middle-aged can hardly find "strength to preach twice of a Sunday."

In the fall of 1847, Mr. Ballou, then in his seventy-seventh year, attended the Universalist convention in New York city, where he delivered a sermon before the brethren assembled there, which created no small degree of notice, and was pronounced by those who heard it to be one of extraordinary power and force. Some of the brethren at once called upon him for a copy for publication; but when he told them that he had no copy himself, and that it was entirely extemporaneous, their surprise was great. That one of his advanced age could deliver a discourse of so remarkable a character, with every point arranged in the most exact order, abounding in powerful and well-sustained argument and varied phases, unless assisted by notes, seemed almost impossible.

So much sensation did this discourse create, that Mr. Ballou acceded to the earnest solicitations that besieged him, and wrote it out for the press, and it was published in pamphlet form. He remarked to us, concerning the matter, that it was much harder for him to write it than it would have been to have written two sermons from a given text, since he had to *recall* what he had spoken extempore weeks before. But this was done so exactly as to create surprise in those who had listened to it from

30

the pulpit, for its correctness and likeness to the oral delivery.

We subjoin a short sketch from this sermon, because it is so characteristic of the spirit that actuated Mr. Ballou at all times; a spirit of the utmost simplicity,—one of the striking peculiarities of real genius,—both in his public teachings and private life, and also as a specimen of his purity and force of style at this period of life. The contrast drawn between the gospel of Christ and the polished creed of the schools is striking and obvious.

"With all the pomp, with all the glory, with all the "wealth, and all the learning of the schools, among both "Jews and Gentiles, let us, for a moment, compare the "simplicity that was in Christ. Born in a family which "was supported by mechanical labor, brought up in "laborious habits, destitute of wealth and the honors of "the schools, he commenced his public labors. To "assist him in the ministry of his doctrine, a few fisher-"men, and others of useful occupation, were chosen. "The doctrine which Jesus taught was as simple and "easy to understand as the common affairs of life. "His sermon on the mount, containing the sublimest "beatitudes, and all the duties of life, requires but "ordinary talents to understand. His manner of teach-"ing by the use of parables communicated truth in the "most simple manner. When he justified his favor to "publicans and sinners, of which he was accused by the "Pharisees and Scribes, how simple was his method! "'What man of you, having an hundred sheep, if he "lose one of them, doth not leave the ninety and nine in "the wilderness, and go after that which is lost, until he "find it? and when he hath found it he layeth it on his "shoulder, rejoicing. And when he cometh home, he "calleth together his friends and neighbors, saying unto "them, Rejoice with me; for I have found my sheep "which was lost.' And how sublimely simple, if I may "so say, was his application of his parable! 'I say unto "you, that likewise joy shall be in heaven over one "sinner that repenteth, more than over ninety and nine "just persons, which need no repentance.' On foot, see "him travel from city to city! Fatigued and weary of "his journey, see him resting himself by Jacob's well at "Sichar; and mark the simplicity of his conversation "with the woman of Samaria! To set his disciples an "example of humility, behold him who gave sight to the "blind, hearing to the deaf, healing to the sick, sound-"ness to the maimed, and life to the dead, gird himself "with a towel, and wash their feet!

"How poorly has the simplicity which is in Christ "been maintained by the Christian church! Read its "history, in which we learn its conformity to such "worldly institutions and customs as are pleasing to "human ambition, and all the vain pride and corruption "which characterized pagan idolatry. That subtilty "with which the serpent beguiled Eve is constantly at "work, persuading us to seek to render religion popular "in the eyes of the world. That spiritual wickedness "may be maintained in high places, high places must be "established and supported. So deeply is the love of "popular esteem rooted in the heart, that it is to be "feared many are inclined to concede to opinions and "customs inconsistent with their better judgment, for "the sake of that shining phantom."

We remember an incident which occurred to Mr. Ballou in January of 1848, which he related to us at the time. He had occasion to enter an omnibus to proceed from one extreme of the city to another, when, having scarcely become seated, an elderly woman, who was occupying a seat immediately opposite, said to him,— "Mr. Ballou, do you not constantly preach to your con-"gregation, 'O ye generation of vipers! how can ye "escape the damnation of hell?'" Mr. Ballou turned his keen, piercing eye upon her, and seeing that some bigoted and fanatical individual had recognized him, and desired to commence an argument, replied,—"No, "madam; that class do not attend my church!" The woman had not anticipated so decided an answer, and, shading her eyes with her hands, contemplated the floor of the coach the remainder of the passage.

So little self-pride had Mr. Ballou, and so little comparatively did he think or care about having any biographical sketch appear of him after his death, that it was with the utmost difficulty that we persuaded him to attempt a manuscript of even a few pages, that a more authentic record might be preserved for the aid of the subject when it should be taken in hand. But all that we were able to procure from him the reader will find duly credited in these pages. Mr. Ballou had an ambition, however, that his written works should be preserved after him; for in them he had labored for the good of mankind, and he hoped those labors might not prove unavailable. His wish was highly gratified, in this respect, during his life, by the very wide circulation they attained, and the numerous editions of them which were published, showing that they were largely read and valued by the Christian world.

Having partially yielded to our reiterated solicitations for some few pages of manuscript, if only relating to the simplest affairs, he sat down, and commenced a sheet of paper in the same humorous vein in which he was always sure to treat the idea of writing of himself. This commencement was as follows:

"I have never learned that there were, before my "birth, any prophecies delivered by any one, or that any "one had dreamed anything concerning myself. If there "happened, at the time of my birth, an earthquake, or "the appearance of a comet, or any other phenomenon "of nature which indicated anything relative to me, or "signified what manner of person I should become, in "what employment my life should be spent, whether I "should become useful to society or a nuisance, the fact "has never come to my knowledge."

The life of Mr. Ballou is so intimately woven with the annals of Universalism that the account of the one must be an almost complete life of the other. He nursed the first dawn of belief in impartial and free grace to all mankind, and lived to see the blessed doctrine grow and spread over the land, like the day, from its breaking to the meridian. He was the pioneer, the leader, the propagator, of Universalism.

During April, 1848, he visited and preached in Philadelphia, New York, &c., and on his return expressed himself as he always did of the brethren in those cities, and that he had been made most happy in his communion with them.

About this period, an infatuated preacher of future punishment, somewhere in the northern part of New York State, while in a high state of excitement, declared to his audience that Universalists and Infidels always renounced their belief before they died, and absolutely instanced old Hosea Ballou, as he termed him, who had *lately* died, penitent and fully repentant for his evil life, entirely refuting all his former belief, and praying to be saved from the wrath to come. Equally ridiculous allusions were made to his wife, who was said to have showed more consistency, and to have died stubbornly adhering to her old principles. This ridiculous assertion was reported in a paper published in the vicinity, and a copy marked and sent to Mr. Ballou.

We asked him if he had not better address a brief letter to the editor, just to confound the propagator of the falsehood. "No," said he; "I have learned, by experience, that libels, if neglected, are forgotten; if resented, "they too frequently pass for merited satire."

In the month of June, 1849, Mr. Ballou visited Troy,

N. Y., for a few weeks, and preached there and in the neighborhood, with his accustomed vigor and mental power. His clear, musical tones of voice were as perfectly modulated as ever, and his mental and physical vigor was the occasion of remark by all who listened to him.

One of Mr. Ballou's latest impromptu efforts at versification was elicited by a request for his autograph, by a young lady, who presented her album for this purpose, and in which he wrote the following lines:

THE MAID I PRIZE.

"The maid I prize may not be one
  Whose beauty dazzles vulgar eyes;
Those glowing folds 't were wise to shun,
  Where death in hidden poison lies.

The maid I prize may not rely
  On costly robes my heart to win;
The rose's blush, the lily's dye,
  Can ne'er commend a breast of sin.

The maid I prize has tears for grief,
  And soft compassion for the poor;
'T is her delight to grant relief;
  Where want resides she knows the door.

The maid I prize hath chosen that part
  The golden Indies cannot buy;
And garnered in a pious heart
  A treasure far above the sky."

As late as December, 1851, and January, 1852, Mr. Ballou passed five weeks in the city of New York, preaching to the societies there frequently three times of a Sabbath, and at conference meetings during other days of the week. He was often called upon for lengthy remarks, which he most cheerfully and heartily gave. He was never so happy, never so well, as when engaged about his Master's business; and though, at this age,—eighty-one,—his form was a little bent, and his step less firm than of yore, yet in the pulpit he stood as erect as at fifty. His whole soul seemed to dilate, and his firmness of voice and body to be like iron; so much so, indeed, that it was usual to hear remarks to this effect, from all quarters, wherever he appeared.

During this his last visit to New York, he wrote to us as follows:

"MATURIN: A kind Providence brought me safely "hither in due course, and I have already made several "appointments and promises relative to my services while "I tarry here. As in years gone by, I find the same "cordial hospitality here, and brotherly love extended 'towards me still. I need hardly say how grateful this "is to my feelings. We grow, perhaps, more sensitive, "as we advance in age, as to these little kindnesses and "attentions, that unitedly go to make up the quiet peace "and happiness of private life.

"Our Heavenly Father has smiled upon the sacred "cause in this place, and the churches flourish here "exceedingly. Even now I am about to proceed to "New Jersey, to dedicate a new temple, raised to the "service of the living God. To me, the increase of the "denomination with which I have so long been identified "is a source of peculiar satisfaction. My bodily health "is fully as good as when I left Boston; and, by the "blessing of Divine Goodness, I trust again to be at home "in a brief period, to enjoy the society of those near and "dear to me. Please tell your mother to duly regard "her health, and remember me kindly to all the family.

"Affectionately,

"HOSEA BALLOU."

"After the singing of another anthem," says the correspondent of the Trumpet, in a letter from Newark relative to the dedication referred to, "came the sermon, by "our venerable and beloved Father Ballou, from the fit-"ting words recorded in 1 Chron. 16 : 29. The audience "was not large, but respectable in number; and from the "first moments when the gray-haired speaker stood up "before the people till he sat down again, the most "marked and almost breathless attention was given. "The speaker believed that 'the name of the Lord' "expressed all the attributes of His adorable character. "He proceeded to notice some of those attributes, with "wonderful power and simplicity, enforcing the truth that "*goodness* must be coëxtensive with *wisdom* in the "Divine character. He illustrated the workings of the "law of love, as opposed to the law of fear, by the exam-"ples of the grateful offerings of our people to the beloved "Washington and Lafayette. The people honored them, "not because a terrible penalty was threatened should "they refuse to yield the tribute, but because they loved "them. Worship, true worship, cannot be *bought;* it "must be *free.* It can be offered only to a God infinite "in goodness and mercy. Father Ballou affectionately "exhorted the people to give unto the Lord, in the neat "temple they had reared, the glory so justly due for all "his revelations of good will to the children of men. "As children, filled with gratitude, should they come "into his courts. A severe, yet *kind*-spirited rebuke, "was administered to those who go to church simply to "display fine apparel, or because it is fashionable. In "doing our duty, we are happy, we offer unto the Lord; "while they who serve fashion and popularity have just "their reward, *and no more.*

"I have never listened to this aged servant of God "with greater delight and profit than on that occasion. "It hardly seemed possible that so clear, and forcible, "and eloquent a production, could come from the mouth "of one who has borne the brunt of eighty-one years."

At the age of four score, Mr. Ballou preached before the New York Convention of Universalists, at Boston, in September, 1851. Concerning this occasion, Rev. A. C. Thomas, in the autobiography before quoted from, says: "He (Mr. Ballou) is an exception to the 'labor and sor- "row' affirmed of those who, by reason of strength, at- "tain that period of life. He was, indeed, feeble in body; "but 'his eye was not dim, nor his natural force abated.' "He saw as clearly as ever into the 'root of the matter,' "and largely exemplified his peculiar force of argumentation. Was there ever a clearer or more forcible illustration than the one he presented regarding a mother and her child?—'Your child has fallen into the mire, and its body and its garments are defiled. You cleanse it, and array it in clean robes. The query is, Do you love your child because you have washed it, or did you wash it because you loved it?'"

Mr. Ballou's contributions to the press largely increased during the latter years of his life, and the articles he wrote, at various times, during this period, will bear the most critical examination, as it regards the soundness of their doctrinal points, the excellence and purity of their style, and the Christian spirit they invariably show forth in every line. These contributions to the press have appeared mainly in the "Trumpet and Universalist Magazine," the "Universalist Quarterly," and the "Christian Freeman."

In 1851, at the solicitation of Rev. Mr. Usher, book publisher, Mr. Ballou edited a collection of his sermons, and wrote some original articles, which were published under the title of "A Voice to Universalists." This book also contained a collection of Mr. Ballou's fugitive verses, published many years since, and written for the poet's corner of his paper. We can, perhaps, give no better review or reference to this book, than by copying Rev. Sylvanus Cobb's published review of it, which we subjoin.

"The '*General Epistle to Universalists*' is itself

"worth the price of the book. Tell us not that this "might have been published in tract, or any cheap form. "It would never have served its mission thus to be read "and thrown away. It should have been where it is, in "a large, splendid book, to grace our centre-tables, and to "be taken thence and read as often as once a month.

"The same remarks may be made in relation to the "'*Advice to Young Men who design to enter the* "*Ministry.*'

"The '*Short Essay on Universalism,*' '*The Doc-* "*trine of Universal Salvation shown to be included* "*in the Divine Commands,*' and '*The Utility of* "*Evil,*' are likewise valuable mementos of their author; "and so are the two *Convention Sermons.*

"And then, in respect to the metrical compositions, "we could not spare them from this book. True, the "author, as he modestly says in a note to the reader, "makes no pretensions to being a poet; yet his poetry is "to us exceedingly precious. It is in this we discover "more clearly the moral likeness of the man. In the "frontispiece we have a satisfactory likeness of the outer "man; and how should we consent to tear from the book "this no less accurate likeness of the soul? In these "hymns we see the author in his characteristic meekness "of spirit, self-abasement, pure and ardent devotion, and "all-sustaining faith in the wise and perfect government "of God. Here, too, in these hymns and poems, are "specimens of the author's clearness and precision of "intellectual discernment, and his argumentative acumen.

"The work shall go down to posterity as a memento of "Father Ballou."

The article in this book entitled the "Utility of Evil" is one of great power and force. Mr. Ballou's theory is, that what *we* call evil does not exist without the wise permission and appointment of the infinitely good and gracious God. In the article on this subject he says:

"Reader, do not be offended at the title of this short "article, and call it impious. Will you say you never "before heard that evil is useful? Will you say the "suggestion is wicked, and could be made by no other "than one who is wicked? Well, suppose all which you "imagine be true, may it not be well to be calm, and "deliberately consider that, though you have never "before heard of this thing, it may, notwithstanding, be "a divine truth? If you will be candid, and bring your "mind into a suitable condition to be reasoned with, we "will call you to the consideration of questions which, if "properly answered, will lead us into the true light of "our subject. 1st. Is evil self-existent? If no one will "allow this, there is no need of argument to disprove it. "It follows, of course, that evil had a cause which pro- "duced it; this is self-evident. 2d. Is it not equally "self-evident that the cause which produced evil is good? "If we say that the cause which produced evil was evil, "we thereby say that evil existed before it existed! "When these several points are understood, we are "prepared to state the following axioms:

"1st. That which had no beginning had no cause to "produce it. 2d. If we should say that good had an "origin or a cause, we should be compelled to say that "that cause was evil! 3d. If we allow that evil had an "origin or cause, we must allow that the origin of evil is "good." pp. 115, 116.

From the commencement of 1852 until within a week of his death, we find him constantly active, with the weight of fourscore years and more; yet he never for a moment faltered in his mission. During the last year of his life he preached in seven different states, and in about forty different places. His pen was still as busy as ever. One Sunday found him in Maine, the next in New Hampshire, the third in Vermont; now he is in New York, New Jersey, or Rhode Island, preaching the word with unabated zeal and surprising effect in all directions. The copy of the Trumpet that announces his death contains two articles from his pen, commending to the order two lately published biographies, showing forth as illustrations of what a true and noble aim will empower the soul to do amid the humblest circumstances, one of the strongest illustrations of which is his own life. His last paragraph reads thus: "We need not look forward "to the good time, for it is now come, when ministers are "esteemed for their knowledge of divine truth, and their "ardent love for the same, together with their faithfulness "in dispensing it to the people, and their living and "walking in the precepts of Jesus." At the time of his death he had two appointments already arranged, one in Massachusetts and one in New Hampshire, besides several under consideration.

"Verily, he was at his post to the last," says Rev. T. B. Thayer, in his eulogy upon Mr. Ballou; "and when "the messenger came, he was ready. He fell in the full "armor of God, with the helmet of salvation on his head, "his spotless heart covered with the breastplate of "righteousness, his feet shod with the preparation of the "gospel of peace. In one hand he held the shield of "faith, and in the other the sword of the spirit, which is "the word of God,— the sword which he had for sixty "years wielded with such success in his multiplied battles "with error and sin, and by which at last he was, through "Jesus Christ, made conqueror, and more than conqueror, "over death and the grave. Verily, the old man died, "as he had lived, faithful, courageous, serene, victorious, "to the last."

It was in these ripened days of his experience that his counsel was eagerly sought by all, laity and clergy, in private and in public. His activity and anxiety to be about his Master's business carried him constantly into the midst of all important denominational assemblies; and here he was ever received, both his presence and his counsel, with profound respect. If there was contention, misunderstanding, or difficulty of any sort, all eyes were turned upon him who sat so quietly and thoughtfully in their midst; he was their peace-maker, his calm voice stilled the tempest, his finger pointed the way towards the right. As Mr. Thayer says in the eulogy just quoted from:

"It will be a long time before we shall get accustomed, "in our associations and conventions, to the absence of "that venerable form, those gray hairs, and that voice of "wisdom, and gentleness, and love, which came like oil "on the troubled waters of debate, and drew out the "entangled threads of thought, and by quaint queries, by "questions which answered themselves, questions plainer "than most men's answers, penetrated to the heart of "every subject, and showed us, as by a flash of light, the "exact point where the truth lay. We shall often desire "in our councils his presence, his clear thought, his "persuasive language, his gentleness of manner, and his "conclusive logic."

Mr. Ballou had a most remarkable faculty of seeing through any abstruse question or subject that came up for discussion before any body with which he was sitting in fellowship, and could at once seem to set all right in their midst, by a few shrewdly-uttered words. Another brother has said of him in this respect:

"It was wonderful how he would put the needle in "amid the tangled skein of reasonings, in a debate, and "untie the knot just where the whole might be wound off "without any difficulty; and how he would hold to the "essential point in an important discussion, and dissipate "every obscuration that threatened to darken and eclipse "it, was astonishing, and showed where his power as a "master reasoner lay. Such was the man."

We must now turn from these desultory remarks and references, to describe the end of his earthly mission.

CHAPTER XV.

END OF HIS EARTHLY MISSION.

How shall we speak of the close of that life which we have so feebly succeeded in portraying,— how depict the sunset of his soul upon earth,— how describe the unfeigned and unbounded sympathy and mourning of a whole denomination,— how refer to the appropriate ceremonies — the funeral obsequies — that were so beautifully and tenderly performed by the society over whom he had so long held such heart-sway, and whom he loved better than all else on earth, save his family? How shall our feeble pen portray these striking and long to be remembered scenes? Throughout this entire subject we have written tremblingly, and with a full realizing sense of the magnitude of the theme, and the humble ability of our pen. But here we feel our hand indeed too feeble, our sensibilities too acute, and shall call to our aid stronger minds and abler pens.

In no more appropriate place than here can we refer to his parting with the loved companion of his bosom. His wife had been confined to her chamber for some weeks, by severe indisposition, just previous to his own last illness, nor was she able to leave it until some time after the last obsequies in honor to his memory. On the morning that Mr. Ballou was taken ill, he came to her from his own dressing-room, kissed her tenderly, and bade her adieu, with all the gentle and affectionate solicitude with which a young husband might have left his bride; and, passing down stairs to the parlor, was preparing to depart for the scene of the convention at Plymouth, when he was suddenly taken in a fainting fit. A couch was immediately removed to the room where he was taken so suddenly ill, and he was not removed from it until he fell quietly asleep in death. Little did the fond wife and companion of his bosom think, when he bade her thus farewell, that it was for the last time; — that it was the last time she should ever behold, on this earth, that countenance that had never been turned upon her save in love and tenderness,— that noble brow that had been her pride and glory in its sublime truthfulness and purity of expression,— those eloquent lips that had been such a well-spring of heavenly truths! But such it was. Herself too ill to be removed from her chamber, she never saw him afterwards; and she still cherishes his memory as associated with that fond and endearing look that accompanied his last kiss and farewell!

In relation to the manner in which he had prepared the mind of his wife for the event which he seemed so clearly to foresee, Rev. Mr. Miner, in his farewell sermon, said: —

"He had often exhorted his companion to hold herself "in readiness for his departure, forewarning her that "every separation from her might be the last. But a "few days previous to his death, he had renewedly im-"pressed this upon her mind. What a sublime specta-"cle was this! At more than fourscore years of age, "braving the rigors of mid-winter and the extreme heat "of summer, and regardless of the dangers that attend "the rapid conveyances of our time, this veteran preacher "'takes his life in his hand,' and goes forth continually "to promulgate the everlasting gospel!"

We must not omit to give the reader a brief article which Mr. Ballou left among his papers, relating to the close of his earthly career. It was folded in with his accounts, will, and other important papers, and was written in his usual legible hand. It was in the spirit of a preface to the will which followed, and in which every matter had been plainly arranged, with that regard for impartiality, strict justice and completeness, that was in accordance with his nature, and all that he did or said in relation to any subject in which he engaged.

"In view of that solemn event, which must unavoida-"bly take place, which will end my mortal days and "close my labors on earth, I make this serious and im-"portant declaration: I humbly and earnestly pray that "the Father of the spirits of all flesh may, in that mercy "which he has revealed in our Lord Jesus Christ, forgive "all that in my whole life he sees amiss in me. This "prayer is offered in that *faith* for which I adore him "who hath given it to me.

"I heartily regret that I have not been a better hus- "band, a better father, and especially a better and more "useful minister of the gospel of divine grace. For my "faults in these particulars I ask the forgiveness of the "kind and faithful wife of my bosom, of my dearly- "beloved and dutiful children, and of the discerner of "my heart and thoughts, to whom I offer devout and "unfeigned gratitude, that, by his favor, I have been "enabled to do as well as I have in the relation of a hus- "band, and father, and minister of the gospel of Christ. "I sincerely return thanks to all my brethren in the "common faith, for all their kindness to me. I sincerely "thank the great fraternity of Christians, united with me "in the precious faith in which we believe, and especially "the church and society with whom, for more than thirty "years, I have lived in love, and with whom I have "labored in word and doctrine, for all their numerous "favors. HOSEA BALLOU."

"A great man has fallen," says the editor of the Trumpet. "There have been but few such men as "Father Ballou. We can truly say that those who "knew him best loved him most. Those who had heard "him preach the oftenest, and who had read the most "thoroughly what he had written, felt more than others "the power of his mind, and were more deeply convinced "than others that he was intellectually, as well as relig- "iously and morally, a great man. His life was pro- "tracted beyond fourscore years; he enjoyed a very large "share of health and strength through that whole time. "He was never idle; he worked, up to the last week of "his life, in the harvest-field, and actually died with the "sickle in his hand. He was taken sick at his own "house; and, after six days of comparatively light suf- "fering, he gently fell asleep in death, quietly as an "infant falls into slumber, and at the moment when he "seemed to be putting his body in the posture for the "coffin.

"It is in vain for us to attempt to give, in this brief "sketch, an account of the travels of Father Ballou; "the small but interesting and instructive incidents of "his life,—his sermons, his controversies, the different "books he wrote, the judgment of impartial men con- "cerning him,—all these things must be left to be "described at a time and under circumstances when full "justice can be done to the illustrious man. His charac- "ter, too, must be drawn. For ourself, we say, most "unreservedly, we never knew a better man. We say "this, after having lived in his family under his imme- "diate tuition, and since that time spent more than thirty "years side by side with him, 'in journeyings often,' in "mutual consultations, and in very frequent interviews. "If we ever saw a person equally amiable, kind, upright, "gentle and true, it is the aged widow who survives him.

"If he was more than a father to us, she was more than "a mother. She can never be honored too much for her "goodness. To her must be attributed much of the ease "and quietness he enjoyed in life, and without which he "could not have accomplished the full measure of the "good for which he is now beloved and reverenced. So "much for the moral qualities of this venerable man and "woman. There remain yet to be described (but it can-"not be done here) the childlike simplicity of the man; his "benevolence; his blindness to the faults of others; his "open eye to their virtues; his strong sense of rectitude; "his remarkable and long-continued habits of justice; "his wonderful mind, so clear, so strong, to the last; his "eagle-eyed sagacity; his strong faith in God and his "word,— a faith like a mountain for its towering height "and firmness; his devotion to the truth; his love of the "work of the ministry; his truly religious character; his "susceptibility to deep devotional feeling; his love of con-"ventions and associations for the seasons of public wor-"ship they gave him so many opportunities to enjoy; his "love of conference meetings; his power over the people; "his closing sermons at conventions; his prayers at the "separation, when all, old and young, male and female, "clergy and laity, would be melted into tears; — ah! "who shall attempt to describe all these things?

"For myself (for I will throw off the editorial style), "I acknowledge that I feel most deeply the loss of this "steadfast friend. I mourn, not for him, but for *myself.* "To me he had been a father. He found me in my "early manhood, and drew me out from seclusion. He "taught my lips to pray. He turned my attention to "the ministry; and he sought and obtained the means to "support me, when I had not a cent with which to help "myself. He was in the desk with me when I stood up "tremblingly (in the town-house in Roxbury) to preach "my first sermon. He introduced me to the society in "Milford, Mass., where I had my first pastoral charge, and "where I formed the tenderest relations of human life; "and he was the cause of my being invited, in the year "1822, to settle at Cambridgeport, where I ever since have "lived. For six years thereafter, I was associated with "him in conducting the 'Universalist Magazine;' and "from that time to his death he has been a constant con-"tributor to the columns of the 'Trumpet,' refusing for "the last ten years all pecuniary compensation, although "repeatedly pressed upon him. He has been the ear-"nest, steadfast friend of my wife and children; my "earthly guide and counsellor, who has reproved me, but "not too often; my teacher to the end of his life; a man "of whom I have learned more concerning God and the "divine word, and the relation between God and man, "than I have learned from any other human source. "How can the event of such a man's death transpire, "without exciting in me extraordinary sensations? And "yet I am not inconsolable. When I reflect upon what "he was, upon the length of his life, upon the great "measure of good he accomplished, upon the fact that he "was permitted (although so much away) to die at home, "surrounded by his most exemplary and loving children, "after a very brief sickness, and to die so gently, almost "in the act of binding sheaves in the harvest-field,—I "cease to mourn. I thank God for what he was; and if "I could call him back to earth, I should not dare to do so. "I thank God that I saw him within an hour of his death, "and that he knew me, and extended his hand, and that "I was permitted to take it and kiss it. And now, "although there never will be, for there never can be, "another man to me like Father Ballou, I will be recon-"ciled. And I will close this brief sketch with the "words of Job,—'The Lord gave, and the Lord hath "taken away; blessed be the name of the Lord.'"

Passing over the feelings of sorrow, yet of calm resignation, that exercised the aged widow and mother, and the large circle of devoted and loving children, who have so fully realized the solemn character of this bereavement, we wish to give here the series of resolutions presented to the mourning family by the second Universalist society, over which Mr. Ballou had presided for a period of so many years. They were communicated to the family in the same delicate and feeling manner in which all else relating to the melancholy event had been performed by those engaged in it. They are as follows:

"WHEREAS it has pleased Almighty God to call to "himself our venerable father in Israel, Rev. Hosea "Ballou, the senior pastor of this society, who departed "this life on the 7th day of June, 1852, aged 81 years; "and whereas, in recurring to the events of his long and "memorable life, we bring to mind the time when he "first appeared as the fearless advocate of what he then "and ever afterwards felt to be God's truth as revealed "in the Holy Scriptures; the moral courage with which "he sustained that truth amid all the assaults of learn-"ing, bigotry and tradition, continuing faithful to the "last in the path that was revealed to him as the path of "duty; therefore,

"*Resolved*, That the present prosperous aspect of the "Universalist denomination, and the gradual infusion of "its principles into those of other Christian denomina-"tions, are monuments of honor to its pioneers, of whom "Hosea Ballou was one of the chief.

"*Resolved*, That the denomination of Universalists "have therefore lost, in this dispensation of Divine "Providence, a champion whose latter days they have "delighted to honor; a practical example of the working "of the faith once delivered to the saints; and one who "has most ably worn the breastplate of righteousness "and borne the shield of faith, and who has gone down "to the grave 'full of years and full of honors.'

"*Resolved*, That as sole pastor of this society during "a period of about twenty-seven years, and as senior "pastor for about eight years, his career has been uni-"formly marked by a wisdom and kindness, in all his "intercourse with its members, both individually and col-"lectively, which prevented even the approach of any "discord between them; and by a large and broad "charity, which made all mankind his brothers, and chil- "dren of the same paternal God.

"*Resolved*, That in the death of this venerable Chris- "tian, whom we have so long looked up to as a pastor, "yea, even as a father, this society especially has met "with a heavy loss; and while we feel deeply the weight "of this afflicting bereavement, yet we would gratefully "acknowledge the kindness of an all-wise Providence in "having spared his life and continued his usefulness in "so signal and uninterrupted a manner, during the pro- "tracted period of his connection with us.

"*Resolved*, That in the simplicity of his daily life, "which was most truly a life without guile, we see a "proof of his devotion to principle worthy of all honor; "and in his inflexible integrity he has left an eloquent "lesson, which all, young and old, may read with profit.

"*Resolved*, That we sympathize most sincerely with "the afflicted widow, children and other relatives, of our "deceased pastor, in their bereavement; that we feel the "poverty of language to administer consolation, and can "only point them to the sublime truths of gospel grace "which their departed relative spent his life in teaching; "that we fervently commend them to Him who 'tempers "the wind to the shorn lamb;' and, while we can hardly "expect to assuage their grief with the wound yet so "fresh, we would bid them sorrow not as those without "hope, but remember how many a weary soul has found "rest from the teachings of him they now mourn, and "direct them to the glorious faith that he is 'not lost, but "gone before.'

"*Voted*, That the foregoing resolutions be signed by "the Moderator and Clerk, and published in the 'Trum-"pet' and 'Freeman,' and that a copy of the same be "forwarded to the family of our deceased pastor.

"G. W. GAGE, *Moderator*.

"NEWTON TALBOT, *Clerk*."

It still remains for us to describe the funeral ceremonies; and here again we copy from others. The description is as it appeared in the Trumpet.

"The funeral of this venerable man, and faithful old "Christian teacher, took place on Wednesday, June 9th. "Prayer was first offered at the house, in the hearing of "the widow, who had not left her chamber, and scarcely "her bed, for some thirty days. This part of the ser-"vices was strictly private. The corpse was then taken "to the church, with the members of the family in car-"riages.

"The church had been very appropriately put in "mourning for the occasion. The large portrait in the "vestry was shrouded in crape, showing nothing but the "figure of the aged preacher, as he stood in the pulpit. "In the great chapel, the pulpit, and the recess back of "it, were dressed in drapery of black crape. The entire "front of the gallery, all around the house, was fes-"tooned with black. The organ, also, was appropriately "dressed in mourning, in good keeping with the other "arrangements.

"The house was thrown open for the public at two "o'clock, at which time large crowds were waiting at the "doors; and for a full half-hour before the services were "commenced, every seat and foothold upon the floor, "aisles, window-sills and recesses, excepting reserved "pews, were occupied. At three o'clock the corpse "arrived. The clergy, numbering somewhere between "sixty and a hundred, proceeded from the vestry to the "pews assigned them. The members of the Second Uni- "versalist Society also had their appropriate places. "The corpse was borne to the position in front of the "pulpit, the bearers proceeding in the following "order:

"Rev. Dan'l Sharp, D. D.,	THE BODY.	Rev. Edward Turner,
"Rev. S. Barrett, D. D.,		Rev. S. Streeter,
"Rev. S. Cobb,		Rev. T. Whittemore,
"Rev. L. R. Paige,		Rev. Josiah Gilman.

"During the entrance, the organ gave forth a mourn- "ful prelude. The sight was a most affecting one,—so "vast a multitude with such an expression of sorrow "upon their countenances.

"1. The services were introduced by a funeral chant, "after which

"2. Scriptures were read by Rev. O. A. Skinner.

"3. The following hymn was sung, many of the con- "gregation joining their voices to that of the choir.

HYMN.

"On Zion's holy walls
Is quenched a beacon-light;
In vain the watchman calls,
'Sentry! what of the night?'
No answering voice is here;
Say, — does the soldier sleep?
O, yes, — upon the bier,
His watch no more to keep.

Still is that heaven-touched tongue,
Pulseless the throbbing breast;
That voice with music strung
Forever put to rest.
To rest? A living thought,
Undimmed, unquenched, he soars,
An essence, spirit wrought,
Of yon immortal shores.

Peace to thee, man of God!
Thine earthly toils are o'er;
The thorny path is trod,
The Shepherd trod before.
Full well he kept his word, —
'I'm with thee to the end;
Fear not! I am the Lord,
Thy never-failing friend!'

We weave no dirge for thee, —
It should not call a tear
To know that thou art free;
Thy home, — it was not here!
Joy to thee, man of God!
Thy heaven-course is begun;
Unshrinking thou hast trod
Death's vale, — thy race is run!"

"4. Prayer, by Rev. Thomas Whittemore.

"5. Hymn, 'Vital Spark of Heavenly Flame!'

"6. Sermon, by Rev. A. A. Miner, junior pastor, "from 2 Cor. 5 : 1,—'For we know that if our earthly "house of this tabernacle were dissolved, we have a build- "ing of God, a house not made with hands, eternal in "the heavens.'

"7. Hymn, 'Unveil thy Bosom, Faithful Tomb.'

"8. Concluding Prayer, by Rev. Sebastian Streeter.

"9. Benediction.

"During the singing of the last hymn, persons began "to press around the coffin, to get a last view of the "departed. Notice was therefore given, at the close of "the service, that the coffin would be placed in the entry, "and all would have an opportunity to see, as they passed "out; but, on account of the great number, each must "content himself with a brief farewell view. The funeral "procession was formed in the following order: 1st. "Bearers, in carriages. 2d. The body. 3d. The com- "mittee of the society. 4th. The clergy of the Uni- "versalist denomination, amounting to nearly a hundred. "5th. The members of the Second Universalist Society. "6th. The friends from the neighboring towns. 7th. "The mourners, in carriages.

"This procession extended from the head of School- "street to the corner of Boylston-street, being nearly "half a mile.

"An immense body of people had arrived at the ground "previously to the funeral procession. The corpse was "borne to the temporary resting-place, in the burying-"ground at the foot of the Common, where it was depos-"ited. The lid of the coffin was raised, and those who "desired passed by once more, and then the solemn scene "was closed."

The last Sabbath that Mr. Ballou preached was on the 30th of May, 1852,—eight days before his death,—at Woonsocket, R. I. The texts were the following:

"FORENOON.—Ecclesiastes 12: 13, 14. 'Let us "hear the conclusion of the whole matter: Fear God, "and keep his commandments: for this is the whole duty "of man. For God shall bring every work into judg-"ment, with every secret thing, whether it be good, or "whether it be evil.'

"AFTERNOON.—Titus 2: 11, 12. 'For the grace "of God that bringeth salvation hath appeared to all "men, teaching us that, denying ungodliness and worldly "lusts, we should live soberly, righteously and godly, in "this present world.'"

The fact of Mr. Ballou's having preached his last sermon in Rev. John Boyden's desk, a brother who had once been an inmate of his family as a student of divinity, has elicited the following letter, which seems particularly appropriate here:

"DEAR SIR:—

"I rejoice most sincerely to learn, as I do this day, "that you are so soon to give us a memoir of Father "Ballou. And, if it be not asking too much, I should "be glad of a little space, that I may record my tribute "of filial affection. He was to me a father, indeed; and "to him I owe more than to any other man,— and, per- "haps, all others,— for the little good I may have accom- "plished as a minister of Christ. He was my teacher "when he knew it not.

"When I was about fourteen years old, I heard him "preach, in the town of Brookfield; and I am sure the "impression that sermon made will remain to the end of "my life. It was designed to unfold the riches of Christ "Jesus. As the theme opened, the audience became "intensely interested; and, as the preacher gathered and "arranged the sacred testimony, to unfold the gracious "purposes of our Heavenly Father as manifested through "the Redeemer, we seemed like hungry children, watch- "ing the maternal hands that feed them. And when he "laid the precious burden before us, he would exclaim, in "all his wonted earnestness, '*Do you see the unsearch- "able riches of Christ?*' Again he would go forth, "gathering other fruits of the divine love, and again "repeat, as a part of his text, 'Do you see the unsearch- "able riches of Christ?' This was the conclusion of "each division of the discourse; and it served not only "to rivet it in our minds, but, by the involuntary mental "response which it induced, made us almost co-workers "with the speaker, and thus gave us growing interest in "the theme.

"From that hour, and from the influence of that single "discourse, I had a strong desire to aid in unfolding the "'unsearchable riches of Christ' to my fellow-men. My "young heart felt, for the first time, that there was a "fulness in the provision which our Father had made for "us that the world had not known; and it seemed to me "I *must*, some time, preach that blessed gospel. Not "more than three or four years after that time, I heard "him preach one of his masterly sermons, in Charlton, "which fired my soul anew with a desire to enter the "ministry. His text was, 'For we preach not ourselves, "but Christ Jesus the Lord,' &c. After reading the "text, he carefully folded his glasses, put them in his "pocket, as was his custom, and, while the audience "were waiting with breathless attention, that they might "secure the first word that should fall from his lips, he "began thus:—'The text *supposes* that there *is* such "a thing as a man's preaching *himself*.' The audience "*breathed*,—a token that they already possessed the "key to the sermon. But it was a remarkable charac- "teristic of his sermons, that, though you might early "anticipate the conclusion to which he was coming, yet "you could not foresee the *process* by which he was to "lead you, since that was peculiarly original. That "sermon strengthened my conception of the glory of the "gospel as we understand it, and especially when he con- "trasted with it the fading and sickly glory of all forms "of partialism. He made us understand how easy and "agreeable a duty it was to preach Christ; because in "him there was neither inconsistency, partiality nor "cruelty. A sermon from this text, I know, has been "printed; but *that* sermon I have never seen on paper, "nor can my poor pen describe the heavenly glow of "feeling expressed by the countenances of that assembly. "Perchance the record is in heaven.

"On the fourteenth day of May, 1829, I entered his "family as a student; and let me here say it was *home*. "There were my adopted father and mother, brothers "and sisters; and never were the beautiful relations "indicated by these endearing words in a single instance "marred. God bless them, for the words of sympathy "and encouragement that fell upon the ear of the timid "young man! The recollections of my experience in that "family tell me that no man knows the good he is doing, "if his heart be right. There is a world of power in a "single word, when it falls on a needy and congenial soil.

"During the last week of that month, and when I had, "as yet, written but one sermon, Father Ballou engaged "with Father Leonard, of Gloucester, that I should sup-"ply his desk the following Sunday. I remonstrated. "I had never spoken in public, except to declaim as a "school-boy; and it seemed to me I *could* not stand up "alone and preach all day, and especially so soon after "formally commencing my studies. But to all this his "reply, in substance, was, that the gospel was very easy "to be understood; that the matter of it was all furnished "to my hands; that I was only a *steward* of God's grace, "and had only to give to the people what was given to "me in the divine word. Well, I told him I would go, "if he said so; but he would have to bear the responsi-"bility, if I failed.

"In the morning, before leaving for Gloucester, I read "my last sermon to him; and then it was that he gave "me a word of commendation, that was like a generous "shower upon the parched ground. And this was fol- "lowed by the well-remembered injunction: 'Brother "Boyden, I have only one word to say in reference to "your labors, and that is, *be in earnest*. Don't speak "one word without making the people understand and "feel that you believe it with all your heart.' This was "the only charge he ever gave me, till, at my ordination, "in Berlin, Ct., in 1830, he enjoined it upon me to "carry the spirit of our holy religion into all my labors, "and especially when I should go to the chamber of sick- "ness, and to the house of mourning. The tremulous "words, as they fell from the lips of the father upon his "son, stirred the whole audience with emotion. They "were treasured in many hearts, and often repeated, both "by the old and young, who waited on my ministry.

"For myself, I must say they made a lasting impres- "sion on my mind; and often, since that time, as I have "visited the sick and dying, has that venerable form pre- "ceded me, renewing the tender injunction, 'Come in the "spirit of the blessed Redeemer.' I trust those words "were not thrown away. And when, as will happen with "most men, my wearied frame has imparted languor to my "speech, I have sometimes been aroused by the sudden "recollection of that stirring appeal—'Be in earnest.' "I know it has often quickened and warmed my zeal; and "when I remember that it was the motto of his life to the "last, I pray that it may be to me as a live coal from the "altar.

"*Punctuality* is another of the sterling virtues that "cluster around that name, and his example has been of "special service to me. It characterized all his labors. I "have known him much for twenty-three years, and I "never knew him to be late in fulfilling any engagement, "and he always took time, so as not to be in a hurry. On "the occasion of the installation of Bro. A. Bugbee, of "Charlton, some years ago, he delivered the scriptures "and gave the charge. In the course of his address, he "dwelt upon the above-named virtue with no little feeling. "'Bro. Bugbee,' said he, 'when you come to church, "*come in season*. Don't let the people come here and "wait, and wonder within themselves, saying, Where is "Bro. Bugbee? Is Bro. Bugbee sick? And O, don't "forget to take time, before you commence your services, "to put up a silent prayer to God, that he may aid and "assist you in the discharge of your sacred duties.'

"I know that that occasion was one of peculiar joy to "many hearts, and it was as the blessing of God on my "soul. The religious spirit within us was quickened; and "many a time since, in my humble efforts to preach the "gospel, that 'silent prayer' has brought celestial fire "from heaven, and imparted new life to my spiritual being. "Doubtless there are many in the ministry whose experi-"ence accords with my own in these things, and whose "usefulness may be in a good measure attributed to the "personal influence of that great and good man, who, "great as he was, could not have comprehended the vast "results of which his unostentatious life was the agent. "And may we not all be encouraged to hope, that, if we "live good lives, the harvest will extend beyond the ken "of the sower?

"But the most interesting fact, to me, in the life of my "spiritual father, is, that he closed his public services in "my own pulpit, in the presence of a delighted congrega- "tion, and, as I believe, of an approving God. His last "sermons are well remembered, even by *children.* He "has never preached here with greater zeal, power, and "comprehensiveness. We accept his services as the bless- "ing of a dying hour, and our veneration for the man is "mingled with gratitude to the everlasting Father, for so "great a gift to our world.

"Fraternally yours,

"J. BOYDEN, JR.

"*Woonsocket, July* 6, 1852."

The following is taken from the report of L. W. Ballou, superintendent of the Sabbath-school attached to the Woonsocket Universalist Society, which school the subject of this biography visited and spoke before on the day referred to. It is especially interesting as being connected with his last public efforts.

"On the thirtieth of May it was our privilege to be "visited by, and to receive the last public instructions of, "our venerable Father Ballou; for in one week from the "time he left us 'the golden bowl was broken,' and that "voice to which we had so recently listened, and which "had breathed life and joy into so many souls, was "hushed forever. But in his works, in his example, in "the glorious doctrines which for more than sixty years "he labored to establish, he still lives and speaks, and "will live and speak for ages to come. Long, I trust, "shall we remember that venerable form, that cheerful "and benevolent countenance, and the words of encour-"agement and hope with which, for the last time, he "addressed us, rejoicing that we were no longer taught "as in times past, and as some are even now, that by "nature we are children of wrath, and under the curse "of God; but that God is our father, our benefactor, our "best friend,—that he cares for and is blessing us always. "Thus did our aged father close his public ministrations, "in proclaiming the same great doctrine which he had "spent his life to establish,—the unbounded, universal, "and unchangeable love of God to man.

"Let us be as faithful to the truth, and in the perform-"ance of our duty, in the sphere in which we move, as "he was in his, and the same rich blessings will "attend us."

The subject of this biography entered most heartily and sincerely into the spirit of Sabbath-schools; and since their general introduction in our societies, throughout the order, he has taken peculiar satisfaction in improving every suitable occasion for addressing and encouraging both teachers and scholars in the object which engaged them, wherever he was called to preach. In his own society he had seen the great good to be derived from such an institution, as it regards the rearing of the tender mind in the garden of the Lord; and he often mingled professionally with children and teachers. The able and feeling remarks of the superintendent, Mr. Goddard, as given herein, will show the appreciation in which the members of the school had been taught to hold their pastor, and the spirit that actuated the hearts of the teachers towards him, under whose Christian teachings they had, most of them, been brought up from childhood.

The following verses, an invaluable legacy to Mr. Ballou's family, and to all those who really loved him, were written by him in anticipation of the closing hour of his life. The date we cannot give, as the original paper bears none; but, from accessory circumstances, and remarks which he made to his wife, that he felt he was "nearly worn out," and that she must be prepared to hear of his decease at any hour,— perhaps, even, away from home, —they may be supposed to express his feelings more particularly within a very few days of the close of his life. They require no dedication from us. They are priceless, and beautiful in the extreme.

The verses are thus introduced: —

"A minister, experiencing certain infirmities of body which strongly
"suggested to him that he might be suddenly called away, wrote the
"following

FAREWELL ADDRESS.

I.

No more thy beams mine eyes delight,
Thou golden sun! the shades of night
Are o'er my vision cast.

Adieu to thy bright, cheering rays,
Thy morning light, thy noon-tide blaze,
Thy settings in the west.

II.

And thou, sweet moon, whose silver beam
Did on my evening rambles gleam,
I need thy light no more;
And you who twinkle in the skies
No more shall set, no more shall rise,
To me, as heretofore.

III.

Ye waves of ocean, fare you well;
Adieu to mountain, hill and dell,
Rich fields and gardens too;
Your flowery robes and fragrance sweet
No more my peaceful walks shall greet;
I bid ye all adieu.

IV.

Ye murmuring streams, whose winding way
Through flowery meads and woodlands lay,
And every limpid rill,
And all ye feathered tribes of air,
With voices sweet and plumage fair,
Accept my last farewell.

V.

Adieu, sweet Spring, the time of flowers!
Thy zephyrs soft, thy falling showers,
No more have charms for me;
Maternal Summer, too, adieu! —
These eyes no more thy beauty view,
Nor thy rich treasures see.

VI.

Autumn and Winter's social glee
Afford their charms no more to me, —
They but a moment last;

For life's short season now is o'er,
I taste its joys, its griefs, no more, —
The transient scene is past.

VII.

Ten thousand friends, and more, farewell!
With gratitude affections swell
Within this breast of mine;
And you, my foes, although but few,
Do share in this, my last adieu, —
May mercy on ye shine!

VIII.

Thou sacred desk, where oft I've stood
To plead the cause of truth for God,
To you I say farewell;
That I've been faithful to my Lord
I call for witness on his word, —
His word he will fulfil.

IX.

And you, my congregation dear,
Kindly regard the farewell tear,
So freely shed for you;
For all your favors to your friend,
May Heaven blessings to you send,
And every grace renew.

X.

One struggle more shall end the strife; —
My children dear, my loving wife,
Ye dearest joys of earth,
Accept this last, this fond adieu;
While I have lived I've lived for you,
But now resign my breath.

XI.

That Power which does for birds provide,
And clothes the grass in all its pride,
Much more shall nourish you ;
On that kind arm in peace recline,
Submissive to the will divine, —
Believe his promise true.

XII.

And now my work on earth is done,
To thee, my Lord, my God, I come,
Still trusting in thy grace ;
As earth recedes may I arise,
To be with Jesus in the skies,
And see his lovely face!"

CHAPTER XVI.

CONCLUSION.

A MODERN writer says, after a visit to the splendid tomb of David Hume, at Edinburgh, "When I looked "upon the spot, I could not forget that his best powers "had been deliberately exerted to load the minds of men "with doubts of their God."

> "To poison at the fountain's source
> The stream of life throughout its course."

Let us contrast the feelings thus naturally arising in the mind, as it contemplates the life of the English historian, with those that will spring up spontaneously in the heart of him who looks upon the last resting-place of the subject of this biography. His whole life was a practical plea for the glorious character of his Heavenly Father, and every power of his nature, both mental and physical, was entirely devoted to and expended in bearing witness of God's love and impartial grace. Who covets the world-wide fame of the infidel historian? Who would not leave behind him the glorious memory of the true Christian? Greatness may build the tomb, but goodness must write the epitaph.

> "Only the actions of the just
> Smell sweet, and blossom in the dust."

We have thus brought the narrative of Mr. Ballou's life down from its commencement to its close. In the execution of the task, it is feared that many imperfections and deficiences will be detected; but we have the consolation of reflecting that, at least, we have not been guilty of exaggeration, and throughout have sought only to present the truth in the clearest light, and with the same simplicity that the subject of these pages would have commended. We have most ardently endeavored to make manifest the pure character, consistent conduct, the high intellectual ability, the unaffected piety, and laborious and unremitted services of the deceased to the great cause he espoused in early life. Had he placed a higher estimate upon his own labors, he would have left behind him a complete record of his toils, that would have interested the most careless and worldly reader. But, while he never spared himself, he appears to have seen no unusual merit in his unexampled labors; he was simply discharging his duty to his Maker and his fellow-men. The thought of challenging admiration for his sacrifices of comfort, for his exposures and trials, seems never to have occurred to him; and hence the minutes of his personal adventures are brief and imperfect. He has only given us enough to enable us to guess at the extent of his toil. For the result of his labors and travels, we have only to look around,—to behold the multiplied churches springing up where he first preached in school-houses, dwelling-houses, or even beneath the fruit-trees, to numerous congregations that have found faith and hope through his ministrations, who fondly regard him as the father of their order, and who rise up to bless his name. Though his lips are now sealed forever, yet his doctrine, a precious legacy, is left for us still, in his own language; and, with the example and influence of his pure life, we may find the surest guide to the understanding of the gospel as it is in Christ.

It is true that the bow is broken; but the arrow is sped on its message, and will pierce the heart of error. The subject of these pages was not a man for his own time alone; he has lived for all time. We find in the pages of history actors upon the stage of life peculiarly fitted for the immediate period in which they lived; men active, bold, successful, and ever ready for any emergency; men governed by principles and incentives peculiarly adapted to the day and hour, without whom it would have been difficult to realize the seeming destiny of man, and the results and history of the times. Yet those persons, if they were to exist now, would be out of their element; there would not occur the same exigencies to call forth their particular endowments of courage and endurance. They illustrated tangible matter, and performed deeds of personal prowess; but Mr. Ballou enunciated, defined, elucidated and illumined, a great principle, a fundamental truth, something that will live through all eternity,— not the ephemeral act of an hour, which, however timely and important at the moment, is forgotten with the casualty that gives it birth. No! Mr. Ballou was not for his own time alone,— he was for all time.

His advent in the religious world was the commencement of a new era in the church; and from that day and that hour the little glimmering of the light of truth which was seen as afar off grew daily larger, and brighter, and clearer, as, in the onward journey of his years and his understanding, he came to behold the gospel as it is in Christ, and to preach it to the world. Nature about him had taught this impartial grace and goodness of God for ages and ages, but the tongues of men had been fabricating and declaring another creed. It was no new truth that he illustrated and believed; but he gave it oral form, and depicted it before men's eyes.

Our task draws now to its close; we have recorded the closing incidents of that life on whose eventful record we have reverentially dwelt, and we must soon resign the pen with which we have feebly depicted the story of departed worth. It remains for us to give a rapid retrospective glance at the career we have traced, with a brief recapitulatory view of the subject. The author has made no attempt at fine writing, and has sought only to present a "plain, unvarnished tale," in keeping with the unostentatious simplicity of the subject of his pages. In these busy and stirring days, most readers crave an exciting book of thrilling incident. In preparing the life of a distinguished warrior, or a bold adventurer, startling incidents and scenes crowd upon the writer, till the task of condensation becomes both imperative and difficult. The turbulent stream, rushing from its mountain home, tumbling amidst rocks and dashing over precipices, affords a picture at every point of its progress; while the course of a river, that rises in some placid lake, and pursues its pathway noiselessly and tranquilly, till lost in the world of waters that swallows up its individuality, however pleasing an object of contemplation, is little fitted to figure in an elaborate personal record, or to minister to the restless eye of the lover of the bold and startling in nature.

The life of the subject of these pages may be compared to that of a quiet streamlet, making itself felt by the verdure and freshness it diffuses around it, but not startling the ear by the tumult of motion. Hence, those who merely take up a book for amusement or excitement, will find themselves disappointed with this biography. It was not, however, for such tastes that the book was designed. It is rather a medium of communication between filial affection, and that scarcely colder feeling of friendship and respect, shared by a large and increasing denomination of Christians, whose common love for the subject of these pages will secure indulgence towards the author.

They will rather follow the delightful traits of Christian character he evinced, will admire the truth and genuineness of his nature, the sweet simplicity of his soul, and the magnitude and glory of his doctrine, than pause to criticize the simple garb that has clothed these special and important matters. It will be the kernel, not the shell, that our readers will discuss; and if we have, in our humble way, succeeded in so portraying the life of our parent as to place it any more clearly and faithfully before men's eyes, then we have done a good work, and our labor has not been in vain. If, by the exhibition of his happy faith, and the application of his own arguments, we shall have succeeded in confirming even one soul in the sacred and cheering faith he advocated, we shall have sufficient reward in our own heart for the toil of this work. He would have labored continually and unceasingly to lead a soul in the straight and narrow way; no fatigue, no disappointment, was ever any hindrance in his path, when duty held the lamp. His eyes were turned onward and upward; they overlooked the rugged way, strewn with rocks and quicksands, over which he strode towards the great goal of his life, in promulgation of God's fatherly love to man.

More fortunate than many whose works have enriched the world, we have seen that Mr. Ballou lived long enough to enjoy an honorable fame. Long before he died the voice of calumny was hushed. He had accomplished what Burke had advised for the refutation of slander,— he had "lived it down." The shafts of malice fell harmless from the shield of his unspotted conscience. He had achieved a greater triumph yet than the surviving of the assaults aimed against his reputation as a man; he lived to behold the truth he had so advocated, in which and for which he lived, adopted by hundreds of thousands as the staff of their lives and the rock of their salvation. It would be difficult to find, in any age, the record of a greater victory of intellectual power.

As we have fully shown, Mr. Ballou started in life with no aids for the development of his mental energies. His circumstances were such as would have completely crushed a majority of gifted minds. Isolation, privation, the want of mental stimulus, surrounded him. The example and aid of elder scholarship was wanting. The steps to the temple of knowledge were hewn by his own hands out of the rugged and unyielding rock. He had no strong hand to grasp his own, and bear him up, and stay his tottering footsteps. Yet, with an iron grasp, he seized upon the rudiments of knowledge, and made them his own. And, while satisfying the cravings of his nature, he neglected no duty of life. Those who had claims upon his industry suffered no injury or loss from this source, for the hours devoted to his early studies were heroically subtracted from hours of repose. When others rested from bodily toil, he was wakeful and toiling mentally.

The energy displayed in his pursuit of knowledge, under such extraordinary difficulties, prepares us for the yet greater energy exhibited in his subsequent course. Accustomed to accomplish his purpose by severe labor, we find him continually proposing to himself questions of difficulties to be solved only by severe intellectual exertion. He cultivates his moral intellectual nature so rigidly, that he is not lightly satisfied on any subject. But we are most impressed with the beauty of his spiritual nature. Most energetic minds are, we think, prone to scepticism. They doubt, resolve their doubts, and then cling firmly and forever to the truths they have established.

It is said, "A resolved doubt is the strongest proof." Paul began by opposing religion, and ended as one of its champions. But with Mr. Ballou there was no necessity of going through with this usual process. His existence and his belief were identical. He recognized his Maker in his words and in his works; faith was his earliest companion, and she was with him to the last. Her light illumined his earliest and his last step; as it beamed upon him with its morning radiance, and cheered his noontide with its glow, so it was the broad, unshadowed sunset of his life.

We have seen how early his inquiring and steadfast mind began to pierce the shadows and darkness with which dogmatism had obscured the true nature of God, and the spirit of his law. The clouds were not dispelled all at once. By degrees they rolled away, as his vision strengthened, until, at length, his eyes beheld the full glory of God in its effulgent splendor. The moment when the last veil was withdrawn, and he beheld the glorious form of Truth embodied in the creed which he ever afterwards professed, was the crown and summit of his existence. Then he found and grasped a treasure which the world could not take away. Years might pass before the many would embrace his doctrine; but he knew that it must eventually make its way to men's hearts and understanding, and that it would be universally recognized and triumph in the end.

From the moment of his discovery, his mission was decided, his calling confirmed, his path through life traced out as clear as daylight. He felt called upon and inspired to preach the gospel of love to all mankind; and he went forth upon his mission, resolved to fulfil it to the utmost of his strength and talent. Surely no man ever more faithfully performed his allotted task. In the discharge of his duty, we behold him fearing no toil, sparing no exertion, shrinking from no obstacle. A man loving peace and quiet, yet he hesitated not to assume the weapons of controversy when his doctrines were assailed. With him, indeed, the truth was everything,—himself nothing. Hence, we are left no record of his many journeyings, his lonely wayfarings, his midnight labors. He accounted these things as nothing, as dust in the balance, weighed against the service he espoused, and the gospel interests which he strove to advocate.

The following letter addressed to us from Manchester, N. H., a few years since, now lies open before us, and will serve to show the reader the indomitable perseverance that the subject of these memoirs brought to bear upon his professional duties;—how little he spared himself in the prosecution of his great mission; how totally he disregarded bodily ease or comfort, when brought in opposition to the prosecution of his sacred mission on earth. It is also another of those brief, meaning and affectionate epistles such as he ever wrote, exhibiting the same reliance upon Divine Providence that ever exercised his bosom: —

"MATURIN: Last Sabbath was to me a day of severe "trial. Early in the morning I was attacked with a "sudden illness, which so weakened me by meeting-time "that, although I made two determined efforts to go on "with my discourse, the last was as unsuccessful as the "first, and I was finally compelled to yield to my bodily "weakness, giving the people to expect my services in "the afternoon. Dr. Colburn kindly conveyed me to his "house, and he and his good lady so nursed me that, by "meeting-time in the afternoon, I walked to church and "went through with my usual services, sparing myself "the labor of reading the hymns. Through the goodness "of an all-ruling Providence, that has ever sustained and "supported me in every trial, I am now recovering, and "am quite as well as before this attack, save that I am "very weak.

"The reason I have written you particularly is, that "your mother and the family generally may not be "alarmed by the report which will very naturally reach "you before I can return home. Please send me a few "current newspapers. Affectionately,

"HOSEA BALLOU."

He neglected no means for the advancement of truth;

discourses from the pulpit, colloquial discussions, written essays, poetical effusions, all were brought to sustain the one great idea he advocated. Though his oral instructions were poured forth on every occasion, he well knew the mighty power of the press over the minds of community, and he wielded this agent with vigor and effect. As his example in the pulpit was followed by a host of disciples, so did his essays in the press give birth to a race of vigorous literary champions of the gospel. But, above all, was the "daily beauty of his life" the strongest evidence of the sincerity of his convictions, and the truth of his doctrine. The example that teaches better than precept was manifested in his social existence. His cheerful deportment, his resignation under trials, were proofs of a "peace which the world cannot give."

His principles forbade him to teach or to show that this beautiful world was created as a gloomy prison-house to the sons of men. Late and copious extracts from his own pen, in these pages, will abundantly show this. He delighted to point out the radiance of the raiment with which our Heavenly Father has gladdened our temporary abiding-place. He loved to trace the "smile of the Great Spirit," in the gushing water-courses, the verdant meadows, the bright skies, the murmuring woodlands, the flower-enamelled fields, and the blue arch that bends over all, enclosing it within a crystal sphere. He was no enemy to social enjoyment; no frown of his ever checked the joyous laugh bursting from young lips, or dimmed the brightness of the domestic fireside. In the relations of husband, father, friend, he was loved and revered,—how dearly and deeply, let the sorrow that has fallen on our hearts at parting speak!

He has gone from our midst! His stately form will no more gladden our eyes, the music of his voice will no more warm our hearts, the pressure of his hand will no more answer responsively to ours. But he has departed, full of years and fame, to that bright world above, whose glory was the theme of his existence. Emulating the virtues which his well-ordered and beautiful life exhibited, cherishing the gospel truths in all their purity, simplicity and attractiveness, as he taught them, may we improve our own lives by the recollection of his, and open our hearts to the still yet eloquent sermon he now preaches to us from the silent tomb! And let that sacred belief, which he taught us to rely upon and to hold as most dear to our hearts, fill us with a hope and assurance of a final and happy reünion with him in heaven! In his own family he fully succeeded in implanting a spirit of belief in and entire reliance upon God's love to his children; and, could the reader behold the influence that this belief now exercises over the heart of his aged widow, what a tower of strength and calm resignation she realizes from the faith he impressed upon her, he would find fresh reason for Christian fortitude, and new hope and faith in the gospel.

And now, ere the reader closes these pages, permit the author to ask for the book a kind consideration, and to solicit the lenient judgment of the public for these records of a parent's life, written and compiled amid the arduous duties attendant upon his editorial calling. The work has little else to recommend it, save the homely truthfulness of its record, and the sincerity that has dictated its composition.

To the many friends of Mr. Ballou, and more particularly to the denomination, clergymen and laity, with whom he has so long held fellowship, the author trusts this book may prove an acceptable memento of one whom they delighted to honor.

NEW EDITION

OF THE

BIOGRAPHY OF HOSEA BALLOU,

WRITTEN BY HIS YOUNGEST SON,

MATURIN M. BALLOU.

The steady demand which this valuable work has met with, from the first week of its publication, speaks more for its intrinsic merit than any review could do. It is a worthy monument, reared by a filial hand, to the memory of one whom a whole denomination delighted to honor. The Biography commences with the boyhood of the subject, and brings him step by step, and year by year, up to the close of his long and useful life. The labors of faith, of mental culture, of physical endurance, and of public application, are thoroughly delineated.

The following notices of the work will exhibit the spirit with which it has been received by good judges :

"It is, indeed, all that we can desire as a Biography of the loved, departed saint." — *Ch. Freeman, Boston.*

"Mr. Maturin M. Ballou has discharged his filial task in a most able and acceptable manner; with unaffected candor, and no disposition to magnify his mission." — *Boston Evening Transcript.*

"The writer has aimed to let his father become, as far as possible, his own biographer; and wherever the patriarch himself speaks, there is wonderful consistency, in the modesty, humility, and plainness of expression." — *Ladies' Repository, Boston.*

"It is a fortunate circumstance, that the work is written by one who knew the subject of it at home." — *Rev. O. A. Skinner.*

"It may be commended, as a vivid painting of the career of a rugged and determined mind, grasping successfully with adverse circumstances, and making its mark on society at every stage in its progress." — *Yankee Blade.*

"The author has so admirably performed his work, as to present the full proportions of his father's character." — *Rev. G. W. Montgomery.*

"It is from the pen of Maturin M. Ballou, editor of Gleason's Pictorial, and evinces a fine taste and great discrimination." — *Boston Evening Gazette.*

"Few writers have better understood the true aim of biography than has our author, as shown by this work." — *Rev. A. A. Miner.*

"The style of the author is smooth, cultivated, and finished; no straining after highly-wrought, flowery diction, and no descending to lightness or frivolity." — *New York Ch. Ambassador.*

"The work is history, faithful narrative, graphically and truly recorded." — *Olive Branch.*

"Those who have heard 'Father Ballou' discourse, or who have read his sterling works, will be sure to obtain the present publication. It is accompanied with an excellent engraving of the good man." — *Boston Bee.*

"The Biography is recorded in a lucid, easy and natural style, at times radiant with flashes of that eloquence which characterized 'the old man eloquent,' the eloquence of simplicity, the voice of nature, and the outgushing of feeling." — *Rev. C. F. Le Fevre.*

"The present volume embodies the history of his public, as well as his private trials. The gist of his doctrines and preaching is here set forth in a manner as creditable to the biographer, as suitable to the excellence of the venerable subject." — *Boston Post.*

"The biographer is well known as one of the most vigorous and successful writers connected with the Boston press, and the present volume will add much to his well-earned reputation." — *Boston Daily Ad.*

"We seem to see him in this book, as he appeared to us in life, — a man of a mild, gentle, unassuming, benevolent disposition, with the simplicity of a child, and the wisdom of a sage." — *Vermont Ch. Repository.*

GRACES AND POWERS OF THE CHRISTIAN LIFE.

By Rev. A. D. Mayo. 12mo., about 300 pages. Price 75 cents.

This is a series of twenty sermons, by Mr. Mayo, on the above subject, which cannot but prove a valuable acquisition to our Denominational Literature.

"This is a beautifully printed book, and its interior life and its ideal corresponds with its actual. * * The style of the author is modern and graceful, and the moral influence of the work cannot be otherwise than safe and good."— *Banner.*

"Mr. Mayo's composition reveals a pure spark of genius, gleaming, if it does not blaze, running like a bright thread and clue through the labyrinth of thought, and bringing to light many a blessed region of truth and peace." — *Christian Register.*

"We have been greatly charmed in reading it, both by the earnestness and depth of its thought, and the sweetness and purity of its style."— *Blade.*

"Its influence, wherever it circulates, will be most elevating and sanctifying."— *Christian Ambassador.*

"We take pleasure in saying that this volume of sermons has our hearty fellowship, and the prevalence of the spirit in its pages would enlarge vastly the communion of liberal Christians."— *Christian Inquirer.*

LIFE-SKETCHES OF REV. GEORGE H. CLARK.

By his Brother. With a fine likeness. 16mo. 160 pages. Price 50 c.

Sketches of the eventful life of this early-fallen brother were written by the request of many friends. The volume embraces a rapid succession of scenes and incidents, drawn from numerous papers left by the deceased, and portrayed by one dearly familiar with him from early life. Father Ballou's note of this work is as follows :

"This brief memoir of our young and esteemed brother in the ministry of God's universal efficient grace commends itself as an affectionate tribute to the memory of the departed, from the pen of a loving brother. It must also be grateful to the whole family circle, who survive the departed son and brother, to have in their possession so valuable a treasure.

"This work will be read with interest and profit by youth in general, and especially by such as think of devoting their lives to the ministerial profession. When such shall learn the fact, that moderate circumstances and limited means do not necessarily prevent a young man from becoming a minister and a pastor, highly esteemed and beloved by a good and respectable church and society, they need not shrink from a hope of success.

"We need not look forward to the good time, for it is now come, when ministers are esteemed for their knowledge of divine truth, and their ardent love for the same, together with their faithfulness in dispensing it to their people, and their living and walking in the precepts of Jesus."

"The subject of these memoirs died young. He had been in the ministry but a few years. He had lived, however, and labored, a sufficient length of time, to prove himself to be an able and eloquent preacher of the gospel, and to become endeared to all who formed his acquaintance. It abounds with incidents in the life of the deceased."— *Christian Ambassador.*

"The book abounds in incidents, and is very interesting."— *Banner.*

"The book is one of thrilling interest."— *Freeman.*

"The book is a record, traced with a loving, sympathetic, and brotherly hand, of the trials, hopes, joys, sorrows, life experiences and death, of a professional as well as a natural brother."— *Springfield Republican.*

"This is an affectionate tribute to the memory of a worthy man, — one of the many instances where high aims are unfortunately united with slender means, rendering life not so much 'a battle and a march,' as a perpetual struggle. We respected the brother whose life is here sketched, and have thoroughly read the volume with interest."— *Ladies' Repository.*

GLIMPSES AND GATHERINGS,

During a Voyage and Visit to London and the Great Exhibition, in the Summer of 1851. By Rev. W. A. Drew, Commissioner of the State of Maine. With a Portrait. About 400 pages. Price $1.

The undersigned issues, in connection with the publishers of the *Gospel Banner*, the above work. It is one of the most attractive and instructive volumes of travel ever published.

"This volume consists of letters written by the author to the *Gospel Banner*, of which he is the well-known editor, during his recent visits to Canada and England. During their original publication they were read with keen interest by the numerous patrons of that paper, as well as by the Maine public generally ; and it was a happy idea to gather them into a volume for more distant readers, as well as for future perusal and reference. The author has a sharp eye for observation, as well as great felicity in description; writes in an easy, off-hand, yet vigorous style; and, on the whole, has placed before us the clearest and most graphic picture of London and the sights in the Crystal Palace that we have yet met with. Not the least interesting portions of the volume are the descriptions of Montreal, Quebec, and their environs, to the accuracy and felicity of which we can testify." — *Yankee Blade.*

"An interesting series of sketches."— *Univer. Quar.*

"It is highly attractive in narration of incidents, scenery and sights. What makes it more valuable to us is a very natural likeness of the author, executed with much skill and beauty."— *Christian Ambassador.*

THE WORKS OF REV. HOSEA BALLOU.

The death of this Patriarch of the Universalist Ministry gives additional value to his Works, and especially to those written in the years of his strength and vigor.

The subscriber is the publisher of those works, and will furnish sets of the same, or single volumes, issued in the best style of typography and binding.

I. **Notes on the Parables of the New Testament.** One vol. 12mo., 297 pages. Price 50 cents. First published in 1804.

II. **A Treatise on the Atonement.** One vol. 12mo., 328 pages. Price 50 cents. First published in 1805.

III. **Series of Twenty-six Lecture Sermons.** Delivered in the School-street church, Boston. One vol. 12mo., 375 pages. Price 62½ cents. First published in 1818.

IV. **Twenty-five Select Sermons.** Delivered on various occasions, from important passages of Scripture. One vol. 12mo., 360 pages. Price 63 cents. First published in 1828.

These are the works in which the convictions of Father Ballou are best expressed, and circulation should be given to them by all who are desirous of diffusing the wisdom of that sainted man. The "Notes on the Parables" are remarkable examples of Scripture interpreting Scripture ; the "Treatise on Atonement" is a piece of mental reasoning intelligible to the humblest capacity ; and the "Lectures" and "Select Sermons" are rare expoundings of the divine word, and the great principles of Scripture truth

The subscriber is also preparing to issue a fine edition of the above works, to be bound in a uniform style with the Biography ; and the whole will then be sold at $4 per set.

A. TOMPKINS

BOSTON, August, 1852.

☞ AGENTS WANTED TO CIRCULATE THE FOREGOING WORKS

www.ingramcontent.com/pod-product-compliance
Lightning Source LLC
LaVergne TN
LVHW020102110826
845151LV00001B/47

* 9 7 8 1 4 2 5 5 4 4 7 9 9 *